# The Evolution of Consciousness

# The Evolution of Consciousness

Euan M. Macphail
*University of York*

Oxford New York Tokyo

OXFORD UNIVERSITY PRESS

1998

Oxford University Press, Great Clarendon Street, Oxford OX2 6DP
Oxford New York
Athens Auckland Bangkok Bogota Bombay
Buenos Aires Calcutta Cape Town Dar es Salaam
Delhi Florence Hong Kong Istanbul Karachi
Kuala Lumpur Madras Madrid Melbourne
Mexico City Nairobi Paris Singapore
Taipei Tokyo Toronto Warsaw
and associated companies in
Berlin Ibadan

Oxford is a trade mark of Oxford University Press

Published in the United States
by Oxford University Press Inc., New York

A catalogue record for this book is available from the British Library

Library of Congress Cataloging in Publication Data
Macphail, E. M. (Euan M.)
The evolution of consciousness / Euan M. Macphail.
Includes bibliographical references and index.
1. Consciousness. 2. Consciousness in animals. 3. Mind and body.
4. Language acquisition. 5. Infant psychology. 6. Psychology.
Comparative. I. Title.
BF311.M186 1998 126–dc21 98-4426
ISBN 0 19 850325 3 (Hbk)
ISBN 0 19 850324 5 (Pbk)

1001454649

Typeset by Hewer Text Limited, Edinburgh
Printed in Great Britain by
Bookcraft (Bath) Ltd,
Midsomer Norton, Avon

For Kate and her menagerie, all of whom remain to be convinced.

# Preface

My aim in writing this book has been to pose questions rather than to answer them—to provoke discussion, not to end it. As my title indicates, the questions concern the evolution of consciousness, and include such questions as, for example, Which animals, other than humans, are conscious? and What do we gain by being conscious? I hope, too, that the book may serve as propaganda for the claim that experimental psychologists—and, in particular, psychologists working with non-human animals—are generating work that is of fundamental importance to our efforts to understand the human mind.

No-one can hope to be a specialist in all the areas (philosophical, psychological, and neurological) that I venture into in the book and I have attempted to write it at a level that will, I hope, be readily accessible to non-specialists. Specialists in one area may find that I have, perhaps, oversimplified some of the issues (and may detect errors that, despite the efforts of my immensely helpful readers, still remain). I shall nevertheless feel justified if they find that my account of areas in which they are non-specialists succeeds in giving them a new perspective on their own fields.

I begin the book by making out in Chapter 1 the case that there are real problems with the common-sense assumptions that at least some non-human animals enjoy consciousness and that consciousness—feeling pain, for example—does have an obvious adaptive role. My approach to these issues is that of an experimental psychologist with a particular interest in differences between species (including humans) in intelligence: my object is to see whether there are psychological observations that can be used to answer questions about consciousness.

Before empirical findings can be brought to bear, a theoretical framework of basic ideas, that can be supplied only by philosophers, has to be erected. Chapters 2 and 3 therefore concern philosophical notions of consciousness and, in particular, of consciousness in animals. These chapters give basic ideas with which to work but may not be regarded as essential reading for those who want to see what psychology has contributed or could contribute to the debate.

The succeeding four chapters explore findings from a variety of research areas in experimental psychology all of which, I believe, are clearly relevant to consciousness, even if they do not point to an unequivocal conclusion. I do not, of course, expect that my readers will necessarily adopt the interpretations that I advance. My purposes will be well served if I persuade them that the research areas are of real interest and if I provoke psychologists into pursuing further the philosophical significance of their results and provoke philosophers into exploring psychologists' work more deeply.

The final chapter concentrates again largely on philosophical issues. After introducing contemporary approaches to the philosophy of mind, I provide a brief account of a way in which the emergence of language may have paved the way for the emergence of consciousness. It seems to be my misfortune that, despite using what seem to me entirely conventional principles in the assessment of findings, I arrive at conclusions that contradict common sense. Most people find it hard to credit my (long-standing) suggestion that a goldfish may be as intelligent as a chimpanzee; and I have a suspicion that not many readers will follow me here in thinking that dogs (not to mention babies) may be no more conscious than clocks. There is, however, surely some virtue in arguing a position that, precisely because it challenges common sense, stimulates questioning of the basis of what seems intuitively obvious. Nothing would please me more than the discovery of arguments or findings (particularly findings) that show me wrong: and if I thought that the arguments made out here had contributed in however small a way to such discoveries, my posing of the questions would prove worth while.

Numerous friends and colleagues have helped me both through informal discussions and by commenting on chapters at various stages of development. Three members of the philosophy department here in York—Marie McGinn, Joseph Melia, and Tom Baldwin—read through all the sections concerned with philosophy and saved me from numerous inaccuracies (I am particularly indebted to Joseph Melia for his advice on the philosophy of mathematics); and Gordon Finlayson made useful comments on Kant. Derek Bickerton made helpful suggestions on the first draft of the early chapters, and Dorothy Hourston and Mark Ungless both read the entire first draft. Dorothy was recruited as a non-specialist reader, but showed a positively alarming degree of acuity in detecting flaws in arguments, as well as merciless exposure of infelicities in grammar or style. Mark, at that time a postgraduate student, obligingly took time out from his explorations of the intellect of garden snails, and the second draft was much improved by his and Dorothy's comments. That draft was read my Tony Dickinson and Celia Heyes, and I benefited considerably from their extensive comments in writing the final draft, which was read by John Pearce, Jennifer Hornsby, Nick Mackintosh, and Bernard Balleine. I am grateful to all of them for both general and specific guidance: the book is certainly clearer and contains fewer errors as a result of their considerable efforts. I should also like to thank Gavin Phillips and Simon Killcross for bringing their computer graphics expertise to bear in preparation of several of the figures; Simon also made helpful comments on some knotty problems in contemporary theories of instrumental conditioning. Sandie and Ann Lindsay found for me the marvellous cover picture by Victor Brauner, and I was fortunate to have had throughout the encouragement and advice of Michael Rodgers, my editor at the Press.

My wife Kate as ever continues to make my life—even when working on books—endlessly pleasurable (and has provided on her minifarm endless examples of intelligence and emotion for me to pore over). Finally, I would like to acknowledge here my debt to the sorely missed Séan Hudson, a fine photographer and good friend, who, through a long chain of chance events, was ultimately responsible for my becoming an experimental psychologist.

# Contents

# 1

## Body and soul

### An old question

Some things are conscious; some are not. Most of us believe that non-living things are not conscious and some living things are conscious. Not *all* living things: most of us do not believe that bacteria, mushrooms, or trees are conscious; we are certain that some animals[1] are conscious, but are not quite sure whether all animals are conscious. Living things are basically collections of cells of various kinds. Cells in turn consist of non-living, non-conscious components. How is it possible to assemble non-living and non-conscious components to produce conscious beings? What is it about the body of conscious beings that allows the emergence of the mind? These questions, in one form or another, have been at the centre of Western philosophy since its origins more than two thousand years ago.

The mind–body problem has traditionally been the province of philosophers who relied on logic and arguments rather than on observation and facts. Psychology began as an experimental discipline some hundred years ago, and the specific aim of the first experimental psychologists was the scientific study of consciousness. Those early psychologists studied human consciousness, but before the end of the century exploration of the animal mind had begun. A key motive for the original interest in animal psychology was the general acceptance of Darwin's theory of evolution by natural selection, which led to the realization that our human mental life must have evolved from some mental potential of our ancestors.

The aim of this book is to see whether light may be thrown on the problem of consciousness by facts unearthed by psychologists. Much of the emphasis on experimental work will be targeted on animal studies, in the hope of finding answers to such questions as 'Are any (or all) animals conscious?' and 'If so, at what stage in evolution did consciousness appear, and what novel function did it serve?'

## Two aspects of consciousness

It is reasonable to expect a definition of consciousness before trying to explain its existence. But consciousness is one of those ideas (like beauty or truth) which are happily used by us all, but which are surprisingly difficult to define. I believe that I mean by consciousness what most of us mean, and instead of making a forlorn attempt at a formal definition, will draw attention to two features of human consciousness.

### Self-consciousness

We human beings distinguish between ourselves and the rest of the world. In a general way, we regard ourselves as being everything contained by our skin. We know that anything that impacts on our bodies is likely to have an immediate effect on our experience, that our eyes have to look in a certain direction for events that occur in that direction to be registered visually, and that we can will our limbs to move in a direct way that is quite unlike moving some object distinct from our bodies. If some part is lost, say a finger is amputated, we know that that special direct communication is lost, and see the finger as now part of the rest of the world, no longer part of ourselves.

However, we know not only that we own a body with which we have a direct form of communication, but also that, in a similarly direct way, we have special knowledge of some of the processes that are going on within ourselves. We know that we know things; we know what we intend to do; we know our expectations, our hopes, and our fears. We know also that our access to what can loosely be called 'mental states' is privileged. Other people can observe as well as we can the positions of our limbs and our movements; but they cannot directly observe our mental states, and do not have the seemingly infallible knowledge of them that we do.

This 'cognitive' aspect of consciousness is known as self-consciousness; but it is, of course, not all that we mean by consciousness.

### Feeling-consciousness

Human beings feel things. We experience colours, smells, hot and cold, touches and tickles—the products of our sensory systems. We also experience internal states like anger, love, hunger—emotions and motivations. Some feelings are sought after; some avoided.

This second aspect of consciousness—what can be called 'feeling-consciousness'—is one that most of us believe is to be found in many (if not all) animals. We might doubt whether, for example, dogs know that they know things (or even whether they know anything), but nevertheless be confident that dogs do have feelings. So, a complete account of human consciousness would have to deal with both self-consciousness and feeling-consciousness.

It seems at least possible, however, that one of these aspects of consciousness could develop in some being even if the other aspect is absent. This brief foray into the definition of consciousness raises then an interesting question—'Is there a link between self-consciousness and feeling-consciousness, or do some creatures show one aspect but not the other?'

## Primacy of feeling-consciousness

Of the two aspects of consciousness just outlined, feeling-consciousness is much the more difficult to investigate but is, in fact, the more important and interesting—partly because the notion of self-consciousness is less concrete and immediate. Any one of several possible definitions of self-consciousness might seem acceptable: some organisms, for example, may have evolved so that they do discriminate between the external world and themselves (and so, to that extent, are self-conscious), but do not have either an idea of 'self' or a concept of an 'inner self' whose mental activity influences bodily actions. I shall at the end of this book opt for a definition of self-consciousness that *does* require the existence of a 'self-concept', but even that reasonably circumscribed notion is not so readily understandable as that of feeling-consciousness.

Animals either do or do not have feelings. We may think that some feeling animals feel less than we do, but we do not doubt that the world is divided into beings that feel and beings that do not feel. This is brought out most clearly when we think of pleasure and pain—the affective aspect of experience. An animal either feels pleasure and pain, or it does not.

This in turn has greater implications for the importance of decisions about consciousness, since ethical issues are closely associated with the existence of pleasure and pain, of states or experiences that matter to the organism in that it prefers some conditions to others. So, most of us believe that it is impossible to do wrong to a clock because it has no preference for one given state over another; we do not believe that clocks *prefer* being intact to being damaged (although, of course, we would think it was wrong if damage to the clock was likely to upset a human being). And the question of whether we think it possible to do wrong, for example, to a tree, or a frog, or a monkey, hangs on the belief of whether the organism is capable or not of feeling pleasure or pain. In other words, if an organism is not feeling-conscious then what happens to it does not matter to the organism (however much it may matter to some human beings).

Because of the immediacy of the feelings of pleasure and pain, and because their meaning is further clarified by their ethical relevance, I shall focus on them when discussing feeling-consciousness. But I should make clear that I include within feeling-consciousness all aspects of sensation— the ways in which we experience such things as colours, tones, tastes, and smells. Many of the difficulties encountered in trying to establish the existence of pleasure and pain apply equally when trying to establish the existence of any conscious sensation whatsoever. In effect, I shall assume that if we cannot convince ourselves that an organism experiences pleasure or pain, then we should assume that it has *no* experience—that it does not enjoy consciousness in *any* form. Such an organism may react to stimulation of various kinds, but there will be no implication that it *perceives* that stimulation as we might do—any more than, say, a video camera perceives the light that it transforms into a digitized stream of information. I shall, in other words, pursue the issue of pleasure and pain as a way of testing the existence of perceptual awareness in general.

So, I shall be concerned with consciousness in both its aspects, but will use as the acid test whether an account of consciousness is successful in explaining pleasure and pain. I shall pass by some of the problems that have exercised certain philosophers and assume, for example, that (adult) human beings are conscious (and not puzzle over the existence of other minds), that sticks and stones are not conscious, and that there is a world outside us of real objects—a world that corresponds pretty well to that which our senses paint for us. Finally, I shall assume that Darwin's theory of evolution by natural selection provides a valid account of the evolution of species, including the human species.

I should give clear warning, however, that there is one common-sense assumption that I shall *not* adopt—that is, the idea that at least some animals are conscious. Instead, I shall devote much attention—both here and in later chapters of the book—to the search for evidence that might allow us to decide that issue, one way or the other. It is, unfortunately, extremely difficult to find experimental support for any particular view of feeling-consciousness, and most of the work that I shall discuss will concern cognitive aspects of consciousness. That should not, however, obscure the fact that the long-term goal is to provide an account, based on evidence, of both aspects of consciousness.

## Feeling-consciousness in animals: the problem

If, as I surmise, most people believe that at least some animals do feel pleasure and pain, what is the point of pursuing the question as to whether they really do possess feeling-consciousness? If we are ready to consign to professional philosophers the debate about the existence or non-existence of consciousness in other humans (essentially on grounds of common sense), why not similarly abandon worrying about the equally common-sense notion that cats and dogs feel pleasure and pain?

The answer to this question is that the notion that animals do have feelings itself leads to notions that, from another point of view, equally clash with common sense (and this is the hallmark of all the eternal philosophical problems: common sense supports two mutually contradictory ideas). There are two likely basic arguments that most of us would use for believing in the feelings of animals, and I shall consider them with particular reference to what is probably the strongly held common-sense conviction—namely that animals (or some animals) feel pain.

The first argument is based on the 'feeling-like' behaviour seen in animals: their reactions to noxious events are similar to those of humans (and I use 'noxious' to refer to stimuli, such as blows or shocks, that would be painful if humans were subjected to them). It is because we humans feel pain that we react as we do, and so, presumably, animals that react in the same way must feel pain too. The second argument appeals to the function of pain: if animals did not feel pain, they would be poorly equipped to avoid potentially injurious stimulation. But neither of these arguments is quite as straightforward as might at first appear.

### The significance of feeling-like behaviour

There are both behavioural and physiological parallels between the human and the animal response to noxious events. If a needle is jabbed into the leg of either a human or a non-human mammal, likely responses are:

a)   vocalization—cries, squeals, and other utterances (that may or may not include words);

b)  'involuntary' responses such as increase in heart rate, dilation of the pupils, sweating;
c)  the rapid withdrawal of the limb.

And of course the human, if asked, will report the experience of pain. It is because of the overall parallel in the responses (excluding the verbal report) that we suppose that the animal too feels pain.

### Is vocalization necessary?

Must an animal show all of the non-verbal responses typical of our reactions to pain in order for us to ascribe pain to the animal? Presumably not. Vocalization, for example, does not seem a reasonable criterion for the experience of pain: whatever we may suppose about the existence of pain in fish, it surely is not a good argument to claim that a fish does not feel pain simply because it does not squeal, yelp, or make any other noise in response to noxious stimulation.

### Are the 'involuntary' responses necessary?

What of the 'involuntary' responses? In mammals, these responses are brought about by the activation of a specific part of the nervous system (the sympathetic division of the autonomic nervous system). This system uses adrenalin, and responses to pain and other stressful events are potentiated by the release of adrenalin into the bloodstream. Fish do not of course sweat, but a similar division of the nervous system is found in fish, and noxious stimulation does activate a response (for example, the heart rate changes). There is, on the other hand, no such system in invertebrates. Would we therefore deny pain to invertebrates simply because they have no clear parallel to the autonomic nervous system of vertebrates? Again, probably not, perhaps because it is obvious that these 'involuntary' responses are not in themselves sufficient for our experience of pain: the same responses occur, after all, in a number of situations (following energetic exercise for example) that do not involve pain.

### Is withdrawal necessary? Is it sufficient?

What of the rapid withdrawal of the limb? That, we might well think, *is* necessary to our ascription of pain. If an animal did not rapidly withdraw from a supposedly dangerous stimulus, then (unless the animal was paralysed in some way) we would generally not believe that the stimulus was causing pain. But that is not likely to be observed: animals (vertebrate and invertebrate) *do* show rapid withdrawal from dangerous stimuli.

If rapid withdrawal, or escape, from noxious stimulation is necessary for us to ascribe pain, is it sufficient? Do we suppose that *any* organism that shows efficient escape does feel pain? If we do, we have to conclude that virtually *all* animals—vertebrate and invertebrate—feel pain. That conclusion may seem to stretch the analogy argument rather far—for example, worms react vigorously to a needle, therefore they feel pain. The difficulty is admirably clarified by Julian Jaynes, the Princeton psychologist-turned-philosopher:

> Most people will identify with a struggling worm. But as every boy who has baited a fish hook knows, if a worm is cut in two, the front half with its primitive brain seems not to mind as much as the back half, which writhes in 'agony'. But surely if the worm felt pain as we do, surely it would be the part with the brain that would do the agonising. The agony of the tail end is our agony, not the worm's; its writhing is a mechanical release phenomenon, the motor nerves in the tail end firing in volleys at being disconnected from their normal inhibition by the cephalic ganglion.[2]

Unease with withdrawal as a criterion may be further increased when we reflect on the behaviour observed by the British physiologist Sir Charles Sherrington[3] (1857–1952) in spinal dogs (dogs whose spinal cords had been severed from their brains). He found that the same spontaneous withdrawal from a sharp object that is seen in an intact dog is seen in a spinal dog. And in case we are tempted to suggest that perhaps the spinal cord (which is, after all, an extremely complex component of the central nervous system) may in itself be sufficient for the experience of pain, it is worth reflecting that the same reaction is found in spinal humans—a human whose spinal cord has been severed also shows normal limb withdrawal reflexes to noxious stimuli of which the person is entirely unaware. Are we to suggest that the human's spinal cord *does* feel pain, although the person whose spinal cord it is feels nothing? Surely not: one mind per body is the most that we will accept.

One way of resolving the spinal cord problem might be to argue that a degree of complexity—necessitating the involvement of the brain—is necessary for feeling-consciousness. But how should we specify *what* degree of complexity is necessary? It seems pretty clear that such specification has to use a behavioural (and not an anatomical or physiological) criterion: it is surely entirely arbitrary to decide that feeling is only possible when either a certain number of nerve cells are active or when a certain number of interconnections exist in the brain. Perhaps we should then pursue the analogy argument by considering other, more complex, behavioural features of our human response to pain.

## Is learning a sufficient criterion?

One suggestion, which enjoyed support around the turn of the century, is that although the existence of reflex responses to stimuli is not sufficient to indicate mental life, the ability to *learn* about dangerous stimuli (so as, for example, to anticipate them on the occurrence of a signal) *is* sufficient to demonstrate conscious experience. But this proposal does not take us far: work over the last decade or so has shown that the spinal cord of both humans and animals is capable of learning in the absence of any contribution from the brain. In one study[4], the learning capacity of the spinal cord found a clinical application for a man with complete transection of his spinal cord. This patient could neither feel any sensation from the lower part of his body nor control any muscles there. To give him control of his bladder, a weak shock stimulus to the skin of his thigh was repeatedly given shortly before a strong shock to his lower abdomen. The strong shock (which would have been extremely painful to a human with an undamaged nervous system) caused his bladder to empty. In other words, the weak shock was a signal that the strong shock was imminent (just as Pavlov[5] used a bell for his dogs as a signal for food). After a number of pairings of the weak and the strong stimuli, presentation of the weak stimulus alone (a stimulus that the man could deliver himself by using movements of the upper half of his body) resulted in the emptying of his bladder (just as Pavlov's dogs salivated when the signal for food was heard). The 'learning criterion' of complexity does not therefore allow us to exclude consciousness from the spinal cord.

## Emotion as a criterion?

Another feature of our response to pain is that we don't simply learn to anticipate painful events but rather that that anticipation also gives rise to fear—a central emotional state that affects our responses to a whole range of stimuli, and not just those of which we have had training experience. As there seems no reason to suppose fear exists in the spinal cord, might evidence of such an emotional state provide a useful behavioural criterion of consciousness? We can explore this proposal by considering an unlikely candidate for emotional life—the slug. Since slugs are invertebrates, this will enable us incidentally to explore the suggestion that some structure found only in more 'advanced' brains (for example, the neocortex—a surface layer of the brain found only in mammals, which in humans is much convoluted and envelops the entire hemispheres) may be essential for consciousness.

Much attention has been focused in recent years on a sea-dwelling slug, *Aplysia californica*. One of the reasons for the interest in this animal is that there are in its central nervous system only about 20 000 nerve cells (in contrast to our ten billion human nerve cells). This animal is closely related to ordinary garden slugs, which it resembles both in general appearance and in nervous anatomy. Slugs do not appear to the casual observer to be particularly good candidates for feeling-consciousness, and we might suppose that we could rule out mental life in them on the grounds of simplicity of both nervous system and behaviour. Nevertheless, tests to reveal emotional experience have shown that slugs *do* exhibit the same kind of behaviour as vertebrates.

In one study[6], a solution of shrimp extract (a taste stimulus) was released into an *Aplysia's* tank a few seconds before the *Aplysia* received a strong electric shock to its head. The shrimp taste served, then, as a signal that a shock was imminent. Subsequent tests showed that defensive responses to weak noxious stimuli were strengthened in the presence of shrimp extract. For example, a weak shock to the tail resulted in the *Aplysia* 'inking': the minimum strength of tail shock needed to obtain inking was lower in the presence of shrimp extract (in the absence of previous training, shrimp extract did not affect the inking response). One explanation of this finding—the explanation that would be widely accepted for a similar outcome using a mammal—is that as a result of its pairing with shock, the *Aplysia* now reacts to the shrimp extract by showing fear, a central motivational state that potentiates *all* defensive responses. Striking support for this account comes from another observation—a reward-driven response (biting at a piece of seaweed) was inhibited in the presence of the shrimp extract. In vertebrates, stimuli that are supposed to induce fear both potentiate responses (such as withdrawal) to aversive stimuli and inhibit responses (such as approach) to rewarding stimuli. This account has an intuitive plausibility: we can well imagine being less enthusiastic about eating when fearful, and indeed it is difficult to imagine any *other* reason for the slowing-up of the biting response.

*Choice as a criterion for preference*

Another criterion for feeling-consciousness has been proposed recently by the Oxford zoologist Marianne Dawkins[7]. This criterion does not relate specifically to pleasure or pain, but to the somewhat more general issue of whether animals prefer some states to others. If we decide that they do have preferences, we could worry less about whether their experiences of pleasure and pain are the same as, or even similar to, ours. The fact that an organism prefers some states above others implies experience; no one supposes that clocks prefer one state to another but, if we did, then whether or not we believed that clocks feel pleasure or pain, we would be concluding that they did have a mental life—consciousness—of some kind.

How then are we to decide whether an organism prefers one state to another? The proposal is that we should allow an organism to *choose* between two conditions. If an animal consistently favours one set of conditions over another, then we should conclude that the animal does indeed prefer those conditions: an animal could not demonstrate a preference if there was in fact no preference.

A pertinent example of the impact of this criterion comes from work on the substrate that should be used with factory-farmed chickens. Some years ago, the Brambell Committee was set up in the United Kingdom to consider how conditions for farm animals might be improved. One of their recommendations was that the flooring of chicken cages should consist, not of a fine mesh of thin chicken wire, but of strands of thicker, more substantial wire. The rationale was that the thicker wire should feel more comfortable to the chickens' feet than the thinner wire. However sensible this humane proposal may have been, when experiments are carried out in which chickens can choose how long to spend in each of two environments—one with a fine mesh floor; one with thicker wire—they consistently spend more time on the thinner wire.

Experiments having a similar rationale have further explored animals' preferences by giving them choices between working or not working for some reward, or between a large reward that is accompanied by a noxious event and some other small reward. The consistent results of these experiments allow comparison of different rewards in terms of the 'costs' (that is, work or aversive events) that the animals will tolerate to obtain them.

The outcome of these experiments can surely be taken to show that if, for example, chickens *do* have a preference for one type of wire over the other, then their preferred wire is the thinner wire. But does the demonstration of consistent choice show genuine preference—a preference that implies mental life?

A problem with the choice criterion is that it is hard to conceive an animal that could learn—and successful learning has been shown in a huge range of invertebrates—but would not show choice. One interesting experiment on choice by an invertebrate species studied bumble bees[8]. Individual bees were allowed to explore a large arena in which there were 200 artificial cardboard 'flowers'—100 yellow, 100 blue. Each blue flower contained two drops of nectar which the bee could consume; two-thirds of the yellow flowers contained no nectar, but the other third contained six drops of nectar per flower. So, on average, the amount of nectar obtained would be the same whether the bee visited blue or yellow flowers. In fact, however, the bees visited far more blue flowers than yellow flowers (about 84 per cent of visits were to blue flowers). This preference for blue flowers was reversed when the conditions were changed so that the blue flowers were now 'risky' and every yellow flower contained the constant small amount of nectar.

This study is interesting because humans also show a preference for reliability of outcome—a phenomenon economists refer to as risk aversion. Bumble bees, then, can learn to select according to the rewards associated with different colours (and in this case showed a sensitivity to a rather sophisticated difference between rewards). Many other examples of consistent choice by invertebrates (including slugs and worms) are available, so that if we are to use choice as a criterion for genuine preference (and so, for mental life), we shall have to conclude that invertebrates are conscious. In effect, the choice criterion differs little from the learning criterion, and may in fact seem to paint with too broad a brush.

*Versatile adaptability*

A final behavioural criterion for consciousness has been suggested by Donald Griffin (who, as a research student at Harvard in 1938, demonstrated for the first time that bats emit ultrasonic sounds and use their echoes for navigation). The criterion is somewhat less specific than those already considered, but probably enjoys widespread informal support. It is, that consciousness should be inferred when an animal adapts its behaviour flexibly to 'changing circumstances and challenges'[9]. Griffin rules out the implication that such behaviour would inevitably involve learning; adaptable but instinctive behaviour could well, he suggests, reflect conscious thought. This is, therefore, a criterion that applies primarily to cognitive aspects of consciousness, but would in the eyes of many apply equally well to feeling-consciousness.

The very generality of this proposal makes it difficult to provide an overall assessment of it. Griffin offers a wide variety of examples of versatile behaviour, and, whilst it would be tedious to consider each in turn, one is examined in Chapter 5 (where in fact I shall reject the suggestion that consciousness should be inferred).

At this stage, it is worth making one general point. However much we may wonder at the ingenuity of some particular behavioural adaptation, it is difficult to see that we would understand it any better by supposing that it was accompanied by consciousness. If we want to conclude that an action necessarily implies a conscious agent, we should ask how consciousness has contributed to it—what function is consciousness playing and where does it enter the chain of causality? If we cannot see a clear and necessary role for consciousness, then we should not (or at least need not) infer its presence. When approached in that way, Griffin's proposal faces much the same difficulty of conceiving a function for pain and pleasure that I shall detail in the following section.

*Summary*

The various versions of arguments based on parallels between our reactions to pain and those of animals do, then, run into problems. There are some preparations, like the spinal cord, that show many features of the analogous behaviour, but to which we would definitely not ascribe consciousness; and there are animals, like slugs, that convincingly show analogous behaviour, but to which we may nevertheless have strong doubts about ascribing consciousness. Underlying all these problems is the equally common-sense knowledge that the criteria that we have looked at— the various types of behaviour that we show in response to pain—are accompaniments or consequences of pain; they do not constitute the pain itself. An actor could reproduce all these symptoms without feeling any pain at all, and that, in essence, is why none of these criteria is entirely convincing.

## The function of pain and pleasure

It seems obvious that the function of pain is to motivate us to avoid potentially dangerous stimuli. Similarly, the function of pleasure would seem to be to encourage activity that is good for us. So, we avoid sharp edges because cuts hurt, and we eat what we do because our preferred foods taste good and 'inedible' items do not. An organism that did not experience pain or pleasure would be less well-equipped to avoid dangerous things or to seek out beneficial things.

Built into this common-sense account of the functions of pain and pleasure is the equally common-sense idea that things that give pain *are* dangerous and things that give pleasure *are* beneficial. The fact that we can readily think of things that are painful but not dangerous and—even more readily—of things that are pleasant but not beneficial, should not worry us here; these are exceptions to the rule. We can surely agree that it makes good sense, and especially good evolutionary sense, to assume that pain and pleasure should have become 'attached' to dangerous and beneficial stimuli. So, a light touch on our skin does not trigger pain responses, but a sharp blow, or touching a hot surface, does. This presumably is because a light touch is in general not dangerous, whereas blows and burns are. If burns were not dangerous (in the sense of being likely to lead to serious tissue damage) then, presumably, they would not hurt. The nervous system would not have evolved so that burning sensations were painful—we would have experienced sensations associated with burning, but those sensations would not have been painful.

We can clarify the idea of the distinction between the neutral, 'informative' aspect of a sensation and its affective aspect by considering an experiment on pleasant sensations[10]. Human volunteers tasted a sucrose solution, and were asked to rate it on a five-point scale from very unpleasant, through neutral, to very pleasant. Immediately after this, they consumed a 'glucose load' (a fairly large drink of concentrated glucose solution). One hour later, the subjects again rated the sucrose solution. Initially, all the subjects rated the sucrose solution as 'pleasant' or as 'very pleasant'. But when it was rated for the second time, after the glucose load, the subjects rated it as much less pleasant—in most cases, as actually unpleasant or very unpleasant. This result strikes a bell—strawberries may taste delicious, but we can well imagine that after some bowlfuls, their pleasantness would be very much reduced, even though the *taste* (perfectly discriminable from that any other fruit) might remain the same. And *why* should sweet things taste less pleasant on a full stomach than on an empty one? Surely it is because there is a basic physiological need for carbohydrates when the stomach is empty. Foods taste pleasant when there is a need that their ingestion would satisfy; much less pleasant when there is no need.

It makes sense, therefore, that sensations that provide neutral information concerning what is 'out there' should be 'classified' according to their potential beneficial or harmful effects. Once classified in this way, their detection should automatically encourage behaviour that either promotes or avoids contact with the source of those sensations. In other words, potentially dangerous stimuli should, once detected, activate a pattern of behaviour that would terminate and avoid them; potentially beneficial stimuli should activate a system that should prolong and actively approach them. The same general pattern of activity is called for by *all* potentially dangerous stimuli—they should all be terminated and avoided; similarly, all beneficial stimuli should be sought after. So, all (potentially) dangerous stimuli result in the same affective response—pain; and all beneficial stimuli, in pleasure. Pain activates an action system that can be characterized as an 'avoidance' system; pleasure activates an 'approach' system.

The logic of this common-sense account runs, then, as follows. Sensations caused by the impact of external events are 'classified' by the nervous system as pleasant or painful (or as neutral). This classification is the consequence of natural evolutionary processes—so that, for example, animals that ignored cuts and burns, or did not prefer sweet tastes to less sweet tastes, tended to be less successful in rearing offspring. The experience of pleasure or pain activates the approach or the avoidance action system, and this contributes to the survival of the individual.

What is odd about this account is that there does not in fact seem to be any need for the experience of either pleasure or pain. The essence of the idea is that the nervous system discriminates between beneficial, dangerous, and neutral stimulation, and that the outcome of that classificatory process may activate either the approach or the avoidance system. Why should the organism experience pain before the avoidance system is activated? What *additional* function does the pain serve that could not be served more simply by a direct link between signals from the classificatory system and the action systems?

One popular idea is that the experience of pain confers an urgency on the sufferer to act; that it stimulates behaviour in a peculiarly effective way. Pain may result, for example, in a whole host of those 'involuntary' responses that so disrupt normal behaviour as to make it almost impossible to do anything except tackle the business of ending the pain. But, again, it is not clear that the experience of pain is necessary for these effects. What is required is that signals from the sensory classificatory system that indicate potential danger are accorded high priority, so that they take precedence over ongoing behaviour. Of course, the same must apply in relation to the response to pain—pain, that is, has to be a high-priority signal for it to be effective. And the avoidance system itself should activate the involuntary response system for the same reason that pain does. The involuntary system, by pumping out adrenalin, prepares the body for emergency behaviours (like fight or flight) that are likely to be required in response to dangerous stimuli.

*The evolution of pain*

The notion that pain may not be necessary for efficient escape from dangerous stimuli can be drawn in a different way if we concoct an 'armchair' evolutionary scenario.

It is now generally supposed that the basic building blocks required for self-sustaining life forms—amino acids and proteins—evolved by chance reactions in some primordial 'soup' of simpler molecules. These building blocks came together to form the first true organisms that could reproduce themselves (bacteria-like entities, bound within some limiting membrane).

These first organisms were, presumably, chemical machines, and most scientists are content to believe that standard chemical reactions are sufficient to account for their emergence. They find no need to suppose that any special form of energy—a life-force, for example—has to be invoked to explain the obvious difference between living and non-living matter. For present purposes, we can leave aside the issue of whether there may or may not be a critical factor missing in this 'standard model' of the evolution of life, provided that we can agree that these first organisms were not conscious. This is hardly controversial since there is general agreement that consciousness is to be found only in animals (and not in other living organisms such as bacteria, fungi, or plants).

Now consider the development of these chemical machines. As multicellular organisms evolved, there occurred a division of labour so that different types of cell specialized in different activities. So, all multicellular animals (except sponges) show distinctions between such types as nerve cells, muscle cells, and sensory cells. Sensory cells detect stimuli in the environment outside the confines of the animal's body. Activity in sensory cells promotes activity in nerve cells, and activity in nerve cells may result in activation of muscle cells—of movement of the animal's limbs and body. A sensory system is, then, linked to a motor system via a nervous system.

Now suppose that primitive, free-moving animals, living in the sea, encounter a region that is dangerous—an area of unusually warm water, or having a high concentration of a toxin. Since the sensory cells will have evolved so as to signal events of significance to the animal, we can assume that they will detect the change in temperature (or toxic chemical). Those animals that respond to the sensory signals by moving away from the area will be more likely to survive and produce offspring than those that do not. Eventually, the species will evolve so that every individual withdraws from dangerous stimulation of any kind, provided only that it is detected by their sensory apparatus.

This evolutionary sketch is, naturally, much oversimplified. It suggests, for example, that the detection of 'significant' events would precede the formation of links between the sensory system and the motor system. In fact, of course, those two systems and their interconnections would inevitably coevolve—there would be no advantage in having a sensory system that detected significant events if there was no link between it and the animal's behaviour. And the most primitive system for minimizing dangerous stimulation probably did not involve anything as sophisticated as direct withdrawal from the source but rather something as simple as increasing movement in general (in whatever direction). This technique ('orthokinesis') is in fact fairly effective: woodlice, for example, move more rapidly in dry than in damp surroundings, with the result that they collect together in damp regions[11]. Details are not, however, important here. The point is, that it is easy to envisage the rapid early evolution of links between sensory systems and motor systems that would result in withdrawal from disadvantageous areas and of similar systems for approach to advantageous areas. It is equally easy to see that this scenario has proceeded without any appeal to notions of pain or pleasure.

Taking the development of the animal another step forward, imagine it in an environment in which one colour—red, for example—was consistently associated with a rich food source. Animals that learned the association between 'red' and 'food', and approached red preferentially, would be at an advantage compared with animals that did not detect the association. It makes very good evolutionary sense that animals should develop a learning capacity so that they approach stimuli associated with beneficial events, and avoid those that signal dangerous events. Details of precisely what animals learn have been highly contentious (some rival accounts will be discussed in Chapter 4); but the point to be made here is simply that one can envisage the evolution of learning without invoking notions of pleasure and pain.

Similar armchair scenarios could obviously be developed for the evolution of motivational states, such as fear, that have widespread effects on behaviour, but they are perhaps not necessary. The point would remain the same—those scenarios would not require the introduction of feeling. The causal chain between noxious stimuli and appropriate behaviour would be longer and more complex, but it would remain a 'mechanical' chain, with no apparent function for feeling.

The evolutionary approach has this far, perhaps, merely recapitulated the function argument from a slightly different point of view: if the experience of pain serves no necessary function, it is difficult to see how it could have evolved. But thinking about the evolution of pleasure and pain forces us to look at other aspects of the problem.

Evolutionary considerations do not only allow us to conceive how efficient approach and avoidance *could have* evolved without the experience of pleasure or pain, but they lead to the strong supposition that something of the sort *must* in fact have happened. Surely at least some animals must have evolved in precisely that way (perhaps those, like slugs, to which many of us are unwilling to grant mental life). And if some animals evolved approach and avoidance systems that did *not* involve pleasure or pain, how could we possibly distinguish between them and other animals that *did* evolve feeling-consciousness?

It is not simply that evolutionary considerations provide no *need* for the evolution of those affective experiences; it is equally difficult to conceive *how* they could have evolved—even if a need could be established. We can readily understand, at least in principle, the gradual development of the sensory apparatus, the nerves, and the muscles, so that animals could efficiently approach and avoid good and bad stimuli. That development would reflect changes, coded in the genes, in the properties of the cells—changes that we could, in principle, detect if we examined the physiology of the cells and their connections with other cells. But what change could result in the experience of feelings like pleasure and pain? Suppose that we did see a virtue in the taste of a beneficial substance being pleasant, *how* could the collection of cells change to make that possible? In effect, what I am asking here is the old question in a new guise—how could consciousness emerge from a collection of nonconscious components?

## Language provides a criterion

Arguments about the function and evolution of pleasure and pain seem to point to the common-sense conclusion that pleasure and pain *could not* have evolved. But of course we humans evolved, and since I take the common-sense view that humans other than myself have conscious minds, and *do* experience those feelings, so I conclude that pleasure and pain *did* evolve. A reasonable objection which now emerges is—if it is so difficult to find an instance of animal behaviour that proves consciousness in non humans, why are we so sure of consciousness in humans (other than ourselves)? Why is it necessary to accept the existence of other human minds, but not the existence of animal minds?

The answer lies in what we humans do that confirms to each other that we share comparable mental experience—we *talk about* our intentions, our beliefs, our emotions, our feelings. It is because babies do not talk that we find such difficulty in deciding what it is like to be a baby—and even in deciding whether new-born babies feel anything (an issue that will be discussed in Chapter 6). There is no such difficulty with adults: we share our experiences through language, and one effect of this is that the question of whether minds other than our own exist is of little concern or interest to most of us. The absence of language means that the one clear window into other minds is closed for both animals and infants. We have to consider other sources of evidence in trying to establish the nature of their experience.

The relationship between language and consciousness will receive much attention in later chapters, and it is perhaps important to emphasize the obvious here—although language provides the most persuasive evidence of consciousness in other organisms, the fact that only humans talk is in itself no reason to suppose that only humans are conscious.

## Three questions

The contrast between the conclusion that feeling-consciousness *could not* have evolved and the fact that it *did* evolve suggests the three questions whose exploration will be central to the remainder of this book: first, when did feelings evolve? Second, how? Third, why?

### Evolution of theories of consciousness

A natural starting-point for any attempt to answer these questions is to consider the various solutions to the mind–body problem proposed by philosophers, to see whether any of their proposals provides a satisfactory account of the evolution of consciousness. Notions of consciousness, the mind, and the soul, have been current in the Western world for (at least) two and a half thousand years. Although many different accounts of consciousness have emerged, they can be seen as numerous variations on a relatively small number of basic ideas. I shall trace the introduction and early development of those ideas in Chapter 2, looking at the ways in which they might be used to answer questions about the evolution of consciousness. I shall argue that none of those theories succeeded in providing a universally acceptable account, and Chapter 3 will show how dissatisfaction with them led naturally on to the experimental investigation of how the mind actually works, in the hope that this might throw light on the problem of consciousness. Chapters 2 and 3 will, then, provide the historical background to the development of experimental psychology; few experimental findings will be introduced, and no recent research will be discussed.

Readers who are impatient to get to grips with empirical findings that have a bearing on the evolution of consciousness may prefer to skim through (or skip) those chapters and rejoin the argument in Chapter 4, in which behaviourism is discussed. Behaviourism provided, in the early years of this century, experimental psychology's first major contribution to theories of consciousness, and Chapter 4 will trace the development of the various schools of behaviourism, introducing more recent experimental and theoretical advances that have led to the widespread rejection of the behaviourist account of the mind.

## Evolution of consciousness

Chapters 5, 6, and 7 will explore a number of diverse topics, each of which has a bearing on the evolution of consciousness, and will concentrate on discussion of experimental work. Chapter 5 will consider potential differences in intelligence among animal species, and between animals and humans. Attention will focus on the role of associations in animal cognition, and on the acquisition of language by animals and humans. Chapter 6 begins by looking at the role of associations in human thought, and moves on to consider evidence for both unconscious cognition and unconscious perception in humans. It ends by tackling the question of when human infants become conscious—a question that is approached through a discussion of infantile amnesia.

The claim that at least some animals possess a 'theory of mind', and so are self-conscious, will be assessed in the first part of Chapter 7; the second part of the chapter concerns feeling-consciousness and asks whether parallels between the physiology of mammalian sensory systems should lead to the conclusion that non-human mammals must experience pain and pleasure in the same way that humans do.

Although the experimental material discussed in Chapters 5, 6, and 7 is, I believe, relevant to all theories of consciousness, it cannot be claimed that it gives unequivocal support to any particular account: Chapter 8 returns to the mind–body problem, now seen in the light of the facts garnered in the preceding chapters. This final chapter begins with a critical survey of contemporary philosophical approaches to the mind–body problem and argues the virtues of a 'functionalist approach'. The book ends by sketching out a specific functionalist theory of consciousness based on the experimental findings introduced in Chapters 5, 6, and 7.

As a preliminary to embarking on the search for an understanding of consciousness, two further related issues should be briefly introduced. First, is consciousness necessarily confined to living organisms (as opposed to man-made machines)? Second, what criteria can be used in weighing the strength of one theory as compared to another—what would it be to have a satisfactory account of consciousness?

## Minds and machines

A major focus of this book will be upon experimental studies of what we might call the mental skills, or cognitive capacities, of humans and animals. Those studies will be explored to see whether there appear to be significant contrasts between their thought processes. Another preoccupation of psychologists, particularly evident in the computer age, is whether human thought processes could be reproduced by machines, specifically, by computers.

The simulation of thought is an issue of central importance to the nature of consciousness—as we can readily see if we review some of the potential behavioural criteria discussed in the context of the question of whether animals feel pain. We could easily construct a machine that uttered some noise—'ouch', for example—in response to a violent blow. No one (at least no sensible person) would suppose, however, that the machine now felt pain. Similarly, we could construct a machine that would withdraw a 'limb', that learned, that made choices, and so on. We would not suppose in any of these cases that the resultant behaviour was sufficient to guarantee feeling in the machine (we would in fact suppose quite the opposite). Considerations such as these may help to clarify what it is that we need to solve the riddle of consciousness.

Suppose that we succeed in producing a computer whose performance of some 'mental' process—playing chess, for example—could not be distinguished from that of a human, and suppose that there were no solid reasons why human performance should not be qualitatively identical (that there were not, for example, too many calculations carried out in too short a time)—then we would surely have to conclude that the computer performed in the same way as a human. The program that underlay that activity would provide a full explanation of that human cognitive process, and we would *know* how non-conscious components could be assembled to produce that activity.

In order to program a computer successfully to reproduce some aspect of human performance we would, of course, have to understand how humans themselves achieve that performance; conversely, if we did understand correctly the nature of some mental activity, then we should, at least in principle, be able to show how a program to reproduce that activity could be constructed. (Some psychologists believe that a full explanation of any human cognitive process would consist precisely in producing a program that would obtain human-like performance.)

Nothing of the sort has, of course, yet been achieved. Computers can play chess well enough to beat almost all humans—but we know that good computer performance is *not* achieved in the same way that humans achieve good performance. Similarly, computers have been programmed to allow them to carry out fairly simple 'conversations' with humans; but no computer can yet conduct a sensible conversation on unpredictable topics, as any human can readily do. The fact is that we do not yet fully comprehend how humans play chess or learn language, and this is reflected in our inability to write programs that successfully simulate human performance or to understand why we cannot do so.

These considerations apply equally to feeling as to cognition: just as if we understood thought we could build a machine that thinks, so if we understood feeling we should either be able to build a machine that feels or understand why we cannot build such a machine. This notion, then, gives us a way of deciding whether or not to accept accounts of human mental processes, involving both cognition and feeling.

## Criteria for a successful account of consciousness

No theory of consciousness has yet been successful in the sense of obtaining universal acceptance. Since it is more than likely that the theory to be sketched out at the end of this book will be no more successful using that criterion, I should make explicit two criteria that I shall use in attempting to decide whether a theory succeeds or not.

There are, of course, general criteria, such as comprehensibility and plausibility, that are presumably adopted by everyone that assesses any theory. But the following two criteria are specific to the problem of consciousness. The first is, that the account must provide a method of deciding which living organisms enjoy consciousness, and which do not. More specifically, it must allow us to decide whether a given organism feels pleasure and pain. If a theory fulfils this criterion, it will effectively be able to answer the question '*when* did consciousness evolve?' The second criterion concerns inanimate objects—a successful account must either show (at least in principle) how to make a machine conscious (in particular, to be capable of feeling) or show why it is impossible to do so. Any theory that satisfies this criterion will be able to answer the question '*how* did consciousness evolve?' And any theory that successfully fulfils these two criteria will surely succeed in answering our third question '*why* did consciousness evolve?'

## Notes and references

1. I shall throughout the book use the word 'animals' to refer to non-human animals only; this is for convenience, and should not be taken to encourage the supposition either that humans are not animals (of course we are) or even that humans are a special type of animal (except that all my readers will be human).
2. Jaynes (1993), p. 6. Julian Jaynes' book, *The origin of consciousness in the breakdown of the bicameral mind* (originally published in the USA in 1977 by Houghton Mifflin), by far the most entertaining book yet published on consciousness, also gives an account of various criteria for the demonstration of consciousness in animals.
3. Sherrington (1906). Sherrington used his analysis of reflexes in spinal animals to deduce principles of organization of the central nervous system. He introduced the term 'synapse' for the region at which one nerve cell makes functional contact with another.
4. Ince, Brucker, and Alba (1978).
5. See Chapter 4 for a discussion of Pavlov's conditioning procedure.
6. Walters, Carew, and Kandel (1981).
7. Dawkins (1993).
8. Real (1991).
9. Griffin (1984), p. 37.
10. Cabanac and Duclaux (1970).
11. A detailed account of the use by animals of kineses can be found in Fraenkel and Gunn (1940).

# 2

## Concepts of mind

### Philosophies of mind

Notions of how the mind works—of the nature of consciousness—have evolved over some two and a half thousand years. Until the emergence of experimental psychology, these notions were developed by philosophers. Once psychology was established as an academic pursuit, there began an interplay and an exchange of ideas between philosophers and psychologists. Many of the concepts with which psychologists work have their origins in the writings of the early philosophers, and in this chapter I trace the evolution of major themes in the philosophy of the mind before scientific psychology began. Although I shall concentrate on accounts of the nature of the mind, we can best make sense of those accounts when given at least a sketch of their philosophical background. Therefore, I include sufficient information about the general philosophical position of each philosopher to make his account of the mind comprehensible.

### Concepts of the mind in the ancient world

One theory of the nature of the mind has dominated European thinking for two thousand years and more—it is that the mind or the soul[1] (the seat of what we now call consciousness) is formed from a substance different from that which forms material bodies, living or non-living. There are, then, two quite different types of entity—material things and non-material things. This basic notion, conventionally known as dualism, has taken many forms, and was first clearly articulated by Greek philosophers (Socrates and Plato in particular) in the fifth and fourth centuries BC.

The alternative to dualism is sometimes known as monism—the idea that all existing things are formed from one basic 'stuff'. Monism can take two forms: the single real substance is either something ethereal like 'spirit' or 'mind' (panpsychism or idealism), or it is matter (materialism or physicalism). The English-speaking world has had little time for versions of the 'ethereal' view, and I will follow that tradition in giving it short shrift—as I stated in Chapter 1, I shall take the common-sense view that there are, as our senses suggest, real objects out there. So, the only alternative to dualism that will receive serious consideration here is materialism, which holds that ordinary matter, composed of the same elements that go to make ordinary material objects, can take on forms that are capable of consciousness. This idea also found expression in early Greek philosophy.

## Plato's dualism

Plato's account of the soul provides a good starting point for this brief history of the development of concepts of the mind, partly because until the teaching of Socrates (Plato's teacher) the Greeks had entertained relatively simple notions of the soul. The Greek word for soul—psyche (ψυχη)—also meant breath, and this reflected their notion (now regarded as somewhat primitive) that living beings differed from non-living beings through being infused with a life force, equated with breath. Non-living things became alive when this force was breathed into them, and died when breath left them. This view attached much importance to living bodies, but little to the soul itself; when the psyche left the body on death, its subsequent existence was of no interest to the early Greeks.

Socrates proclaimed the supreme importance of man's immortal soul, and is reported to have mocked the prevalent view on the day of his enforced suicide (in 399 BC) by suggesting that it would be unwise to die on a windy day in case one's soul, departing the body, should be dispersed all over the place. Socrates left no published work, and our knowledge of his philosophy derives almost entirely from Plato's writings, which took the form of dialogues. Plato was born in 427 BC, and spent most of his long life in Athens, where he founded his school, the Academy, and where he died at 80 years of age. His early dialogues reflect Socrates' views, and the later dialogues, his own maturing views[2].

### The world of ideal forms

Plato's views on the nature of the soul are inextricably tied up with his theory of knowledge—of *true* knowledge that is. As is widely known,

Plato believed in the existence of two worlds—a world of ideal forms, and the earthly world that we inhabit. He lived at a time when Athens had recently suffered a catastrophic defeat in her long war against Sparta, one consequence of which had been scepticism that democracy provided a good system of government (a scepticism compounded by the fact that it was the Athenian democracy that had sentenced Socrates to death). This led to deep concern with the ways in which states—and Athens in particular—*should* be run, and with what was good and what was bad. This was a question, Plato believed, that could be answered by careful thought alone—thought that should be focused on clarifying the true nature of the good.

In the world of our ordinary experience, it is inevitable that no two material bodies—no two logs, for example—could be absolutely equal; nevertheless, we do have a very clear idea of the concept of equality. Since we do not experience equality in the material world, what does it refer to, and how could we acquire the concept? Plato's answer was that there are two worlds—the material world that we know through our senses, and the world of ideal forms, of which things in the material world form poor reflections. The ideal forms include both ethereal things such as goodness, equality, and justice, and more tangible things such as stones, trees, and dogs. Knowledge of the true nature of something in the material world means an understanding of the ideal form reflected in that thing. So, what all dogs have in common—and what makes them dogs—is that each reflects the ideal form of the dog: no one dog is a perfect dog, but by contemplation about dogs, it should be possible to fully comprehend its ideal form and to know the true essence of what it would be to be a perfectly realized dog.

*Innate knowledge*

With the exception of mathematicians (many of whom believe in the independent existence of such mathematical entities as numbers) few people now suppose that Plato's world of ideal forms exists. But one aspect of the theory of forms did enjoy a long and influential history. For Plato's belief in the power of thought (as opposed to observation) was based on his notion that we have innate knowledge of the ideal forms—a knowledge that is obscured following birth by our exposure to the material world. By thinking about goodness, we can stimulate reminiscence, and so recall and perceive clearly again the ideal form of goodness. We would then know without possibility of error what should be done. This then was Plato's solution to the question of how knowledge of ideal forms could be acquired in a world in which no examples exist.

The notion that we possess innate knowledge that is obscured following birth carries with it the implication that the possessor of the knowledge existed before birth—that, in other words, the soul exists prior to its association with a body. The soul can, therefore, be separated from the body and enjoy an independent existence. In this, it resembles the ideal forms; it also resembles them, according to Plato, in being immortal. But whether the soul is to be regarded as a form itself is not clear. We need not discuss Plato's arguments for the immortality of the soul here—they are frankly unconvincing and played little part in the subsequent history of ideas of the mind. Although he is not consistent about what sort of entity or substance the soul is, he is clear that it is not a material thing—that it is quite different from any of the material bodies that we encounter in this world. The non-material soul acts as an intermediary between the world of ideas and the material world; the soul has access to the material world through the senses, and an innate knowledge of the ideal world that is imperfect only because of the corrupting influence of the material world.

The soul that I have discussed thus far is exclusively the human soul, but we have seen that the Greeks believed that all living beings possessed psyche. Do non-human animals then possess immortal souls? To answer this question, we need to consider one final aspect of Plato's theory of the soul—his belief that the soul consisted of three parts. The 'lowest' of these parts is the 'appetitive' part, and the second, the 'courageous' or 'spirited' part. These parts are found in both animals and humans (and since Plato refers in places to the psyche as the 'life principle' it is a reasonable assumption that the first, appetitive part—or something very like it—is found in plants). The third, 'highest' part of the soul is the 'rational' part, found only in humans. None of the three parts of the soul is made from any material substance, but only the rational part of the soul is immortal and has access to the world of ideal forms. Thus non-human living organisms have parts of the soul in common with humans, but they do not have an immortal soul, and are inferior forms of life.

Plato defends the notion that the soul has distinct parts by arguing that if the soul was unitary, then we could hardly experience conflicts between desire and reason—between, for example, a desire to pursue one course of action and the knowledge that some other course ought to be chosen. And, of course, the notion that there are distinct parts to the soul, only one of which is immortal, makes sense of the argument that although humans obviously do have much in common with other living beings, human souls alone are rational and immortal.

*Plato's legacy*

The most influential of Plato's ideas concerning the soul—ideas that have played a large part in the development of current theories about consciousness—are first, that the human rational soul is not formed of any material substance and is immortal; and second, that although non-human animals possess a type of (non-material) soul, they are not rational creatures, and their souls do not survive their deaths. Two other ideas that concern the nature of knowledge will also recur in our discussions of later philosophers: first, that at least some human knowledge is innate; and second, that knowledge of the world can be gained simply by the use of reason. Plato sometimes wrote as though he believed that the material world could in some sense be reduced to numbers, and that all true knowledge could be derived by logical deduction from a set of axioms. This view lies at the core of thought of those philosophers known as rationalists. The major opposing view is the empiricist position that knowledge can be acquired only through the senses—a position that was adopted by Plato's student, Aristotle.

## Presocratic materialism

Materialist accounts of mental life were advanced by early presocratic Greek philosophers, and, in particular, by the 'atomists' Leucippus and his student Democritus[3]. Virtually nothing written by these philosophers survives, and we know their work only through accounts of it by other philosophers, such as Aristotle. Little is known either of their lives, although we do know that Democritus was born in about 460 BC.

The atomists argued that the universe consists of an infinite number of atoms—the ultimate units of matter—and the void in which the atoms exist. Individual atoms are indivisible, impenetrable, and all formed from the same basic 'stuff'. Atoms vary only in shape and size, and all objects and organisms consist solely of 'aggregates' of atoms of various shapes and sizes.

How did the atomists suppose that life could arise in certain aggregates of atoms of matter? Their answer has little appeal for us today—it was, that the 'soul' consists of small, round atoms, well-suited for inducing things to move by their own motion. These 'soul' atoms alternated with 'body' atoms (larger and less regularly shaped) in living organisms, with a concentration of 'soul' atoms in that part of the body where thinking takes place (and it is not entirely clear whether the atomists believed that the thinking mind was in the head or in the heart). The death of an organism resulted in the eventual dispersal of the 'soul' atoms, so that there was no possibility of the persistence after death of any individual's soul. However much sympathy we may now have for the atomists' account of the nature of the universe, we do not find anything of value in their theory of the nature of the mind: the idea that a particular kind of atom subserves consciousness gives us no insight into the mind–body problem. For a lasting contribution to a materialist account of the mind, we have to turn to the very much more sophisticated position adopted by Aristotle.

## Aristotle: substance and form

Aristotle was born in Thrace in 384 BC and came to Athens in 367 BC, where he was a member of Plato's Academy for some twenty years, until Plato's death. Aristotle then left Athens, went on to become the tutor to Philip of Macedonia's son (the future Alexander the Great), and returned to Athens to found his own school, the Lyceum, in 335 BC. He died in 322 BC. To understand his notions about the mind we must, as with Plato, begin by looking at his theory of knowledge[4].

### Perception as the source of knowledge

Aristotle shared with Plato the conviction that true knowledge must be eternal, and that it must therefore involve entities that are, unlike material bodies, unchanging. Unlike Plato, however, he believed that perception is the only source of knowledge. To take an example, through perception of horses, the human mind could come to a knowledge of what was universally true of horses—to an understanding of the unchanging essence of 'horsiness'. These unchanging essences, or universals, are clearly similar to Plato's ideal forms with, however, the critical difference that, according to Aristotle, they do not enjoy an existence independent of the instances in which they are manifested. Numbers, for example, do not exist apart from their manifestation in groups of, say, three things, seven things, and so on.

For Aristotle, the basic data that we have are those of the senses, generated by material objects—a natural position for him to take as a scientist, with a particular interest in living things. His general goal was to study organisms so as to understand their essence, in the belief that once the essence was grasped, the other properties of the organism would be explained (could, in fact, be logically deduced). What, then, is the essence of an organism? This is tantamount to questions like 'what is it to be a frog, or a pig, or a man?'; 'if material bodies (including living beings) are manifestations of eternal universals, how is it that *change* occurs?'; and 'what happens when a plant is eaten and becomes part of an animal?'

## Composite nature of material things

Aristotle's answer is that there are in the universe unchanging basic 'stuffs'—the 'matter' of material bodies on earth, and the near-divine 'quintessential' stuff of which the ether and the heavenly bodies (the planets—including the sun and the moon—and the stars) are made. Earthly matter consists of mixtures of four elements—fire, water, earth, and air (and Aristotle refers to the quintessential stuff as the fifth element). But unchanging matter always goes to make up a particular substance, and substances come and go. A substance is basically a particular object, or an individual organism, and every substance is composite in the sense that it possesses two aspects—the *matter* of which it consists, and the *form* that infuses the matter and determines what sort of thing the substance is. So, when a sculpture is hewn from a rock, the matter is not changed, but is now a sculpture— its essence, or form, is that of a sculpture. Similarly, when the matter of a plant is incorporated into an animal's tissues, the plant ceases to exist, and its matter now belongs to a substance whose matter, but not whose essence, is now somewhat different.

## Soul as the substantial form of the body

Aristotle's notion of quasi-composite substance is relevant here because of the way in which he describes the mind. Like Plato, Aristotle supposed that all living beings possessed a psyche, but unlike Plato, he did not believe that the psyche could exist independent of the body. He argued that the psyche (the soul) is the 'substantial form' of the body; the soul is not the same as the body—it is after all what differentiates a live body from a dead body—but it cannot be separated from a body any more than the wax impression of a seal can be separated from the wax itself. The type of soul that an organism has will determine what sort of living being it is. What types of soul then are there?

A crucial element in Aristotle's scheme was his notion that one major aspect of determining a thing's essence consisted in establishing its purpose, or final cause. For example, an embryo of a chicken is infused with the essence of chicken and its *purpose* is to change into a fully grown chicken— another realization (albeit imperfect) of the 'universal chicken'. Aristotle argues that the soul is to the body as sight is to the eye: if a functional disembodied eye could exist, its soul would be sight. So, in asking what types of soul exist, we are also asking, 'what are the purposes of the various types of souls of living beings?'

The first (and lowest) type of soul is the nutritive type found in plants: plants simply strive to maintain themselves in order to propagate and produce other individuals of their species. The second type possesses both the nutritive power and, in addition, perception and appetition, and this is the kind of soul found in animals. The third type of soul encompasses the powers of the preceding two, plus thought and reason. This highest type of soul is peculiar to humans. The different powers possessed by organisms are effected by organs, each of whose specific purpose is to manifest that power (for example, sight is a power mediated by the eyes, the organ of sight). This is, therefore, a purely physiological account of living activity and very different from Plato's dualist view.

There are clear parallels between this classification of souls and Plato's classification of the parts of souls. One minor difference is that Aristotle supposes that there are different types of souls rather than different parts of a composite soul. The major difference of course is that Aristotle believes that souls are in no sense separable from the body; they are not composed of a different 'stuff'.

### Immortality of the active intellect

Unfortunately, Aristotle's account has now to be muddied somewhat by remarks of his that suggest, first, that there may be different parts of the soul and, second, that one part of the human soul may be capable of an independent existence. For he does not suppose that there is a material organ that has the power of rational thought: thought is divine, and is the only human faculty that arises from a non-material source. Aristotle refers, almost in passing, to a distinction between a passive and an active intellect, suggesting that the latter alone is eternal, divine, and not based in matter. It seems that Aristotle agrees with Plato in seeing rationality as something peculiarly human, in virtue of which we do indeed have a separable, immortal soul.

Where humans are concerned, Aristotle then was a dualist too. But we may best see this as the end-product of his view that there is a *scala naturae* —a ladder of created entities—that rises in an unbroken chain from inert material objects, through plants, to animals having increasingly complex essences, and finally to humans, who form the apex of earthly beings. This view led him to believe that plants have been created to serve animals, and animals, to serve man. His conclusion that the rational part of the human is immortal may, similarly, have reflected his need to achieve a predetermined theological outcome—a link between humanity and a divine being—despite its violation of his general insistence that body and soul are inseparable.

For our purposes, a critical feature of Aristotle's theory of the mind is that he accepted a materialist account of feeling. His composite notion of substance allows for pleasure and pain experienced by both animals and humans as a function of their bodily organs—of matter formed of the same elements as non-living bodies. For Aristotle, the soul is in effect the sum total of the capacities of the organs that embody an organism's faculties, and what we call consciousness reflects the activity of those organs.

## Aristotle and materialism

In rejecting Plato's dualism—at least as applied to plants and animals— Aristotle adopted a position that finds echoes in some modern materialist accounts of consciousness[5]. But, unsurprisingly, some of his thoughts are now universally rejected. His theory of transmission of souls from one generation to the next should be noted here, since it rules out the possibility that a machine could be constructed that had a 'soul' of any kind. Souls belonged to individuals of species whose essences were eternal, and those souls could be transmitted only by parents to offspring (the father contributing the form, and the mother, the matter, of the embryo). A particular type of soul could be infused only into a body that has within it the potential for that soul, and you could no more create a machine with a soul than the mating of two foxes could produce a fox with the soul of a frog.

The idea that the 'essences' of all species were fixed at the moment of their creation is incompatible with the facts of evolution, and was widely rejected even before Darwin proposed his theory of evolution by natural selection. But we may, of course, reject fixed essences without necessarily rejecting the idea that the mind is somehow a reflection of the activity of bodily organs. We should, however, also note the incompleteness of this theory as an account of what we currently mean by consciousness (a concept that is probably relatively recent: in ancient Greece, the crucial distinction was between the living and the non-living). It is not clear whether the activity of *all* types of soul constitutes consciousness (for example, are plants conscious?). Nor is it clear how the activities of those organs that serve the animal soul—the eye, for example—should necessarily give rise to consciousness. Are all of the organs of a given animal necessary for consciousness, and, if not, which are sufficient? This latter question reminds us that Aristotle did single out one faculty—the active intellect—as unique, and that faculty, responsible for rational thought, was not served by a material organ.

## The next two thousand years

The popularity of Plato and Aristotle fluctuated over the centuries following their deaths; Aristotle in particular suffered neglect because his most important work was lost for some three hundred years, resurfacing in Rome in the first century BC. The most influential event for Western thought was, of course, the widespread adoption of the Jewish concept of a personal God, coupled with Christian beliefs. Philosophers were replaced by theologians, who nevertheless showed a wide reliance on ideas derived from the Greeks, modifying them to conform with Christianity. Early Christian theologians tended to be Platonists, partly because much of Aristotle's work had again become generally unavailable. St Augustine (354–430), for example, bishop of the city of Hippo on the North African coast, adopted Plato's theory of ideal forms. But the 'great African doctor' replaced Plato's notion of recollection of innately known forms with the idea that the forms existed in the mind of God, and could be accessed by humans only through a God-given process of illumination; thus the soul need not (as in Plato's system) exist before an individual is conceived, but could be created (by God) at the moment of conception.

When Aristotle's work was reintroduced to Western Europe in the twelfth century, he rapidly became the dominant influence, and was widely known as 'The Philosopher'; thus St Thomas Aquinas (1225–74), the Italian Dominican friar who is still the most influential theologian of the Catholic church, attacked Platonic ideas then widespread among Christian theologians. He adopted Aristotle's notions that the soul is the substantial form of the body, and that only the human active intellect is separable from the body. Aquinas also followed Aristotle in according low status to animals: animals were, in his view, incapable of reason, and were created by God specifically for the benefit and use of humans.

Thus for two thousand years there remained general agreement on several important issues: first, that all living organisms, plants, animals, and humans possessed souls; second, that only humans were rational; third, that the rational element of the human soul was composed of a substance very different from that which formed material bodies; and fourth, that the rational element was immortal. Some agreed with Plato that the souls of non-humans were also composed of a non-material substance that was somehow compounded with matter to form living organisms; others— and this was the dominant view from the thirteenth century onwards— held with Aristotle that non-rational souls could not be separated (except conceptually) from their material organisms, and were formed from a material substance. We should remember, however, that the qualitative difference between living beings and non-living objects was maintained: it was supposed that it was impossible in principle to create a living being—a creature with a soul—from non-living parts. The first major challenge to this consensus came in the seventeenth century from René Descartes.

## Two versions of dualism

### Descartes: interactive dualism

Descartes was the first great modern philosopher. His writing provides a model of stylistic clarity, and has a personal immediacy—partly the result of some of his major work being in the first person—that catches the reader's attention. He was born in France in 1596, and educated at a Jesuit school, La Flèche, where the work of Aristotle and Aquinas formed the greater part of the syllabus. Although he remained a devout catholic throughout his life, he acquired at La Flèche a deep distaste for the arguments used by medieval scholastics and, in particular, for their appeals to the infallible authority of Aristotle. After spending some time as a soldier, and a few years as a socialite, Descartes worked on his philosophy in Holland, leading a reclusive life enlivened by voluminous philosophical correspondence. In September 1649 he reluctantly agreed to visit Queen Christina in Sweden. She insisted on discussing philosophy with him at 5 a.m. and, not surprisingly, he contracted pneumonia and died in February 1650.

Cogito, ergo sum

Descartes is best known for his '*cogito, ergo sum*' argument[6]—the end result of his decision to doubt everything of which he could not be certain. Thus, he could not rely upon the evidence of his senses—he might be dreaming—and could not assume, therefore, the existence of a material world. He doubted also whether such mathematical statements as $2 + 3 = 5$ could be safely relied upon—we do after all make mistakes, and some evil genius might perhaps have induced us to perceive as necessarily true, statements that are in fact false. But of one truth he could be sure: he thought, therefore he must exist. This particular argument carries an intuitive conviction, even though most commentators agree that it has no logical force. For example, the statement 'I think' cannot be true of a real person unless the 'I' exists—so we cannot conclude from 'I think' that

'I exist' because the truth of the former assumes the consequence that is supposedly deduced.

Whatever the technical value of the argument, Descartes goes on to ask why he is persuaded that there can be no doubt of its validity. He concludes that the conviction of the '*cogito*' argument derives from the fact that he clearly and distinctly perceives its truth: he therefore adopts as a general rule that whatever he clearly and distinctly perceives is true. But by 'perceive' he does not mean use of the senses; he remains sceptical of the value of sensory perception. What he means is rather that the truth of the statement is guaranteed by the fact that its contradiction is impossible. It is simply logically absurd to suppose that an organism currently thinking 'I think' does not exist, and that is the sense in which he clearly and distinctly perceives that he must exist.

## The existence of God

Having established that a being who thinks 'I think' must necessarily exist, Descartes uses two arguments to explain how the existence of God cannot be doubted. The first argument—which nowadays seems particularly unconvincing—begins from the observation that he, Descartes, is doubting. Since knowledge is more perfect than doubt, it follows that his being is not wholly perfect—but does, however, have an idea of a being more perfect than himself. What could the origin of that idea be? Descartes argues that this idea must come from some nature that is in reality more perfect. The same general argument holds for all the notions of perfection that he holds, and he goes on to conclude that there must indeed exist a being that possesses all these perfections—God.

His second argument attempts to demonstrate the self-contradictory nature of denying God's existence. He argues that just as the idea of a triangle includes the equality of its three angles to two right angles, so his idea of a perfect being includes the existence of the being. This argument is a version of the 'ontological' argument which was first introduced by St Anselm (1033–1109; Archbishop of Canterbury from 1093 until his death) and widely accepted by medieval theologians. It assumes that the essential nature of God is that He manifests all perfections (and this, we might agree, is true by definition); and a being that did not exist would be less perfect than one that did—therefore, God must exist.

Although these arguments are now universally rejected (Kant achieved the final demolition of all the supposedly logical 'proofs' of the existence of God[7]) their importance here is simply that Descartes took the existence of God as proved, using it in further arguments, one of which gives his reasoning a distinctly circular appearance—for he argued that it was precisely the existence of God that guaranteed his general principle that whatever is clearly and distinctly perceived is true.

## The material world

Another of Descartes' arguments concerns the existence of the external, material world. Although he did not wholly trust the evidence of his senses, Descartes argues that the external world must truly exist because God would not have deceived us into conceiving its existence unless there really was such a world. But what is the nature of the external world? Because of his distrust of the senses, Descartes maintains that all we know is that matter occupies regions of space (that is, has extension), and that motion occurs. Other apparent properties of matter, such as its temperature and colour, are imposed by our senses and do not necessarily reflect the *real* qualities of matter.

Descartes rejects the Aristotelian scheme of elements (earth, water, fire, and air), and supposes that matter is some infinitely divisible substance, all of whose activity can be accounted for in terms of extension and motion. In doing so, he also rejects the Aristotelian notion that the properties of different substances are to be accounted for in terms of their essences—the notorious claim, for example, that the sleep-inducing effect of opium could be 'explained' by supposing that opium possesses (as part of its essence) the '*virtus dormitiva*'. Rejection of the notion that there are qualitative differences between classes of things each defined by its 'essence' was in fact formal recognition of the growing success of scientists in formulating laws that clearly applied to all material objects, irrespective of their 'essences'. Descartes was encouraged by these scientific advances to believe that laws governing the physical world could eventually be deduced, like the truths of mathematics, from self-evident first principles. He recommended, accordingly, that scientific investigation should reduce complex questions to increasingly simple components, until self-evident principles—adequate to answer the question—emerged. He adopted, then, a rationalist theory of knowledge.

## Innate ideas

Descartes also relies upon the existence of God for his account of innate ideas. He asks how he could have derived his notion of God as a wholly perfect being—surely not from the very imperfect evidence of his senses? Using this argument, he concludes that the idea of God must be innate (and, as we have seen, uses the existence of the idea as another proof of

God's existence). Descartes also agrees with Plato that the concepts that form the basis of mathematics are innate. Finally, because of his notion that matter is not 'really' coloured, Descartes was led to conclude that even our basic sensory ideas—such as redness, heat, and so on—are innate. The source of these ideas, including the self-evident principles from which mechanical laws should be deduced, is, of course, God.

## The nature of the self

We can now turn to what is, for our purposes, the most important aspect of Descartes' philosophy—what is the 'I' that he now knows exists? What sort of entity is the thinking self, the mind? In tackling this question, Descartes tries to establish the essence of the idea of the mind, contrasting it with the essence of the idea of body. His way of thinking shows that he did not wholly succeed in throwing off the Aristotelian tradition of which he so disapproved.

Descartes argues that his 'I' is a conscious being that doubts, understands, asserts, wills, senses, and imagines. None of these activities can be thought of as distinct from his consciousness, and he cannot be mistaken about the occurrence of any of them. The essence of his existence—the logically necessary aspect—is, therefore, that he is a thinking being, or, more generally, a being that is engaged in some sort of mental activity. Descartes moves from this conclusion to the argument that because the essence of the mind is to think, to cease to be conscious would, for the self, be to cease to exist. So, humans are never truly unconscious: despite an external appearance of unconsciousness, the reality is that a mind is incessantly active (thus, for example, humans are assumed to dream throughout sleep).

Descartes adopts various arguments to show that his 'I'—his self—is distinct from his body. Although it is *not* possible to imagine that the self is not thinking, it *is* possible to imagine a self without a body. If one can conceive of a mind distinct from the body, then the essence of mind cannot include body. Similarly, Descartes asks whether we can conceive of the self as having extension. Does the mind have a particular shape or size? Is it to be found in a particular location, for example, in the top of the head, or the left side, or the right side? Since, according to Descartes, these questions are not only unanswerable but also logically absurd, we have to conclude that we cannot properly speak of the extension of the mind. The mind cannot, therefore, be a material substance.

When he considers his idea of body, Descartes finds that it comprehends the properties of other material objects—such as being of a particular shape, occupying a certain area of space, being perceived by the senses, and being moved by other bodies. But he finds that the powers of self-movement, of sensation, and of thought do not belong to the essence of body: these are not powers possessed by material bodies. Body and mind are, then, two entirely different entities, and it is logically absurd to suppose that a material object could be conscious.

Descartes therefore adopts, like Plato, a dualistic account of mind and body. But Descartes advances the dualist argument by proposing, first, that much of human behaviour can be explained in entirely mechanical terms, and, second, that there is a specific site in the brain at which the non-material human mind interacts with the material human body.

*Reflexes*

The idea that some behaviour was machine-like sprang from an odd mixture of mechanistic and physiological notions. Descartes was, it seems, much impressed by the feats achieved by complex water-powered machines constructed for the amusement of the public. The way in which a machine could respond to a specified input suggested to him that at least some behaviour (animal and human) could, similarly, be purely mechanical. Descartes was also influenced by the demonstration of the circulation of the blood by the English physiologist William Harvey (1578–1657)—although he quite wrongly disagreed with Harvey on some crucial details of the roles of the ventricles. He therefore attempted a specific mechanical account of the way in which the nervous system could operate so that a sensory stimulus might elicit a behavioural response. The details of his scheme are incorrect, but the basic notion that he introduced is that of the reflex, whose detailed mode of operation was not properly understood until the late nineteenth century.

Nerves were, according to Descartes, hollow tubes that contained 'animal spirits' and a central filament. Animal spirits were produced in the heart from a mixture of air and blood, and Descartes was very clear that, although these spirits were refined and fast moving, they *were* material bodies. They were stored in the ventricles of the brain, and could be directed selectively into certain nerves by the opening of pores that connected the nerves to the ventricles. When animal spirits were infused into nerves, the muscles to which the nerves were attached expanded, and this distension resulted in the contraction of the muscle, and the pulling of the limb to which it was attached.

Stimulation from the external world was detected as a consequence of the movement—a tugging—of the central filament of nerves, which in turn produced the opening of pores in the brain. Descartes believed that all sensory modalities operated in this way—vision, for example, was the result of the movement of invisible material bodies that were activated by the object seen, and whose movement stimulated the filaments of nerves at the back of the eyes. The specific pores opened by a sensory input would determine the flow of animal spirits into other, specific, nerves: thus Descartes provided an entirely mechanical account of what we now know as a reflex, and although the physiology of the reflex is, of course, very different from that proposed by Descartes, the underlying logic has not changed.

### Animals: mere machines

Descartes believed that a mechanical account was appropriate not only for relatively simple behavioural reflexes (knee-jerks, eye-blinks, salivation, and the like) but also for complex 'automatic' behaviour, such as raising an arm to ward off a possible blow. His perception that reflex behaviour might in principle be complex led to one of his most radical proposals—namely that animals (and plants) were mere machines, with no mental life. This was, it need hardly be said, a huge (and at the time dramatic) break with traditional thinking. He has, after all, abandoned the ancient notion that there was something special about living as opposed to non-living things. We now know that all living cells contain the genetic instructions that allow a more or less mechanical interpretation of cellular function; we know also that spores may exist in a state of suspended animation for years before springing into life. But the fact remains that we have not yet conclusively proved that it is possible to create a living organism from inorganic matter—or, at any rate, we have not yet succeeded in doing it. How much greater must the imaginative leap have been in the seventeenth century, when the idea of constructing a 'living' machine must have seemed to so many an absurd idea?

   If all animal behaviour could be accounted for in mechanical terms, why did Descartes not suppose that all human activity was similarly amenable to mechanical explanation? To put the question another way, of what (non-mechanical) activity are we humans capable that animals are not? Descartes' answer parallels that given by Plato and Aristotle—humans are rational, animals are not. But Descartes makes this argument more specific by tying the notion of rationality to language. He claims that animals neither produce nor comprehend language, and rebuts counter-claims by pointing out that, for example, parrots may make word-like sounds without having the least notion of comprehension. We see here the beginnings of an argument that is still alive today, but for present purposes the important point is that Descartes linked language to rationality, equated thinking with being rational, and, in turn, linked thinking to mental activity and so to consciousness. Animals (like other machines) may be capable of complex behaviour, but they are, in the Cartesian view, capable neither of rationality nor of thought, and so, not capable of consciousness.

### Mind–body interaction in the pineal gland

One basic problem facing dualists—those who believe that mind and matter consist of qualitatively different substances—is that of explaining the obvious fact that mental life shows a very close correspondence to material events: external stimuli obtain conscious sensations, and internal decisions are followed by external movements. Descartes attacked this problem head on, by proposing not only that mind and body interact, but also by giving a specific site for the interaction—in the pineal gland.

The human pineal gland—about quarter of an inch long, and so-called because it resembles a pine cone in shape—lies centrally in the brain, in one of the ventricles. Unlike other components of the brain, which are represented bilaterally in both halves, the pineal gland is a unitary structure This feature, along with its general location, encouraged Descartes to adopt it as the site of mind–body interaction. A unitary structure could integrate input from differing sensory sources to obtain a co-ordinated output—for example, images formed by two eyes would be seen, not as two images, but as an integrated whole. (This unitary structure had the added advantage for Descartes that it accommodated the notion that the mind itself is unitary— there was, for him, no possibility of divisions within the thinking self.) And the location of the pineal gland in the ventricles would allow very fine pineal movements to influence the flow of animal spirits to the various possible muscular outputs. So, in Descartes' mechanical scheme, the pineal gland served a central integrating role. It was now a small step to propose, first, that very fine movements of the pineal gland, caused by external events, could influence the mind and obtain conscious sensory experience, and, second, that mental activity could influence the movements of the gland and so translate 'mental' volition into bodily movement.

It is perhaps neither necessary nor fair to go on now to point out that there never was any direct evidence for a pineal role in mind-body interaction: the gland's role remains somewhat obscure, although it is known to secrete the hormone melatonin, which is involved in the control of circadian (and other) rhythms. What is important is that Descartes grasped the nettle, and produced an account of mind-body interaction that, whatever its shortcomings, emphasised the importance for dualism of finding some account of the relationship between the material and the psychic world. Interactive dualists since Descartes' time have occasionally made alternative suggestions, but those proposals have no more concrete support than Descartes' proposal—and it is, of course, extremely unclear what such concrete support would be.

It is, however, not a necessary consequence of dualism that mind and body should interact. Another possibility is that the mental and the physical worlds should proceed in parallel, and this was the solution preferred by Leibniz.

## Leibniz: parallel dualism

Gottfried Leibniz, born in 1646, is best known for his discovery, independent of Newton, of the calculus, and for his philosophy. But during his lifetime he also published works on law, history, and politics. Because he was anxious not to antagonize theological orthodoxy, most of his philosophical work was not in fact published until after his death. Like Descartes, Leibniz ended his life unhappily. He had entered the service of the Elector of Hanover, and was engaged in writing an exhaustive history of the House of Brunswick. But when, in 1714, the Elector became George I of England and left Hanover, Leibniz was not asked to accompany him, and he died in relative obscurity in 1716.

### Necessary and contingent statements

To understand Leibniz's views about the mind, we have again to begin by looking at his theory of knowledge[8]. Leibniz distinguished between two types of statement. One type is necessarily true, in the familiar sense that the contradiction of such a statement is logically impossible. These are statements (such as 'all bachelors are male') in which the predicate is overtly part of the definition of the subject, and mathematical truths, whose demonstration relies upon reason alone. The second type is the contingent statement (for example, 'Caesar crossed the Rubicon') that describes a possible, but not a necessary, state of affairs. Necessarily true statements comprise an important constituent of true knowledge; but, of course, not all contingent statements are true, and Leibniz seeks a way to certain knowledge about the truth of contingent statements.

### The best of all possible worlds

Leibniz's route begins from the existence of God, which is, he argues (adopting the ontological proof) a necessary truth. God, being perfect and omnipotent, must necessarily have brought into existence—out of all possible worlds—the most perfect possible world (the view that Voltaire (1694–1778) was to lampoon in _Candide_[9], his novel, published in 1759, about Candide and his teacher, the Leibnizian philosopher Dr Pangloss, who responded to a series of unimaginable disasters by concluding that this was, nevertheless, the best of all possible worlds). On what principles would God have selected the best possible world? Leibniz's answer to this question reflects the fact that he was a mathematician. It was, that God would choose to act so as to obtain the most efficient outcome—the maximum variety of effects—from the minimum set of causes, just as the unravelling of a simple mathematical function ($\pi$ for example) can be both infinite and complex.

The parallel here with a mathematical function is not simply an analogy: Leibniz believed that there was a very close resemblance between a mathematical function and the nature of an existing substance. For him, the true essence of each created substance contained every property that was true of it. Thus crossing the Rubicon is part of the essence of Caesar, and so true contingent statements are in reality necessarily true— except, of course, that no human, and only God, knows the true essence of the subjects of contingent statements.

Like Descartes, Leibniz was a rationalist in the sense that he believed that all events were the logically necessary consequences of propositions established by God. Unlike Descartes, Leibniz accepted that most of those propositions could be known only by God: the innate ideas that Leibniz allowed were only those basic principles—such as the notion of contradiction—that underlie mathematics and logic.

Thus a contingent statement is true when God has brought into existence a substance whose essence contains the predicates appropriate to the subject of the statement. To omniscient God, it is necessarily true that Caesar crosses the Rubicon, that Charles I is executed, and so on. Leibniz referred to the substances that God created as 'monads'.

_Pre-established harmony_

Since the history of a monad is no more than the unravelling of a series of necessary truths, monads cannot interact—they are 'without windows'— and are entirely independent of one another. How then is it that the world seems so orderly a place? Why, for example, do there appear to be relatively simple laws that govern the interactions of material bodies? The appearance of orderly interaction was ascribed by Leibniz to a pre-established harmony; the fact that the laws are simple provides a demonstration of God's success in generating multiple complex outcomes from simple initial principles.

### Psychophysical parallelism

Leibniz accepted the Cartesian view that the mind is qualitatively different from the body, but rejected the notion that body and mind interact. In rejecting the possibility of the mind being a material body, he introduced a powerful metaphor whose force still weighs against the plausibility of materialist accounts of the mind. Suppose there was a machine, he argued, that did achieve thought, sensation, and perception, then we could conceive of it as increasing in size—keeping its proportions constant—until we could enter its interior, like entering a mill. But if we entered it, we would find only 'pieces working upon one another' and 'never anything to explain perception'[10]. Essentially the same argument can be brought to bear on the currently widespread view (discussed in Chapter 8) that mental activity is simply brain activity.

Leibniz rejected the Cartesian notion of interaction between mind and body as simply inconceivable (as well as being in contradiction with recently discovered mechanical laws of conservation). In his own system, of course, it was impossible for the more general reason that each mind is a monad, as is each bodily substance, and monads do not interact. Bodies act according to mechanical laws ('efficient causes'); souls, according to their 'desires, ends and means' ('final causes'). It is this mode of action that allows monads to make 'free' decisions. One might, for example, argue that since when God created Caesar he created someone who necessarily would cross the Rubicon, Caesar could not have made a free choice. But Caesar's mind acted rationally, according to its desires. A rational decision between alternatives can indeed be predicted by an omniscient God, but the decision is nevertheless free. How then is it that the activities of the mind—a decision to move a limb, for example—are reflected in the movements of bodies? The answer, of course, is that the entire universe proceeds in accordance with a pre-established harmony: there is no interaction, merely a parallelism that reflects this miraculous harmony.

### The souls of monads

Finally, we may ask where animals lie in Leibniz's scheme. The answer is somewhat complicated by the fact that all monads—that is, all created substances—are said to possess the faculty of perception (unconscious or otherwise) and to mirror the universe. All monads, moreover, are immortal: no created substance ever ceases to exist (just as the exposition of $\pi$ is infinite). There appears then to be no major qualitative difference between living and non-living bodies. But Leibniz recognizes one important advance when perception is accompanied by memory (and allows that animals capable of remembering have souls) and a further advance when rationality—found only in humans—appears.

## Predarwinian materialism

Dualism has remained the dominant Western account of the human condition since the beginnings of Christianity, and this is hardly surprising since it is a basic tenet of all versions of Christianity. Opposition to dualism inevitably led to dispute with the church, and when clear statements of a materialist alternative appeared, they came from professed atheists.

Thomas Hobbes (1588–1679) was a fine early example of an outspoken atheist and sceptic, who clearly anticipated with some relish the shock that would be suffered by most of his readers. Hobbes took it as axiomatic that the universe consisted simply and solely of material bodies, and that the business of philosophy and of science was to understand the motions of bodies. Statements that referred to incorporeal substances were self-contradictory, incomprehensible, and absurd. Mental activity, such as perception, imagination, and thinking, consisted of various forms of motion of body and brain matter. So, according to Hobbes, sensation arises when the motions of some external object 'press' a sensory organ, in turn producing motions in us—those motions being the sensation from which we infer the appearance of the object; and pleasure is 'nothing really but motion about the heart', thought 'nothing but motion in the head'[11].

Hobbes' greatness lay in his political writings, and he did not develop his materialist account of the mind sufficiently to show how he could tackle obvious philosophical objections. His account has a distinctly dogmatic ring, and provides no suggestions about how one might, for example, arrange material bodies in motion so that they might experience something. A fuller and more influential statement of a materialist account of the mind was published some one hundred years later, by the Frenchman Julien Offray de La Mettrie.

## La Mettrie

Born at St Malo in 1709, La Mettrie studied at colleges in Normandy and Paris before becoming a doctor of medicine at Rheims in 1733. After a brief stay in Leyden, La Mettrie returned to St Malo to practice as a country doctor, and married there in 1739. The marriage was unhappy, and he abandoned his family for Paris in 1742, where he became a medical officer to the army. He saw action in the War of the Austrian Succession, and in 1744, at the siege of Freiburg, contracted a fever, the effect of which on his thought processes led him to reflect on the close relationship of our bodily and mental states. In 1745 he published a treatise, *Histoire naturelle de l'âme*, in which he suggested a mechanical account of human thought—an account that so outraged respectable opinion, that the Parisian parliament condemned it to be burned. When in 1746 he published another work that ridiculed the French medical establishment, the reaction was such that he thought it safest to leave France for Holland, where he wrote *L'homme machine*, which was published anonymously in Leyden in 1747. There was a huge public outcry against the book, and when the author's name was revealed, early in 1748, La Mettrie was obliged to leave Holland also. He found refuge in Prussia at the court of the anticlerical Frederick the Great, whose other guests included Voltaire. To the immense satisfaction of his religious opponents, La Mettrie died suddenly in 1751 having, it appears, eaten a prodigious amount of a pâté of pheasant and truffles—a clear manifestation of divine vengeance.

## L'homme machine

In *L'homme machine*[12], La Mettrie argued that Descartes had been wrong in asserting that humans, unlike animals, possessed a non-material soul: humans and animals alike were machines. He wrote in a rhetorical style, much punctuated with exclamation marks and derisive comments about the soul. The main strands in his argument were, first, that the state of the body clearly influenced the activity of the mind; second, that human brains differed very little from animal brains; and third, that living matter possessed an intrinsic power of motion.

La Mettrie provided illustrations of the powerful effects of bodily state on human behaviour—behaviour that is presumably the consequence of mental activity. Illnesses disrupt thought processes, making idiots of geniuses; soldiers deprived of sleep snore through the noise of cannons; emotions like jealousy, greed, and ambition prevent any possibility of rest; and opium, wine, and coffee have their various predictable effects on mental activity. La Mettrie attached great importance also to both climate and diet, and attributed, for example, the legendary ferocity of the English to their custom of eating their meat red and bloody, not well-cooked, as in France. Finally, La Mettrie noted the effects of age on both the body and the mind: as the body matures and deteriorates, so does the mind.

Since he believed that the brain was responsible for thought processes, La Mettrie was interested in anatomical studies of the brain, and in comparative studies in particular. There was, he noted, very little difference between the general organization and composition of the human brain and quadruped brains. This provided general support for his belief that there is no qualitative leap between the mental activity of humans and that of animals, such as monkeys and apes, that are anatomically similar to humans. He emphasized this belief by claiming that it would be possible to teach an orang-utan to talk, and that once having mastered language, the animal would be not a wild man, but a perfect man—a little gentleman.

La Mettrie accepted that it was not possible to show specific causal relationships between brain structures and thinking, but was encouraged by the very fact that there are systematic differences in brains between different groups of animals: humans (according to the evidence then available) had the biggest and most convoluted brain, and among animals, larger brains were found in the less wild species. Such observations provided at least a measure of support for the idea that behaviour (and so, mental activity) was closely linked to brain structures.

By abandoning Descartes' claim that only humans are conscious, La Mettrie was faced with a problem that Descartes had avoided—how could a 'machine' (composed solely of material parts) be conscious? How could it come to *feel*? In tackling this, the central problem of materialism, La Mettrie drew attention to a phenomenon that attracted much scientific attention in the seventeenth and eighteenth centuries—the irritability of animal tissue. He cited numerous examples of tissue that continued to move and to respond to stimulation despite being severed from the central nervous system. One peculiarly grisly example was a report of a human heart that leapt a foot and a half in the air after being thrown on to a fire after its removal from the corpse of an executed man; another was the well-known case of the chicken that runs about after being beheaded (by a drunken soldier). But aside from these spectacular examples, La Mettrie was impressed by the many reports of the excitability of isolated excised muscle fibres, and particularly so by the then recent observations (published in 1744) of the Swiss naturalist Abraham Trembley (1710–84)[13] on freshwater polyps (now known as *Hydras*). Trembley showed, first, that these creatures were animals (they are related to marine jellyfish) and, second, that not only do small parts cut from a polyp move, but they also survive and reproduce asexually (by budding). This latter observation was, of course, very difficult for those who supposed that animals possessed a 'soul' of some kind, since it appeared that the soul of a polyp could be split into many souls.

La Mettrie argued that these observations proved that 'each little fibre' possessed its own principle of movement, quite independent of either nerves or the blood supply, and given this 'animated bodies will have all that they need for moving, feeling, thinking, repenting . . .'[14]. This then is La Mettrie's solution of the problem of feeling in machines: living machines possess an intrinsic power of motion, and that power is sufficient to explain consciousness. The argument is not convincing; it seems to imply either that isolated fibres are conscious, or that there is some other principle of organization (not spelled out) that creates consciousness in a community of self-moving cells. And although this may not seem to us too serious a problem, La Mettrie's account also creates a divide between man-made machines and living machines. The whole point of the man–machine metaphor is that it claims to reduce humans to machines, whose properties are well understood. But La Mettrie 'explains' consciousness in terms of intrinsic motion, and that is not a property of man-made machines and so is no better understood through the metaphor. It needs hardly be added that, even if intrinsic motion were satisfactorily explained, there remains still a large gap between the notion of intrinsic motion and that of consciousness.

La Mettrie did, then, succeed in emphasizing the clear links between bodily and mental events, and in drawing analogies between human and non-human brains. These issues pose problems for the Cartesian dualist account. But La Mettrie's proposed solution of the mind–body problem in terms of intrinsic motion of living matter has problems of its own.

## The magic unexplained

In this chapter we have seen the development of ideas that have dominated Western thinking about human nature. There are obvious contrasts between living and non-living things, and between living things that do not (we suppose) have feelings, like plants, and those that do, like humans. The living versus non-living contrast may not now seem so mysterious; but feeling versus non-feeling—conscious versus non-conscious—remains as live a problem today as two thousand years ago.

Dualists believe that some 'magic ingredient' is needed to convert inert material substances into a feeling entity. For them, the magic is provided by the soul—but this is a solution that has two drawbacks. First, the soul itself is incomprehensible—its existence does not clarify the incomprehensible. Second, the apparent effect of the soul on the body (and vice versa) has to be explained; there are two proposed solutions—Cartesian interaction, and Leibnizian psychophysical parallelism. However, no satisfactory scheme of interaction has been offered, and Leibniz overtly relies upon an equally incomprehensible miracle.

Materialists, of course, must explain the magical occurrence of feelings in terms of aggregates of non-feeling components. La Mettrie's intrinsic motion constitutes little advance over the 'soul' atoms of Democritus, and is surely less sophisticated than Aristotle's account. But Aristotle was a dualist where the human mind is concerned, and since it is only human consciousness of which we can be certain, he does not help the materialists explain whether or how animals might be conscious. Materialists, by the end of the eigtheenth century, could, therefore, no more solve the mind–body problem than dualists. So, how can progress towards a comprehensible solution be made?

Western philosophy took a dramatic change of direction with the emergence of the British empiricists, beginning with John Locke. These men asked questions about how the mind actually works, rather than supposing that mental activity is beyond comprehension or explanation. This interest led to the development of psychology—the scientific discipline concerned with mental activity, and now clearly distinct from philosophy. It makes good sense that the mind–body problem (a problem that has changed little over millennia) is more likely to be solved the more we observe and know about mental activity and the mind. Chapter 3 will, then, trace the gradual transition from philosophy to psychology.

## Notes and references

1. 'Soul' and 'mind' are used more or less interchangeably to refer to the seat of consciousness. 'Soul' is generally used by dualists who believe in the immortality of the human soul.
2. There is no substitute for reading philosophers (translations of the original). For the standard edition of Plato's dialogues, see Plato (1953). There are many translations available of individual dialogues, of which the most relevant to his concept of the soul are *Phaedo*, *Timaeus*, and the *Republic*. For a readable general introduction to Greek philosophy, see Guthrie (1967). For a more detailed discussion of Plato's ideas on the soul, see Guthrie (1975).

3. For an account of the views of the atomists, see Guthrie (1965).
4. For Aristotle's philosophical works, see Barnes (1984). The most relevant parts are the three books that constitute his *De anima*. For an introduction to Aristotle's thought, see Barnes (1982) or Guthrie (1967); for a fuller discussion, see: Guthrie (1981).
5. See Chapter 8.
6. For an introduction to seventeenth century philosophers, including Descartes, Hobbes, and Leibniz, see the commentary and extracts in Hampshire (1956). For Descartes' original works, see Descartes (1931–4).
7. See Chapter 4.
8. For Leibniz's major philosophical work, see Leibniz (1902/1957).
9. Voltaire (1759/1947).
10. See Leibniz (1902/1957), p. 254 (section 17 of the 'Monadology').
11. Hobbes (1840), p. 31.
12. For La Mettrie's *L'homme machine*, see de la Mettrie (1953).
13. For an account of Trembley's work, see Lenhoff and Lenhoff (1988).
14. De la Mettrie (1953), p. 180.

# 3

## From philosophy to psychology

### Experimental philosophy

Rationalism and its accompanying system-building style of philosophy has failed consistently to grip the pragmatic English-speaking community. Empiricism—the notion that all knowledge derives ultimately from the senses—has been the dominant trend of British philosophy from the late seventeenth century onwards[1]. But the early British empiricists did not introduce novel solutions to questions about the physical or non-physical nature of the mind. Their importance for us lies in the fact that they directed attention to the *contents* of consciousness, and began the search for laws governing the association of ideas—a search that has played a large part in the history of psychology.

I shall discuss two of the figures who dominated the early development of empiricist philosophy, and who influenced the subsequent development of psychology—John Locke and David Hume. Locke launched the basic empiricist programme with two assertions: first, that all knowledge derives from experience, and second, that the proper business of philosophy is the analysis of the contents of the mind—of ideas.

### Locke

John Locke was born the son of a Puritan country lawyer in the village of Wrington, near Bristol, in 1632. He studied philosophy at Christchurch, Oxford, but was also interested in current developments in science and medicine, becoming a Fellow of the Royal Society in 1668, and taking a degree in medicine in 1675. In 1667 he joined the household of Antony Ashley Cooper (the first Lord Ashley, later created Earl of Shaftesbury) as physician to Lord Ashley and tutor to his son. Shaftesbury was a strident opponent of (and plotter against) the Duke of York, later James II, and eventually fled to Holland, where he died in 1683. Locke himself left for Holland in 1683, and did not return to England until William of Orange drove James II from the throne in the Glorious Revolution of 1688. He lived in London until 1691, when he retired to Essex, as a guest of Sir Francis Masham. He died in 1704, with Lady Masham reading psalms to him.

## Locke's Essay

Locke's major philosophical work, *An essay concerning human understanding*,[2] was first published in 1690. Its genesis was, according to Locke, to be found in discussions with friends in 1671. Those discussions had ended in unsatisfactory puzzlement, which had led to an interest in which issues could, and which issues could not, be resolved by human understanding: 'it was necessary to examine our own abilities, and see what *objects* our understandings were, or were not, fitted to deal with'[3]. Locke's primary concern, then, was with what we might call the psychology of epistemology—the 'nuts and bolts' of the ways in which we acquire knowledge.

### The nature of the mind

Locke's *Essay* begins with a disclaimer—he is not going to discuss the nature of the mind (neither its 'physical consideration' nor its 'essence'); he regards speculation on these issues as curious and entertaining, but as diverting him from his proper path. Later, Locke discusses two possibilities: first, that extended matter might think, and, second, that an immaterial thinking substance was conjoined with a material body. Neither position seemed satisfactory to Locke, who concluded that we could not, without divine revelation, solve the mind–body dilemma. Nevertheless, Locke generally wrote as though from a Cartesian dualist position (he referred, for example, to the brain as 'the mind's presence-room'), and accepted that mental activity does affect bodily motion—although he did not attempt any specific mechanism by which this might take place.

### Innate knowledge denied

There are a number of strands to Locke's attack on the notion of innate knowledge, and a flavour of these can be given by summarizing his arguments concerning universal consent. According to Locke, proponents of innate knowledge claim that the existence of truths that are universally accepted by humans demonstrates that those truths must be innate. Locke gives as an example of such a truth, 'it is impossible for the same thing to be and not to be'. But, he argues, first, the claim is not valid—there could be some factor other than innateness that accounted for universal consent; second, it is simply not true that there are universally accepted truths. Children and idiots, for example, do not perceive these truths—do they not have minds? And, in case it is argued that all *rational* humans accept these truths, surely it is true that children acquire reason before they acknowledge all the supposedly innate truths? 'How many instances of the use of reason may we observe in children, a long time before they have any knowledge of this maxim, that 'it is impossible for the same thing to be and not to be'!'[4]

## Sources of ideas

How then do we come by knowledge? Locke's answer to this question begins with the suggestion that we should examine the contents of our minds, from which, after all, our beliefs and knowledge originate. Those contents are ideas, and the word 'idea' is used in a very general sense to denote 'whatever is the object of the understanding when a man thinks . . . whatever is meant by *phantasm, notion, species*, or whatever it is which the mind can be employed about in thinking'[5].

Locke suggests that the mind at birth should be conceived of as a sheet of white paper, and that 'If it shall be demanded then, *when* a man *begins* to have any ideas, I think the true answer is, *when he first has any sensation*'[6]. Locke therefore rejected not only innate knowledge, but innate mental content of any kind: there are no innate ideas, and all the ideas that enter the mind are provided by experience. Two sources of ideas are available: some ideas—including the first ideas that enter the newly born mind—are provided by the senses; others come from what Locke calls 'reflection'. These latter are ideas provided by the operations of the mind—operations such as 'perception, thinking, doubting, believing, reasoning, knowing, willing and all the different actings of our own minds'[7]. Locke then proceeds to analyse further the nature of our ideas, using no other justification for the analysis than a generally covert appeal to introspection.

## Simple versus complex ideas

Ideas are classified as either simple or complex. Simple ideas are 'unmixed', 'distinct', of 'one uniform appearance', and 'not distinguishable into different ideas'. Some of the examples of simple ideas that Locke cites—colours, tones, smells, and tastes—originate from a single sense. Some are derived from the activities of the mind (the process of reflection), but in apprehending simple ideas, the mind is passive—simple ideas enter the mind via sensation or reflection, and cannot be invented by the mind, nor analysed into components. Other simple ideas, however, are not so simple: those, for example, such as space, figure, and motion, that are derived from more than one sense.

Locke is clear that ideas should be distinguished from the things that give rise to them. He never doubts the existence of the external world, and this is one of many reasons why he achieved a reputation as a 'common sense' philosopher. He adopted the notion that material objects had a limited number of 'primary', inherent qualities—solidity, extension, and motion. Other sensations such as colours, sounds, tastes, and so on, reflected the 'secondary' qualities of objects—qualities that were in effect the power of the primary ('real') qualities of the objects to cause those sensations. So, for example, although the *shape* of an object could never be to one hand circular, and to the other, square, the same water can feel hot to one (cold) hand and cold to the other (hot) hand. For Locke then, as for Descartes, the world of real material objects consists simply of solid molecules of matter occupying particular regions of three-dimensional space, either in motion or at rest. Sensations of temperature, colour, sound, and so on are to be explained in terms of the motions of those molecules and their effects on the mind.

Complex ideas are derived from simple ideas as a consequence of mental activity, and fall into three types: first, simple ideas may be combined to give a new complex idea; second, ideas may be brought together in such a way as to give rise to relational ideas; and third, the process of abstraction may give rise to general ideas. Locke goes on to classify further complex ideas (into modes, substances, and relations), but details of that classification—which led him, as they would us, into troubled philosophical waters—are not pertinent here.

## The nature of knowledge

In the final book of the *Essay*, Locke arrives at his goal—a specification of what knowledge is. His conclusions are, perhaps, somewhat unexpected. Given his insistence that ideas constitute the only contents of our minds, he is obliged to argue that knowledge is no more than the perception of agreement or disagreement between ideas. In pursuing this argument, Locke comes to the rationalist view that the safest pieces of knowledge are the necessary truths of mathematics or logic—truths that are either immediately apparent ('intuitive knowledge') or can be proved by a series of steps each of which is intuitively certain ('demonstrative knowledge').

The only things of whose *existence* we have certain knowledge are first, ourselves, and, second, God. Knowledge of our own existence is intuitively certain (and for this claim Locke relies on Descartes' *cogito* argument); knowledge of God's existence is demonstrative, and for this Locke uses a 'causal' proof of God's existence—we know that we exist, it is intuitively certain that real beings cannot be produced by *nothing, something* therefore must have existed eternally, and so on.

Locke is forced to conclude that the least reliable form of knowledge — 'sensitive knowledge'—is the best that we can attain for the existence of anything other than our own selves and God. None of our knowledge about how the world actually is (furnished by our senses) has the same guarantee of certainty that is enjoyed by intuitive and demonstrative knowledge. But, Locke believes, sensitive knowledge is nevertheless knowledge, and he backs this claim with the argument that we are 'invincibly conscious' that ideas derived from the senses are different from those derived from memory. For example, our perception when actually looking at the sun is different from what we perceive when we remember looking at the sun: thus, we may be certain that external objects, such as the sun, do exist. Whatever the merits of this argument, we know that in order to achieve the common sense conclusion, Locke has to abandon his claim that knowledge consists in the perception of agreement between ideas. He does believe that the evidence of our senses is sufficient to allow us to claim knowledge of an external world.

## Minds of non-humans

Locke's *Essay* includes two claims about the status of non-human organisms. The first is that vegetables are distinguished from animals by the absence of any form of sensation, and thus of any ideas and of any mind. The second is that although animals do have minds, and possess both some reason and the faculty of memory ('the storehouse of ideas'—demonstrated, for example, by the fact that birds learn tunes), they are not capable of forming *general* ideas (that is, complex ideas produced by a process of abstraction 'whereby ideas taken from particular beings become general representatives of all of the same kind')[8]. Locke gives as an example 'whiteness', a general idea abstracted from observations of chalk, snow, and so on, and regards the process of abstraction as the way in which humans form 'universals'. Since non-humans do not form general ideas, they cannot master language (although parrots and several other birds can be taught to make 'articulate sounds').

*Locke's legacy*

We have seen that although Locke's writing has a strong ring of dualism about it, he disclaimed any particular theory of consciousness—dualist or materialist. But Locke did introduce two notions that have been of central importance in psychology: first, that the contents of consciousness are amenable to analysis (by a process of introspection); and second, that all those contents—our ideas—derive ultimately from experience, and from sensation in particular.

## Hume

A second significant figure in the development of psychology was the Scotsman, David Hume, whose work was pivotal in the transition from the empiricists to Kant (the last major philosopher before the emergence of experimental psychology). David Hume was born in Edinburgh, in 1711. Although the son of relatively affluent parents—his father's family was, Hume tells us, 'a branch of the Earl of Home's'—he was, as the younger son, brought up to believe that he would require gainful employment to maintain a palatable standard of living, and his family hoped that he would become a lawyer. He attempted a business career for some three months, but decided that philosophy was to be his dominant concern, and in 1734 he went to live in France (spending much of his three years there in the town of La Flèche, where Descartes had been educated).

While in France he wrote *A treatise of human nature*, which was published in London in 1738. Unfortunately this book, in Hume's words, 'fell dead-born from the press'. Some ten years later he rewrote the first book of the *Treatise*, and published it as *Philosophical essays concerning human understanding*—a title he subsequently changed to *An inquiry concerning human understanding*. In 1751 he published *An inquiry concerning the principles of morals*, which was a new version of the later parts of his *Treatise*. The two *Inquiries*, written in what he had hoped would be a more attractive literary style, were no more successful than the *Treatise* had been, and in fact Hume's rise to prominence was the result of his historical writings.

In 1752, Hume was appointed Librarian of the Faculty of Advocates in Edinburgh—a post which gave him access to a large library. Hume took advantage of this to begin work on his *History of England*, the first volumes of which concerned the Stuarts. Although these books attracted widespread hostility—largely, according to Hume, because he showed some sympathy for the beheaded Charles I—the *History* eventually achieved remarkable success and provided Hume with a substantial income.

Despite the success of the *History*, Hume's philosophical work remained largely unrecognized in Britain, where one attack on his work, *An essay on the nature and immutability of truth: in opposition to sophistry and scepticism*, by James Beattie (a 'bigoted, silly fellow' according to Hume) was so successful that it ran into five editions before Hume's death in 1776. Hume was, however, appreciated in France during his lifetime, and after his death was credited by Immanuel Kant with arousing him from his 'dogmatic slumbers'.

## Experimental nature of philosophy

Philosophy was, for Hume, the science of man—a science that he regarded as 'the only solid foundation for the other sciences'[9]. He argued that this science should be based, like other sciences, on experience and observation. It would, he supposed, be impossible to grasp the powers and qualities of the mind 'otherwise than from careful and exact experiments'[10]. Although we might not regard his own introspective observations as experiments in the modern sense, he set in train a mode of thought that did lead to modern experimental psychology.

## Associations

At an early stage in the *Treatise*, Hume introduces the notion that association is a critical determinant of the way in which the mind operates. The concept that ideas might be associated was not, of course, novel. Aristotle is generally credited with having set out the first set of 'laws' of association—in *On memory* he suggested that one recollection might lead to another that was similar, contrasting, or contiguous (occurring, that is, just before or just after the current recollection). Locke, too, wrote a chapter on the association of ideas in the fourth edition of his *Essay*, in which he noted that custom results in the regular following of one idea by another. He suggested that 'trains of motions in the animal spirits . . . once set a-going, continue in the same steps they have been used to; which, by often treading, are worn into a smooth path, and the motion in it becomes easy, and as it were natural'[11]. But Locke did not assign a large role to association, and in fact was concerned rather to warn against the dangers that might arise from an association that misrepresented the true state of the world—a superstition, for example, based on some coincidental pairing of events. It was Hume who began in earnest the search for what became known as the 'laws' of association.

Hume argues that ideas do not succeed one another in the mind in random order, but that there is what he calls a 'gentle force' that associates ideas. He adopts two of Aristotle's principles of association—similarity and contiguity (in time or place)—but introduces a crucial third principle of cause and effect, which he sees as the most influential of the three.

### Causation

It was Hume's analysis of causation that so shook Kant. Although it now seems unsurprising, its effect at the time was devastating for rationalist philosophies as it seemed to demolish the notion that events in the real world could, even in principle, be derived logically from universally acceptable premises.

Hume asks how we derive the notion of causation, and begins his analysis by finding (by introspection—his experimental method) that two conditions are always satisfied when one event is taken to be the cause of another. First, the two events are contiguous in time and place; and second, the 'cause' precedes the 'effect'. But these two conditions are not sufficient in themselves—two events might be contiguous, and the one precede the other, without our taking the one to *cause* the other. There is a third, and more important, relationship between a cause and an effect—a 'necessary connection'. Hume now asks how we derive the idea of a necessary connection between a cause and an effect, and concludes that this occurs when we observe a 'constant conjunction' between two events that are contiguous and succeed each other in time. Thus the three conditions that give rise to the idea that two events are causally related are contiguity, succession, and constant conjunction.

Hume asks whether it is rational, given that these three conditions have been satisfied, to infer a necessary connection between two events. If the inference is based on reason, then the underlying principle must be that 'instances of which we have had no experience resemble those of which we have had experience'[12]: but 'we can at least conceive a change in the course of nature'[13], so contradiction of that principle is not *logically* impossible. Hume goes on to devote a large part of the first book of his *Treatise* to exploring the nature of the 'necessary connection' that forms an essential component of our notion of causation. He explores—and finally rejects—a number of arguments that might be used to support the idea that there is a *logically* necessary connection between a cause and its effect; and since the laws of nature uncovered by scientists are based precisely on the principle that the course of nature will *not* change (the principle of induction), those laws cannot be *necessarily* true, and a rationalist account of the real world is not possible.

The fact that we infer an effect from a cause is not, therefore, due to any necessary connection between the events. There is, as seems obvious to us now, no logical guarantee that if B has always followed A, B always will follow A. Hume argues that it is, instead, an inference attributable simply to our nature—to the way in which our minds happen to work. It is an instance of the operation of the 'gentle force' of association.

*Animal thought*

Hume is forthright about the animal mind: 'no truth appears to me more evident, than that the beasts are endowed with thought and reason'[14]. He establishes his case in two steps. First, he argues that where the external actions of animals resemble those we ourselves perform, we should conclude that their internal actions are likewise similar. Second, just as our thought processes are based on the association of ideas, so it is obvious that animals too guide their actions by associations formed from experience: 'from the tone of voice the dog infers his master's anger, and foresees his own punishment'[15]. Chapter 4 will show that this view—supposing the general comparability of human and animal thought—was to have a long history.

*Hume's scepticism*

The basic tenet of empiricist philosophy is that mental life consists of a succession of ideas that originate from experience. For Locke, as we have seen, ideas were in some sense 'in' the mind, as objects of thought. Hume wrote that 'the mind is a kind of theatre, where several perceptions successively make their appearance . . .'[16]. But he was not at all certain that there was an audience in the theatre, for he added 'they are the successive perceptions only, that constitute the mind; nor have we the most distant notion of the place, where these scenes are represented, or the materials, of which it is composed'[17].

The idea that the mind is 'nothing but a heap or collection of different perceptions'[18] led Hume to a systematic scepticism about the existence of both the mind (conceived of as something separate from perceptions—as, for example, a substance in which perceptions are supposed to inhere) and material objects (given his analysis of causation, their existence as sources of perceptions was clearly not a necessary inference). This scepticism was restricted to rejecting the notion that the existence of either the mind or the material world could be proved beyond logical doubt. Hume was quite clear that humans cannot in practice doubt the existence of either minds or bodies, and his question is—what is it about our nature that leads us inexorably to such beliefs?

More generally, Hume wrote: 'should it be here asked me . . . whether I be really one of those sceptics who hold that all is uncertain, and that our judgement is not in *any* thing possessed of *any* measures of truth and falsehood, I should reply that this question is entirely superfluous, and that neither I, nor any other person, was ever sincerely and constantly of that opinion'[19]. Hume believes that he cannot wholly accept his sceptical conclusions because 'nature, by an absolute and uncontrollable necessity, has determined us to judge as well as to breathe and feel'[20]. His purpose is, therefore, to persuade his reader 'that belief is more properly an act of the sensitive than of the cogitative part of our natures'[21]. In effect, Hume's aim is to show first, that we cannot deduce logically such universally accepted truths as that minds and objects exist and that there are real causal relations between events, and, second, that the appropriate response to this conclusion is to analyse the function of the human mind so that we can understand the real source of those beliefs.

*Immateriality of the soul*

Although Hume doubted that the existence of either mind or body could be (logically) proved, he did have things to say about non-material objects and of the possibility of their interaction with material objects. First, he argued that non-material things clearly exist: 'an object may exist, and yet be nowhere'[22] (and if it exists nowhere, it is not an extended entity and is therefore not matter). The 'objects' he has in mind are such things as reflections and perceptions: 'a moral reflection cannot be placed on the right or on the left hand of a passion; nor can a smell or sound be either of a circular or a square figure'[23].

Hume goes on to discuss the question of whether such non-material things could be causally related to material objects—what is the *cause* of our perceptions? People, he argues, find it absurd to imagine that, for example, 'the shocking of two globular particles should become a sensation of pain, and that the meeting of two triangular ones should afford a pleasure'[24]—and so conclude that it is 'impossible that thought can ever be caused by matter'[25]. Hume returns to his analysis of causation, noting that there is *never* a necessary connection between a cause and its effect, but that we infer causation as a consequence simply of constant conjunction. The constant conjunction of a material and a non-material event provides just as intelligible a causal link between those events as does the constant conjunction of two material events. Unfortunately, however much we may admire Hume's consistency, what he in effect is telling us is that causation is something that *cannot* be understood in any circumstances. And yet, of course, we have no problem with accepting that there are mechanical laws that govern the interactions of material bodies, nor any problem with the fact that those 'laws' do not have the force of logical necessity. We *do* find mechanical laws intelligible, we do *not* have any corresponding set of laws that describe the effects of material bodies on the mind.

## The missing shade of blue

Hume's greatness lies in the fact that he was, unlike Locke, prepared to follow through the consequences of the empiricist approach even when that conflicted with common sense. Many of the problems of empiricism derive from its insistence that at birth the mind is 'white paper' or a *'tabula rasa'*, whose *only* source of information is the senses. Hume saw that this basic assumption inevitably leads to serious difficulties. At the beginning of his *Treatise*, he raises the following interesting question: suppose someone had in the course of his lifetime experienced all the shades of blue except one, and suppose that he was shown all those shades, arranged from deepest to lightest blue, with a blank in the place of the missing shade, would he be able to 'raise up to himself the idea of that particular shade, though it had never been conveyed to him by his senses?'[26] The question can be put another way: would the person know, when shown the missing shade, that it was blue? Hume has no hesitation in answering in the affirmative, but dismisses the example as being 'so particular and singular, that it is scarce worth our observing'[27].

In fact, as Hume surely knew, the question is critical, and points clearly to the conclusion that our minds are *not* passive receptacles, furnished solely by experience; it is not *experience* that tells us that the various shades of blue resemble each other, but some other 'inbuilt' source of information. Sensory input is actively classified and categorized so that, for example, light within a particular band of wavelengths is seen as blue, light within another band as green, and so on. The similarity that we perceive among wavelengths is not a simple consequence of the physical similarity of stimuli 'out there', but depends as much upon what is 'inside' as upon what is 'outside'. We see light with a wavelength of, say, 610 nanometres as red; if we increase the wavelength by 30 to 640 nanometres, we still see a red hue; but if we decrease the wavelength by a similar amount to 580 nanometres, we see yellow. Physically, light of 580 nanometres differs from light of 610 nanometres no more than does light of 640 nanometres, but the mental experience is very different—and that difference is imposed by the organization of our sensory system.

Although Hume saw the conflict between his brand of empiricism and the psychological realities of perception, he did not resolve it. That was to be the task of Kant, the next major figure in this story.

## Hume's legacy

One general legacy left by Hume was simply his tenacious mode of thought—the example he provided of following arguments to their conclusions, however unpalatable those conclusions might be. His arguments led him to a scepticism that comprehended many common sense beliefs; he accepted that neither he, nor anyone else, could wholeheartedly accept his conclusions, but could not see how his scepticism could be resolved. Many of the real problems, of course, lay in the basic assumptions of the British empiricists—so that in effect he exposed the difficulties not only of rationalism, but also of empiricism.

A more specific legacy to psychology was the attention Hume drew to the importance of associations, and his notion that the laws governing them should be investigated using the technique of introspection. Introspection has had a profound influence on the course of psychology, but has seen dramatic shifts in popularity; and the laws of association have been investigated with particular thoroughness by workers interested in the intellectual capacities of animals. The central role of associations in thought persisted as an important strand in British nineteenth-century philosophy, represented by John Stuart Mill (1806–73), Alexander Bain (1818–1903), and Herbert Spencer (1820–1903)[28]. But experimental psychology was to begin in Germany, and Hume's more immediate legacy was to provide a crucial stimulus for Kant—the last philosopher that we shall discuss before moving on to psychologists proper.

## Kant

Immanuel Kant delights his biographers by having lived such a spectacularly dull life. He was born in Königsberg in 1724, and throughout his long life (he died in 1804) never travelled more than forty miles from that old town, in whose university he spent his entire academic career, from undergraduate to professor. He did not marry, and in later life spent each day in a routine—writing, coffee drinking, eating, walking, lecturing— that was so regular that his neighbours could set their watches by it. He was also, by the standards of philosophers, remarkably slow in developing his philosophical position and in producing the work for which he became famous.

The dullness of his day-to-day life seems the more remarkable in its sharp contrast with the dramatic impact that his work had from the moment, in 1781, that the first edition of his *Critique of pure reason* was published. His goal was to achieve what he called a Copernican revolution in philosophy, and revolutionary he certainly was—so much so that the German romantic poet Heinrich Heine (1797–1856) called him the 'great destroyer in the world of thought' and a man who 'went far beyond Maximilian Robespierre in terrorism'[29].

Although his ideas had a dramatic impact, they were expressed in a heavy and frequently obscure way—a style very different from the readable prose of the British empiricists[30]. In trying to put across the essence of Kant's philosophy, I shall emphasize the psychological importance of his contribution and avoid much of the difficulty that any account of his contribution to philosophy in general would inevitably involve.

### The role of experience

Kant agreed with Hume and the British empiricists to the extent that he believed that all knowledge *begins* with experience, but disagreed that all knowledge is therefore *derived* from experience. Sensory input was necessary, he believed, to activate the mind, but to perceive that input at all it was necessary first to organize it according to two 'intuitions'—space and time. These intuitions are 'a priori', in the sense that they are not derived from experience. Kant's argument is that it is a necessary precondition of any sensory event whatever that it should be perceived as occurring at a particular time and in a particular location.

### Synthetic 'a priori' knowledge

Kant began the *Critique* by distinguishing between 'a posteriori' and 'a priori' knowledge. A posteriori knowledge is knowledge derived from our experience of the world—knowledge that could not have been acquired in any other way. A priori knowledge is knowledge that is necessarily true, is independent of experience, and is universal in its validity.

Kant went on to introduce a further distinction—between analytic and synthetic judgements (or propositions). He used the term 'analytic' to refer to propositions whose predicate was somehow contained in the subject. For example, the statement 'all swans are birds' is analytic because the predicate 'birds' is contained in the subject in the sense that the definition of 'swan' contains the notion that swans are birds. Since Kant's time, the term 'analytic' has been widely adopted to refer to all true statements whose contradiction would be logically absurd. (Kant's 'analytic' truths differ from Leibniz's 'necessary' truths because Kant, although he regarded mathematical truths as necessarily true, did not regard them as analytic.) Kant referred to statements that are not true in that sense as 'synthetic', and true synthetic statements include those that refer to information gained from experience of the world such as events in history (for example, 'Caesar crossed the Rubicon').

Part of Kant's revolution lay, however, in his claim that not all true synthetic statements depend upon experience. Although synthetic propositions are typically, and unsurprisingly, a posteriori—dependent that is on experience—Kant claims that there are also synthetic a priori truths (and proposes mathematical truths an example). He uses the notion of synthetic a priori truths to resolve the problems raised by Hume's demonstration that causal statements cannot be necessarily true. For Kant advances as an example of synthetic a priori knowledge the statement 'every alteration must have a cause', and argues that the notion of cause implies necessity—a necessity that could not (as Hume himself had shown) be derived simply from pairings of events. Our knowledge that every alteration must have a cause is activated by experience, but is not derived from experience: it is, according to Kant, an irresistible contribution of the mind, determined by the structure of the intellect. The a priori truth of the statement 'every alteration must have a cause' provides for Kant the justification of inductive reasoning.

We need not go into the many challenges there have been to Kant's position. One controversial example of an a priori synthetic proposition was that 'in all changes in the material world the quantity of matter remains unchanged'—whereas we now know that matter and energy are interchangeable. But the philosophical validity or otherwise of Kant's arguments is not, particularly for us, the critical issue. What is important is that Kant drew attention to the role that the internal structure of the mind—mental architecture—*must* play in our experience of the world. This is surely true, and provides the appropriate framework for a resolution of Hume's difficulty with the missing shade of blue: perceptual similarities are the consequence of the structure of our minds, a structure that is to a large extent independent of experience. Similarly, Kant's argument concerning the nature of statements about causation can be rephrased into the less contentious claim that we humans are so constituted that we cannot interpret the world except in terms of causation—that the human mind cannot conceive of the occurrence of a change that is not the consequence of some immediately preceding event. As an account of the true source of our notion of causality this has an intuitive plausibility that contrasts with

Hume's associationist analysis (that, as Hume so clearly saw, cannot explain the idea of necessity that seems so central to causation).

## Noumena and phenomena

Kant claimed, then, that although we do not possess innate knowledge, our minds are so equipped that when experience occurs, it is inevitably interpreted in ways determined by our minds. This raises questions about the nature of our picture of the real world—that picture is now viewed as necessarily indirect, an interpretation of sensory input that is constrained by the structure of our intellects. This is indeed the substance of what Kant saw as his 'Copernican revolution': just as Copernicus asked whether it would not make more sense to suppose that the world went round the sun rather than vice versa, Kant asks whether it will not make more sense to suppose that 'objects must conform to our knowledge' rather than that 'all our knowledge must conform to objects'—to suppose, that is, that our experience of the world is shaped by the nature of our minds rather than that the nature of our minds is shaped by our experience of the world. Kant formalized this issue by arguing that the only things of which we can have knowledge are 'phenomena', and that the world of real objects—of 'noumena'—can be known to us only indirectly, and only to the extent to which we properly understand the relationship between noumena and phenomena. Since we do not directly perceive the noumenal world, then in order to know what is 'out there' in the external world we need to understand the nature of the transformations wrought upon it by our minds. And that is a psychological issue.

## The animal mind and the human soul

Kant agreed with the empiricists that—contrary to Descartes' thinking—animals enjoyed at least some conscious experience. He was, however, clear that their experience was very different from ours, and explicitly ruled out for them any capacity for judgement, or for conscious reflection on their experience. Animals might indeed learn, but that would be an automatic procedure of association formation—very different from the powers of conscious reason that the human mind possesses.

Kant's lowly view of the animal mind has to be seen in the context of his belief that the human soul is immortal, and capable of free choice. Although he did not believe that the existence of God could be *proved* by reason alone, he did believe in the existence of God and argued, moreover, that this was a belief that must be held by all rational men. These considerations point naturally to the conclusion that Kant was a dualist, at least as far as the world of appearances—phenomena—is concerned. But since he believed that we have no direct knowledge of the world out there—noumena—he argued that we have no certain knowledge of the ultimate nature of noumenal mind or noumenal matter (nor even of whether there is any substantive difference between them). That being so, he could sidestep the problem of their interaction. Thus although Kant was, to all intents and purposes, an interactive dualist, he offered no solution to the question of how mind and body might interact. His major contribution, from our point of view, was to highlight the active input of our minds to the nature of our experience.

### Kant's legacy

Because of our primary interest in psychology, we have concentrated hitherto on Kant's impact on empiricism. We should now digress briefly, however, to record Kant's final demolition of two of the pillars of previous rationalist systems. First, he showed that nothing of consequence can be derived from the 'cogito' argument. Kant argues that 'cogito, ergo sum' is—as is now universally accepted—a tautology. But he also goes on to show that none of the properties claimed for the 'I' of the argument, for example, that the thinking being is a substance, or that it is simple or unitary, can be demonstrated logically. Second, he demolished the ontological 'proof' of the existence of God (God is the subject of all the perfections; existence is one of the perfections; therefore God exists—an argument relied upon, as we have noted, by Descartes and many others). His particular technical criticism of an argument that has many flaws was that 'existence' is not a 'real' predicate: to add 'existence' to a concept of something does not *add* anything to the concept—you can, in other words, define concepts (such as the concept of a unicorn) any way you like, but you cannot *define* things into existence.

The demise of the ontological argument has meant that, since Kant (who also demolished other, less convincing 'proofs' of God's existence), even theologians have by and large abandoned the effort to prove that God *necessarily* exists. Hume dismissed the notion that there could be a (logically) necessary account of the succession of events in the real world; and Kant ended the idea that there might be logically necessary truths of a metaphysical kind. Kant reinforced the British empiricists' insistence on the primacy of evidence obtained from experience, and added a new emphasis on the independent and crucial contribution to experience of the human mind.

Kant's insistence that only 'appearances' (phenomena), and not 'things in themselves' (noumena), are available to us, led him to the conclusion that the contents of consciousness constitute the proper (the only) subject matter of psychology and, in turn, that psychology, burdened with data that seemed systematically resistant to precise measurement, could never become a science on a par with chemistry. He also had the perhaps bizarre view that introspection—the only method of investigating the contents of consciousness—might be positively dangerous: it might, he thought, lead to mental illness[31].

Despite Kant's scepticism of the possibility of a scientific psychology, experimental psychology began in Germany. His view of the mind provided an appropriate intellectual context in which to think productively about observations—both physiological and psychological—that were made shortly after his death and whose significance (given the notion that the mind contributes actively to the interpretation of sensory input) was readily apparent.

## Experimental psychology

### Wundt: the first experimental psychologist

The first laboratory designed specifically for research in experimental psychology was opened in Leipzig in 1879, and its director (the first scientist to regard himself primarily as an experimental psychologist) was Wilhelm Wundt (1832–1920). Wundt spent the great majority of his early academic career (until 1874) as a physiologist in the medical faculty at Heidelberg. He was, throughout his life, a prolific writer, and in one of his early books (on sensory perception, published in parts from 1858–62) he introduced the phrase 'experimental psychology'. His reputation, however, was established by a later book, *Physiological psychology* (1873/4), the success of which led first to a Professorship at the University of Zürich and then, a year later, to a Chair of Philosophy at Leipzig, where he remained until his death.

The psychological experiments that Wundt and his colleagues carried out were confined to humans, and explored three main areas: perception, psychophysics, and reaction times. Wundt was not the first to investigate these topics, but those who had done so before him were not, first and foremost, psychologists. I shall introduce each area briefly, concentrating in each case on the contribution of one scientist[32].

*Perception: Helmholtz*

One of the first implications of the adoption of a Kantian approach to the mind is that we should look at the ways in which external input is transformed as it is consciously perceived by the mind. The significance of sensation and perception was, therefore, obvious in the early nineteenth century, and an important figure in the study of these (and other) topics was Hermann von Helmholtz (1821–94).

Born in Potsdam, near Berlin, Helmholtz trained as a surgeon, but at the same time studied physics. Having qualified, he practiced as an army surgeon, but maintained his broad academic interests and mixed with members of science faculties at the University in Berlin. His early publications led in 1849 to his appointment to a Chair in Physiology at Königsberg. In 1858 he moved to Heidelberg, where Wundt served as his assistant for six years, and in 1871 returned, now as Professor of Physics, to Berlin, where he ended his career.

Helmholtz's biological work gradually progressed from an early interest in general physiological issues, to sensory physiology, and, finally, to the psychology of perception.

Helmholtz's first major contribution to physiology concerned an issue of wide philosophical interest. The Professor of Physiology at the University of Berlin, at the time when Helmholtz was at the Medical Institute, was Johannes Müller (1801–58) who, although he made major contributions to sensory physiology, held two views that now seem archaic. The first was vitalism—the belief that there is a special source of energy or force in living things, that does not exist in non-living bodies. Helmholtz attacked this idea in a famous paper (primarily directed at physicists) in which he used his knowledge of physics to argue the case for the conservation of energy throughout the universe, and his physiological work on frog muscle to show that the consumption of energy by living matter was precisely that expected from a purely physical system. Not only would a 'life-force' conflict with the principle of the conservation of energy, but there was, in any case, no evidence for any 'extra' force or source of energy in living things. Helmholtz's rejection of vitalism supported the idea that living things are machines, and Helmholtz himself was a thorough-going mechanist, believing that all living things—including humans—operate according to laws of chemistry and physics that are common to all material objects.

Müller's second archaic notion was that the speed of nervous transmission was extremely fast—comparable to the speed of light—so fast, in any case, that it could not be measured. But Helmholtz devised some remarkably simple and ingenious experiments that allowed reasonably accurate measurements to be made of the speed of transmission (in both frog and human nerve). He found that nervous transmission was unexpectedly slow—slower, for example, than the speed of sound. Another obstacle to the idea that the nervous system was beyond scientific investigation of the mind was now removed.

When Helmholtz moved to Königsberg (Kant's university), he turned his attention to sensory physiology, making major contributions in the fields of both vision and hearing. In each area, he followed the transformation of the physical stimulus into a conscious perception. Helmholtz began by concentrating on vision. A first step was to emphasize the importance of a principle known as the law of specific nerve energies (attributed to his mentor, Müller): the modality of a sensation is determined by the activity of a particular sense organ, and not by the type of energy that has activated the organ. So, for example, when sunlight strikes our eye, we experience vision; but when it falls upon our skin, then that same energy is sensed as warmth. And a blow to our skin will result in sensations like touch, pressure, and pain; but the same blow to the eye will cause visual sensations—'seeing stars'. This is an eminently Kantian principle: the sensation does not in any sense 'resemble' the external stimulus, since the same external stimulus produces quite different sensations, depending upon which organ has been activated. Sense organs are normally, of course, activated by their appropriate type of energy; their threshold for such energy is much lower than that of other organs for the same energy—but that does not affect the logic of the principle.

Helmholtz went on to specify the many distortions to the original light input that were caused by the optics of the eye, and correctly proposed that our sensations of colour could be explained in terms of the activity of three classes of receptor (blue, green, and red), each maximally sensitive to a different wavelength. (Helmholtz acknowledged that a similar proposal had been advanced in 1802 by the English scientist Thomas Young (1773–1829), but it was Helmholtz's achievement in showing how this theory could account for such phenomena as colour mixing that led to its widespread adoption.) This too falls comfortably into a Kantian perspective: our sensory experience is necessarily determined as much by the nature of our sense organs as by the objects that impinge upon them.

But when Helmholtz moved from sensation to perception, he found himself in sharp disagreement with Kant's views. Helmholtz argued that sensations could not provide an 'image' of the external world—our sensations of light, for example, do not resemble light energy—but that they do provide signs or symbols that act as a guide as to what is out there in the real world. The task of the intellect in perception is to work out, from sensory signs, what the world is like. Whereas Kant had believed that this step is largely achieved by the given nature of the intellect, Helmholtz believed that the interpretation of sensory input was predominantly based upon previous experience.

Perception, according to Helmholtz, consists in the main of inferences that rely upon previous experience of sensory signs to derive the nature of external stimuli. His prime target was Kant's account of the visual perception of space—an account that Helmholtz described as 'nativist'; he described his own account as 'empiricist', believing, like John Locke, that we learn to see. In Helmholtz's view, we learn from experience of correlations of visual and tactile (and other) stimulation how to interpret visual sensations so as to predict accurately what tactile (and other) sensations will follow from certain movements of our limbs and body—and that, in essence, *is* our sense of space. The process of interpretation of sensations was one of 'unconscious inference', designed to divine what external arrangement of objects would give rise to the set of sensory signals currently present.

The notion that we learn to see led Helmholtz to an interest in the ability of humans to adapt to goggles that distort the visual world (that even invert the world), and he used the notion of a process of unconscious inference to account for the occurrence of visual illusions. These, he claimed, were all due to the eye misinterpreting an input because the input was similar or identical to that which would have been produced by some alternative arrangement of real objects. These are topics that have remained live issues in perception since Helmholtz's day, and the experiments that they have generated—and continue to generate—show clearly both that Helmholtz had the genius to light upon important psychological questions, and that these questions are amenable to empirical investigation.

## Psychophysics: Fechner

In 1846 Ernst Weber (1795–1878), a professor of anatomy and physiology at Leipzig, published the results of studies of discrimination in a number of human sensory modalities (the skin senses—touch, temperature and pressure, hearing, and vision). The most significant findings concerned the smallest detectable difference between two sensations. Weber reported that the smallest perceptible difference (the 'just-noticeable-difference', conventionally abbreviated as the 'jnd') between two weights was a constant ratio (1/40) of the heavier weight—a ratio that was independent of absolute weight. So, a person can tell that a weight of 39 grams is lighter than a 40-gram weight, but cannot differentiate between weights of 39.5 and 40 grams; and weights of 390 and 400 grams can be discriminated, but not weights of 395 and 400 grams. In the first case, a difference of 1 gram is enough to allow discrimination; in the latter case, a difference of 10 grams is necessary—so, it is the relative, not the absolute difference between them that is critical. Similarly, a constant ratio was found to describe the relationship between two lines of visually just-discriminable lengths (1/50 in this case), and between two tones of just-discriminable pitches (1/150).

Weber's work came to the attention of Gustav Fechner (1801–87)—a seminal figure in the history of psychology, but also a distinctly odd man. He spent his entire academic life in Leipzig, where he began by studying medicine, before taking up physics, of which he became a professor in 1834. Some kind of crisis then occurred, which may or may not have been related to damage inflicted on his eyes while staring at the sun (in pursuit of an interest in afterimages), and he resigned his chair in 1839.

Fechner had a habit of offending his fellow academics by writing amusing parodies under a pseudonym, and he adopted a sort of panpsychism which in essence held that there was no difference between mind and matter, and that soul permeated all matter. These views led to a number of bizarre publications (one on the mental life of plants, for example), but also to Fechner's interest in Weber's results—for it seemed to Fechner that Weber's methods could prove that the mental and the physical are indeed identical.

Fechner's goal was to establish a mathematical relationship between a perceived sensation and an objective measure of the physical quantity of the stimulus giving rise to the sensation. He began by formalizing Weber's conclusion as an equation to describe the 'jnd': $dP/P = k$ (where $dP$ is the increase in the physical stimulus $P$, and $k$ is constant). This equation has since become known as Weber's law. Fechner then assumed that within a given modality, every 'jnd' constituted a subjectively equal increment in sensation. This allowed him to treat the 'jnd' as a unit of sensation. Fechner now worked to define a relationship between the scale of sensation (measured in 'jnd') and the scale of the physical stimulus. This he achieved by taking the value of the physical stimulus at absolute threshold (the weakest value at which the presence of the physical stimulus could be reliably detected) as the unit of the physical scale, and by taking the absolute value of sensation at that threshold as zero. These assumptions allowed him—by steps that we do not have to follow here—to derive the following equation: $S = k \log P$ (where $S$ represents the intensity of the subjective sensation). For Fechner, the importance of that equation (Fechner's law) lay in the fact that it seemed to demonstrate the equivalence of the mental and the physical: a given sensation *equalled* a given physical stimulus (just as Einstein's equation: $E = mc^2$ shows that energy and matter are interchangeable).

Fechner's importance lies not in his speculations about the identity of mind and matter, but in the fact that he did provide solid evidence that Kant was wrong in supposing that mental phenomena could not be subjected to measurement. Fechner was a careful experimenter, and extended Weber's findings in the laboratory; in doing so, he introduced techniques that became fundamental to subsequent empirical research in this area. In 1860 he published his findings in *Elements of psychophysics*—and the term 'psychophysics' (introduced by Fechner), reflected his belief that this field of research constituted an 'exact science of the functional relations or relations of dependency between body and mind'[33]. The book, despite Fechner's doubtful reputation, had considerable and rapid influence—particularly on Wundt (who, as we have noted, took up his chair at Fechner's university in 1875).

*Reaction times: Donders*

We can conveniently introduce reaction times with a tragicomic story involving astronomy. In the late eighteenth century, stellar transits (observations of the time at which a given star crossed a point in space, indicated by a wire across a telescope) were calculated by observers who related their visual experience to the beats of a clock that ticked each second. Measurements were taken to an accuracy of a tenth of a second, which involved estimating how far the star was one side of the wire before a tick occurred, and how far the other side after the next tick occurred. In 1796, Nevil Maskelyne (1732–1811), the Astronomer Royal at the Greenwich Observatory—who has recently become notorious for his opposition to John Harrison, the maker of the first marine chronometer[34]—discovered that his assistant, Kinnebrook, recorded transit times that were almost a second longer than those he himself recorded. Kinnebrook was fired.

Subsequent work by astronomers revealed that discrepancies between observers were the rule, rather than the exception, and that discrepancies were relatively constant for any given pair of observers. This led to what became known as the 'personal equation' as a method of standardizing readings across different observers. But it soon emerged that there remained variations in interpersonal timing differences, and that the value of the 'personal equation' varied according to such things as the brightness and speed of motion of stars. Finally, there came the gradual realization that the source of the problem lay in the differing times that individuals took to 'bring together' visual and auditory information. (That this process must inevitably involve some sort of central delay became clear with Helmholtz's demonstration that the speed of nervous transmission was very much slower than had generally been supposed.) And this realization brought the field of reaction times clearly into psychology.

An important early figure in this third area of research in Wundt's laboratory was the Dutchman, Frans Cornelis Donders (1818–89) who, like Helmholtz, was a physiologist with interests in both the physiology and the psychology of vision and hearing. Donders was largely responsible for initiating 'mental chronometry'. His idea was quite simple: measure the time taken to perform some simple reaction; add to the task some further mental demand (for example, a choice); then subtract the time taken for the simple task from that for the complicated task to obtain a measure of the time taken to carry out the extra mental demand. The logic of the procedure is clearly illustrated in Table 3.1, which shows Wundt's use of it as a method for calculating times taken for seven different acts. It should perhaps be added here that although the logic of Wundt's scheme may be attractive, work based on it was unsuccessful in achieving an acceptable mental chronometry, largely because different experiments yielded different values for the various mental acts. This is hardly surprising, given the nature of the acts to be measured: it cannot be supposed, for example, that every act of cognition (or of association, or judgement) is identical and requires the same amount of time for its execution.

*The nature of the mind*

Along with his enthusiasm for experiments, Wundt insisted on introspection as the essential source of data on mental events and, in particular, for the analysis of mental life into elements, whose causal interactions could then be explored; one central agent involved in the causation of mental events was the process of association. In common with other psychologists who argued for the primacy of introspection, Wundt held a dualist view of mind and body. But he was not an interactionist: Wundt believed that mental events had purely mental causes, and were independent of the causally linked events of the physical world.

Wundt believed in psychophysical parallelism: he accepted and indeed emphasized that mental events are correlated with physical events in the

**Table 3.1** Seven reaction times used by Wundt in the attempt to establish a mental chronometry.

| Task* | Nature of task[+] | Name of process[#] |
| --- | --- | --- |
| 1. Reflex | Inherited sensory-motor reaction | REFLEX (1) |
| 2. Automatic action | Learned automatic action | VOLUNTARY IMPULSE (2 – 1) |
| 3. Simple muscular reaction | One stimulus, one movement, with attention on movement | PERCEPTION (3 – 2) |
| 4. Simple sensorial reaction | One stimulus, one movement, with attention on stimulus | APPERCEPTION (4 – 3) |
| 5. Cognition reaction | Many stimuli, each clearly perceived, one movement | COGNITION (5 – 4) |
| 6. Association reaction | Many stimuli, reaction with association | ASSOCIATION (6 – 5) |
| 7. Judgement reaction | Many stimuli, associations followed by judgements | JUDGEMENT (7 – 6) |

*: the name given to the task performed by the subject.
[+]: the nature of the task.
[#]: the name of the process that is timed by the difference between the time taken to perform it and the time taken to perform the preceding, simpler task. (Shown in parentheses are the two reaction times, one to be subtracted from the other).
(From Boring (1950), p. 149.)

nervous system, but held that there was no causal interaction. So, for example, he argued that 'an external voluntary movement is not produced by the internal act of will, but by the cerebral processes correlated with it'[35], and that 'an idea does not follow from the physiological excitations of the sensory centre, but from the processes, sensational and associative, which run parallel to them'[36]. The obvious question—*how* the correlation between mental and physical events comes about—he simply ignored. We are, then, no further forward than we were with Leibniz's account. What seems now very odd is that Wundt's version of psychophysical parallelism was restricted, in that he supposed that our higher mental activities were *not* correlated with distinct physical states:

psychophysical parallelism is a principle whose application extends only to the elementary mental processes, to which definite movement-processes run parallel, not to the more complicated products of our mental life, the sensible material of which has been formed in consciousness, nor to the general intellectual powers which are the necessary presupposition of those products[37].

Although Wundt was a dualist, and believed in the independence of the mental and the physical universes, he had great difficulty in deciding what sort of thing the mind is: he was clear that it is *not* a substance, and that mental events have no need of a substrate that is in any sense separable from those events. He avoided the problem of the audience for the Cartesian theatre by explicitly denying the idea that there is an inner eye that looks at ideas in the mind. Ideas, he claimed, like feelings and acts of volition, are *processes*—not processes *of* something, but processes that constitute all there is to the mind.

*Animal consciousness*

Although no work on animals was carried out in Wundt's laboratory, he took considerable interest in such work, and reviewed the somewhat sparse available data. Given that we cannot obtain data by introspection from animals, Wundt sought a criterion from our human behaviour that might guarantee consciousness. The proposal he came up with was that mental life should be inferred whenever we see in an organism 'external voluntary actions'. Inspection of animal behaviour then led him to conclude that mental life began with the protozoa, and is present in all animals. The difficulties with criteria of this kind have already been discussed in Chapter 1, and we can end this sketch of Wundt's views on animals with two conclusions that have a more modern ring. First, that 'the entire intellectual life of animals can be accounted for on the simple laws of association'[38]; second, that a major intellectual difference between animals and humans is that 'animals lack one function which is characteristic of the intellectual processes, at the same time that it is their invariable concomitant— language'[39].

*Wundt's influence*

Although Wundt, in his voluminous writings, emphasized the relevance and importance of experiments—he (rightly) equated scientific psychology with experimental psychology—it is not for his experiments that he is remembered: modern textbooks do not refer to his discoveries. But he did have an enormous influence, partly as a result of the success of his *Principles of physiological psychology* (the first textbook of experimental psychology, which went through six editions between 1874 and 1922), and partly from the sheer number of psychologists who at an early stage in their careers visited his laboratory and acquired his enthusiasm for experimentation. Those psychologists adopted Wundt's central beliefs about scientific psychology: first, progress can be made only by experiment; and second, the critical data can be obtained only by introspection.

## Functionalism versus structuralism

Although experimental psychology began in Germany and had its roots in European thought, most of the major figures in its subsequent development worked in the United States. This is particularly true—with one major Russian exception—of work on the psychology of animals (a central theme in Chapter 4). Before going on to look at animal psychology, I shall set the scene by discussing the opposing stances of two of the early leaders of American psychology—William James and Edward Bradford Titchener. These were two of many early foreign experimental psychologists who had visited Wundt's laboratory and amongst whom there were disagreements concerning the true nature of human mental life. The apparent impossibility of resolving their differences led to the dominance of the behaviourist school, which in turn led to an emphasis on experiments using animals.

## James: functionalism

William James (1842–1910) visited Wundt's laboratory only briefly, and clearly did not take to Wundt personally: he wrote of him (in 1887) that he 'aims at being a Napoleon of the intellectual world'[40] but that he 'is a Napoleon without genius and with no central idea'[41]. But there are nevertheless similarities between the two men. James' influence was due, like Wundt's, not to experimental findings (James did not in fact enjoy laboratory work), but to the success of a textbook (*Principles of psychology*, first published in 1890); and James agreed with Wundt that 'introspective observation is what we have to rely on first and foremost and always'[42].

James' textbook successfully publicized the work of Wundt and his colleagues. But although James reviewed that work, he was severely critical of a number of Wundt's theoretical assertions, and, in particular, of the notion that mental events—the constituents of consciousness—could be analysed into discrete 'elements'. In fact, James argued, consciousness should be conceived of as a stream, and no two regions of this stream are ever identical. Not only do identical elements not recur in the stream of consciousness, but, in James' account, a given state of consciousness could not even be divided into independent elements: 'however complex the object may be, the thought of it is one undivided state of consciousness'[43].

James did not, then, believe that we should attempt to determine the laws that govern relations between mental elements—indeed, he considered this impossible. In its place, James emphasized an analysis of mental life that would clarify its function. The 'functionalist' school of American psychology had its origins in the enthusiastic acceptance of Darwin's theory of evolution by natural selection. In order to understand any aspect of organic life, we need to understand its function—the benefit that it confers in the struggle for survival. Applied to psychological aspects of living organisms, this general approach resulted, for example, in an interest in America in mental testing, since this was a method that should yield information about the capacities of individuals—capacities that fit the individual for successful competition with other individuals.

*Function and nature of consciousness*

The functionalist approach naturally led James to pose the interesting question: what is the function of consciousness? He observed that much of our normal activity consists of habits—he called habit 'the enormous fly-wheel of society'—and that little or no conscious attention is devoted to habitual actions. Of the 'millions of items' present to the senses, those that we actually experience—that we are conscious of—are those to which we choose to attend. The function of attention is to select items of significance, and, more generally, the function of consciousness is one of selection between courses of action—of choice in those many cases in which decisions cannot be safely left to habit. As this is the first specific proposal that we have encountered for a *function* of consciousness, it is worth noting that it does not help us with the problem outlined in Chapter 1: what James is offering us is an account of a cognitive aspect of consciousness, not an account of feeling-consciousness.

Habits, according to James, were however complex: 'nothing but concatenated discharges in the nerve-centres, due to the presence there of systems of reflex paths, so organised as to wake each other up successively'[44]. What, then, is the nature of consciousness? James considered a number of alternate solutions to the mind–body problem. He believed that consciousness in some sense ' "corresponds" to the entire activity of the brain, whatever that may be, at the moment'[45], but felt that psychophysical parallelism must be rejected because of the (functionalist) observation that it is 'quite inconceivable that consciousness should have nothing to do with a business which it so faithfully attends'[46]. Apparently with some reluctance, James eventually adopted an interactionist approach, and posited a soul which would be 'a medium upon which the manifold brain-processes combine their effects'—a soul 'influenced in some mysterious way by the brain states and responding to them by conscious affections of its own'[47].

Although James rejected the idea that interaction might occur in a specific location such as the pineal gland—for him, the interaction was simply a mystery—his overall position is close to Descartes: a unitary non-physical soul interacts with a body whose system of reflexes is quite adequate for a wide spectrum of behaviour.

### The animal mind

James explicitly rejected the Cartesian notion that animals are not conscious: this opinion, according to James 'was of course too paradoxical to maintain itself as anything more than a curious item in the history of philosophy'[48]. He believed that consciousness increased with the evolution of intelligence and the brain (the neocortex in particular): 'lower' animals, being less intelligent, relied more upon habit and so had little need for consciousness.

## Titchener: structuralism

Functionalists were opposed by proponents of structuralism, and in particular by Titchener, Wundt's leading intellectual heir in the United States. Titchener (1867–1927) was an Englishman who was obliged to go to America (in 1892) because of the strong antipathy to experimental psychology of the University of Oxford (where he had studied philosophy as an undergraduate). He did not object to the claim that the function of consciousness should be explored, but argued that this must be preceded by an adequate analysis of consciousness—an analysis that should identify the ultimate individual mental elements that constitute conscious experience.

Titchener believed that scientific investigations of conscious experience required subjects who were highly trained in the technique of introspection. His work led him to such astonishing conclusions as that there are some 43 000 different elements of conscious experience (more than 30 000 being visual, and 11 000 being auditory). He also became involved in a dispute over the question of whether such a process as 'imageless thought' existed. (Titchener argued that it did not, although he conceded the possibility that there might be 'unconscious thought'.) Naturally, Titchener's insistence on the necessity for technically sophisticated subjects ruled out any possibility of a psychology of children, of abnormal humans, or of individual differences—all areas that had obvious interest for functionalists.

Titchener was always an isolated figure in American psychology, and structuralism died with him. His importance here lies not in the details of his psychology, but in the fact that his frequently acrimonious disputes with his fellow psychologists drew attention to a central problem with the one tenet that they all held in common—that the proper subject matter of psychology is consciousness, data for which could only be derived by introspection. Experimental psychologists, then as now, were concerned that their work should be accepted as scientific, but the difficulty with data obtained by introspection was that different observers might (and of course did) report quite different observations. Such a lack of objectivity was a key difference from data used in such traditional sciences as chemistry and physics. It was the inevitable weakness of reliance on introspection that led to the various behaviourist schools that are the subject of Chapter 4.

## Experimental science and the mind–body problem

We have seen in this chapter that there was an almost seamless transition from the philosophy of mind to experimental investigations of mental phenomena. But although contemporary work by physiologists was consistently producing evidence of strong correlations between brain activity and mental events, no real progress was made by early psychologists in resolving the mind–body issue (as reflected by the variety of beliefs that existed, ranging from Helmholtz's materialism to Fechner's panpsychism). Dualism—either interactionist or parallelist—continued as the dominant view of most leading psychologists, but the difficulties with both types (as James and Wundt made clear) were no less serious than they were when Descartes and Leibniz articulated their theories.

I shall end this chapter by introducing briefly the view taken by Charles Darwin, the man most responsible for the general adoption of the notion that there should be a continuity between animal and human mental life. Darwin himself wrote little in detail about the mind–body problem— probably because he was unwilling to express views that would antagonize the clergy. It is, however, clear that he believed that mental events were *caused* by physical (brain) events. Thomas Huxley (1825–95)—his well-known protagonist ('Darwin's bulldog')—adopted the same view, and explicitly followed through the implication that since physical events occur in accordance with physical laws, mental events are caused just as mechanical events are caused. Huxley therefore concluded that both animals and humans are automata—but not, as Descartes had supposed was the case for animals, *unconscious* automata: we are, he believed, conscious automata. Our mental life is caused by brain events, and we do not in fact possess free will: volition is 'an emotion indicative of physical changes, not a cause of such changes'[49]. Huxley made a brave effort to claim that this was a view that could be reconciled with Christian theology by noting that predestination had figured in the thought of a number of prominent theologians.

We shall return to the idea that brain events cause mental events in Chapter 8, in which recent developments in the philosophy of mind will be discussed. The intervening four chapters will concentrate on experimental work that has a bearing on consciousness, beginning, in Chapter 4, with a discussion of the next major school of psychology—behaviourism—which is of particular interest since it took a specific, novel approach to the mind–body problem.

## Notes and references

1. For an introduction to the British empiricist philosophers, including Locke and Hume, see the commentary and extracts in Berlin (1956).
2. Locke (1947).
3. Ibid., 'Epistle to the reader'.
4. Ibid., Bk. 1, Ch. 2, Section 12.
5. Ibid., Bk. 1, Ch. 1, Section 8.
6. Ibid., Bk. 2, Ch. 1, Section 23.
7. Ibid., Bk. 2, Ch. 1, Section 4.
8. Ibid., Bk. 2, Ch. 11, Section 9.
9. Hume (1956), Introduction, p. 5.
10. Ibid., p. 6.
11. Locke (1948), Bk. 2, Ch. 33, Section 6.
12. Hume (1956), p. 91, Bk. 1, Part 3, Section 6.
13. Ibib.
14. Ibid., p. 173, Bk. 1, Part 3, Section 16.
15. Ibid.
16. Ibid., p. 239, Bk. 1, Part 4, Section 6.

17. Ibid., p. 240.
18. Ibid., p. 200, Bk. 1, Part 4, Section 2.
19. Ibid., pp. 178–9, Bk. 1, Part 4, Section 1.
20. Ibid., p. 179, Bk. 1, Part 4, Section 1.
21. Ibid.
22. Ibid., p. 224, Bk. 1, Part 4, Section 5.
23. Ibid., p. 225, Bk. 1, Part 4, Section 5.
24. Ibid., p. 234, Bk. 1, Part 4, Section 5.
25. Ibid.
26. Ibid., p. 15, Bk. 1, Part 1, Section 1.
27. Ibid.
28. See Boakes (1984) for a lively account of the nineteenth-century British associationists.
29. Cited in Aiken (1956), p. 28.
30. Different introductions to Kant vary in their interpretations of his ideas. For a concise and readable introduction (but one which suggests a different account of the phenomena/noumena distinction from that made out here) see Scruton (1982). For a discussion of his ideas about the mind, see Brook (1994). Although Kant is undeniably a difficult philosopher to read, he equally undeniably is worth the effort: for the standard translation of Kant's *Critique of pure reason*, see Kemp Smith (1929).
31. Brook (1994), p. 10.
32. For a detailed account of the beginnings of experimental psychology, and of its philosophical background, see Boring's classic text (Boring 1950).
33. Cited in Boring (1950), p. 286.
34. Sobel (1996).
35. Wundt (1894), pp 449–50.
36. Ibid., p. 450.
37. Ibid., p. 447.
38. Ibid., p. 350.
39. Ibid., p. 362.
40. Letter to Carl Stumpf, cited in Fancher (1990), p. 240.
41. Ibid.
42. James (1890/1950), p. 185.
43. Ibid., p. 276.
44. Ibid., p. 108.
45. Ibid., p. 177.
46. Ibid., p. 136.
47. Ibid., p. 181.
48. Ibid., p. 130.
49. Huxley (1893), p. 240.

# 4

# Behaviourism: mindless psychology

## The psychology of animals

The widespread acceptance by psychologists of Darwinism, manifested in the functionalist school of the United States, led naturally to an interest in the psychology of animals[1]. Investigations of the mental capacities of living animals might well throw light on the minds of the non-human ancestors of humans, and so help us track the evolution of our own minds. Some early work on animal intelligence was carried out in Great Britain by, for example, George Romanes (1848–94), who was a personal friend of Darwin. But most reports, including Romanes', were mainly anecdotes of the achievements of domestic animals—interpretations of which tended to be markedly overgenerous about the animals' intellects. In the well-chosen words of Edward Thorndike (1874–1949), the first major American worker in animal psychology:

> . . . most of the books [on animal psychology] do not give us a psychology, but rather an *eulogy* of animals. They have all been about animal *intelligence*, never about animal *stupidity* . . . Human folk are as a matter of fact eager to find intelligence in animals. Dogs get lost hundreds of times and no one ever notices it or sends an account of it to a scientific magazine. But let one find his way from Brooklyn to Yonkers and the fact immediately becomes a circulating anecdote.[2]

What animal psychology needed, then, was first, experimental procedures that would produce results that could (as in the traditional sciences) be replicated reliably, and second, the theoretical discipline to interpret the results in as parsimonious a way as possible—a discipline crystallized by the British psychologist Conwy Lloyd Morgan (1852–1936) in his well-known canon: 'In no case may we interpret an action as the outcome of the exercise of a higher psychical faculty, if it can be interpreted as the outcome of the exercise of one which stands lower in the psychological scale'[3].

## Instrumental and classical conditioning

Two types of procedure for the reliable demonstration of learning in animals were introduced at a very early stage in the history of animal psychology—both before the end of the nineteenth century. In the first type, an animal is rewarded (or punished) for making a particular response. The probability and/or speed of the response increase (or decrease) as a result. Because the response is instrumental in obtaining the reward (or in avoiding the punishment), this procedure is now generally known as 'instrumental conditioning'. In the second type of procedure, 'classical conditioning', animals receive pairings of two stimuli, the first of which is neutral (for example, a bell), the second, important—a reward or a punishment (for example, food or an airpuff to the eye). Some aspect of the response to the important event (for example, salivation) is seen in response to the originally neutral stimulus. As is well-known, the Russian physiologist Ivan Pavlov (1849–1936) introduced classical conditioning, which he discovered fortuitously while investigating the physiology of the salivary glands of dogs. The key difference between this type of con-ditioning and instrumental conditioning is that in the former, the responses made by the animal have absolutely *no* effect on the delivery of the reward (or punishment).

Instrumental conditioning procedures were used by Thorndike, whose most influential experiments involved 'puzzle boxes'—boxes from which cats or dogs could escape by performing some relatively simple response, like pushing a lever or pulling on a loop of string. During a series of trials, the animals gradually learned how to escape more quickly from the box. The gradual reduction in the time taken to escape suggested to Thorndike that the animals did not succeed because they had 'understood' the solution (in which case, you might expect a sudden decrease in the time taken to escape), but that some process of trial and error had led to a 'stamping in' of the correct response. Thorndike went on to propose a specific mechanism to explain the stamping in process: he suggested that when, in the presence of a particular stimulus, a response occurred that was shortly followed by a reward, an association[4] between the stimulus and the response was strengthened (the 'law of effect'). The stronger the association between the stimulus and the response, the more rapidly the response was elicited by the stimulus. Both the procedure of instrumental conditioning and the notion that stimulus–response (S–R) associations are formed in such procedures have played a central role in animal psychology.

## The rise of behaviourism

Thorndike's work on problem-solving in animals had led him to some novel views about the ways in which animals and man might learn, but had not produced a radical break with the prevailing view that psychology's function was to explore the nature of conscious life. The results of his experiments allowed him to speculate on the conscious life of cats and dogs which, he concluded, was 'most like what we feel when consciousness contains little thought about anything, when we feel the sense–impulses in their first intention, so to speak, when we feel our own body, and the impulses we give to it.'[5] A dramatic break with the traditional view did, however, occur with the emergence on to the American psychological scene of what became known as behaviourism. Three men—Watson, Hull, and Skinner—dominate the history of behaviourism. They propagated, with an evangelical zeal, the belief that *all* intellectual activity—whether human or animal—was the outcome of a single and relatively simple learning process. For Watson and Hull, that process involved merely the formation of associations between stimuli and responses—S–R bonds. Skinner dispensed with the notion of associations, but for him too, learning involved only a change in probability of occurrence of a specific response given a particular stimulus. For all three, the key idea was, therefore, that *all* learning involves changes in the strength of a specific *response*. This is an extraordinary concept. It is also quite wrong—an extraordinary thing too, given the remarkable influence that behaviourists enjoyed over several decades.

### Watson's behaviourism

John Broadus Watson (1878–1958) began his academic career at the University of Chicago in 1900 and worked with rats—at that time a relatively new laboratory species. It is not for the results of his experiments that he is, however, best known. He achieved fame—or notoriety—for his vigorous advocacy of behaviourism, as expounded in 1913 in his article '*Psychology as the behaviourist views it*'[6]. The article had two principal themes: the first was a total rejection of introspection as a technique, and of consciousness as the proper subject matter of psychology; and the second was the proposal that psychology should instead be solely concerned with the prediction and control of behaviour. He argued that in writing psychology we should 'never use the terms consciousness, mental states, mind, content, introspectively verifiable, imagery, and the like'[7] and that instead we should write of psychology 'in terms of stimulus and response, in terms of habit formation, habit integrations and the like'.[8]

*Rejection of introspectionism*

Watson's attack on introspectionism was entirely justified. As we noted in Chapter 3, disputes had arisen between the various schools that relied upon introspection, when the introspections of one group did not agree with the introspections of another. Watson pointed to the clash between the essentially subjective nature of these arguments and the objective nature of the 'undisputed' natural sciences.

> Psychology, as it is generally thought of, has something esoteric in its methods. If you fail to reproduce my findings, it is not due to some fault in your apparatus or in the control of your stimulus, but it is due to the fact that your introspection is untrained . . .The attack is made upon the observer and not upon the experimental setting. In physics and chemistry the attack is made upon the experimental conditions.[9]

*Rejection of consciousness*

But if Watson's attack on introspectionism was not contentious, his attack on the very notion of consciousness certainly was. Watson in his later writings went on to claim that consciousness was not only 'neither a definite nor a usable concept' but also that 'belief in the existence of consciousness goes back to the ancient days of superstition and magic'.[10] Consciousness is not, then, simply not amenable to scientific investigation: it does not exist, and to suppose that we are conscious is superstitious nonsense.

*Habit formation: the essence of behaviourism*

Watson had been impressed by the learning demonstrated by animals in both Thorndike's and Pavlov's experiments, and regarded all learning as the formation of conditioned responses. What we conventionally term habits are, according to Watson, complicated collections of simple conditioned responses. He agreed with Thorndike that associations are formed between stimuli and responses that co-occur with the stimuli, but, unlike Thorndike, he argued that these associations were strengthened not as a result of reward, but simply on the basis of frequency and recency of the co-occurrence of the stimulus and the response.

So, for Watson, the essential element of all habits was the conditioned response, and conditioning happened whenever a stimulus and a response occurred simultaneously. It is important to appreciate that this theory of associationism differs from earlier ones by specifically *excluding* the possibility of any associations other than S–R associations. So, associations could not be formed between two stimuli (S–S associations): it would not be possible for any organism, animal or human, to associate, for example, a bell and food, so that the bell led to an expectation of food. Similarly, response–stimulus (R–S) associations were ruled out: it *was* possible, in the behaviourist view of the world, for a light, for example, to evoke the response of pressing a bar, but it was *not* possible to associate a press of the bar with food. The idea that all learning involves changes in the strength of *responses* is common to every behaviourist theory, and it is this restriction of the possible content of learning that can be shown to be wrong.

*A behaviourist analysis of thought*

What, then, of those silent human thought processes—like musing, reflecting, day-dreaming—that, to those of us who dare to introspect, seem to continue even in the absence of any obvious stimuli or responses? Watson's answer was straightforward: 'What the psychologists have hitherto called thought is in short nothing but talking to ourselves'[11]. Where do thoughts come from? Watson's reply was simply that the language habits that constitute thought were no different from any other habits. Words uttered vocally or subvocally were responses elicited by stimuli. Trains of thought were initiated by external stimuli, and maintained themselves because the production of each word in the chain produced feedback stimuli—stimuli which, as a result of previous conditioning of language habits, triggered the utterance of the next word in the thought train.

One interesting and ironic feature of Watson's analysis of thought is that he introduced as critical factors both invisible stimuli and invisible responses. This idea, which was to become characteristic of all behaviourist theories, naturally led to difficulties of verification that were just as severe as those that plagued the introspectionists. Although there were studies that supported the general notion that laryngeal muscles show some activity when humans indulge in silent thought, there was never the remotest prospect of any observation of the critical feedback stimuli of those subvocal responses, nor even of any discrimination between the incipient muscular responses that accompanied one word and those that accompanied some other word. Watson acknowledged that 'language habits' were critical to the intellectual superiority of humans over non-humans, but did not attempt to provide anything more than the vaguest hints on precisely how thinking might proceed. He therefore promulgated as dogma the idea that human thinking should properly be seen as the operation of stimulus–response habits.

Although Watson gained early prominence through his extremely effective anti-introspectionist propaganda, he contributed few experimental findings in support of the behaviourist view. This was partly because he became interested in the development of behaviour in children (to the exclusion of work on rats), and partly because of the enforced resignation of his academic post in 1920 (at Johns Hopkins University, to which he had moved in 1913). This occurred as a result of an affair (when married) with one of his graduate students: he subsequently married the student and went on to a financially far more profitable career in advertising.

## Hull's neobehaviourism

Behaviourism began to gain ground as the dominant stance of experimental psychologists in the 1930s and 1940s, when its principal exponent was Clark Hull (1884–1952), Professor at Yale. Like Watson, Hull is best known for his theoretical position (known as neobehaviourism), rather than for his experimental findings[12]. He shared Watson's belief that S–R associations were the only possible type of learning, but introduced a different account of the role of reward in learning. He liked to set his overall view in an evolutionary context, and it is most plausible and most readily comprehended within an imaginary scenario of the evolution of learning.

### Drive-reduction as the principle of reinforcement

In order to maximize its chances of survival, an animal must act to correct any deviation from its optimal state. Systematic deviations from that state are known as needs, and Hull proposed that needs gave rise to internal 'drive stimuli' (hunger pangs, for example). When an animal senses drive stimuli, it should adjust its behaviour, responding first in one way then in another, until those stimuli are reduced or eliminated (as a consequence of the satisfaction and removal of the need). All this seems eminently sensible and the next—and critical—part of the scenario is equally non-controversial: if on some future occasion, in the presence of the same external stimuli, the same need occurs, the animal should repeat the response that had most closely been followed by need reduction. If a hungry animal has had its hunger satisfied shortly after performing action A on a previous occasion in a given context, it surely would make sense for the animal to learn to repeat action A when hungry again in that same context. Hull's basic theoretical position is simply a formalization of that notion. He proposed that learning had evolved so as to strengthen associations between stimuli and responses when the occurrence, in a particular stimulus context, of a response was closely followed by need reduction (strictly, by reduction of the drive stimuli excited by the need state).

Hull believed that the drive-reduction principle applied both to Thorndikian trial-and-error learning, and to classical conditioning. The application to trial-and-error learning is clear, and in the case of classical conditioning, Hull's argument was that, for example, bell–food pairings produced salivation to the bell because the bell–salivation sequence was immediately followed by reduction of hunger.

*A role for pure stimulus acts in thought*

Like Watson, Hull believed that all 'higher' human thought processes were in fact manifestations of S–R associations. Hull did not accept Watson's identification of thought with silent speech, but did adopt the idea that much of human thought was mediated through unobservable responses that yielded unobservable feedback stimuli which elicited, in turn, further unobservable conditioned responses. He dubbed as 'pure stimulus acts'[13] those responses whose sole function was to produce feedback stimuli for responses that had a clear function.

Hull's position on the nature of consciousness was clearly anti-dualist: he made it quite clear that he rejected any appeal to non-physical entities, and was also interested in the notion of creating a 'psychic machine' that would incorporate his principles of learning and would show (or appear to show) such 'mentalistic' phenomena as purpose and knowledge. Although Hull did oddly claim in one article[14] both that consciousness does exist and that the notion of consciousness is a hangover of medieval theology, it is clear that his overall view on consciousness was close to Watson's and that, in particular, Hull believed that human consciousness enjoys no special status over non-human consciousness.

Like many of the early protagonists of behaviourism, Hull was anxious to have psychology regarded as a science on a par with the accepted physical sciences. This led him to present his theorizing in what, in retrospect, seems an almost comic guise as a set of 'postulates', 'theorems', and 'corollaries', many of which were represented as equations. The variables in these equations were 'intervening variables' or 'hypothetical

constructs'—entities that were not directly observable, but whose properties were inferred from behavioural observations. 'Drive' and 'habit
strength' are examples of such variables, but little is to be gained here
by going into further detail. The nub of Hullian theory is clear enough: all
learning and thought consists of the formation and activation of S–R
bonds, and no learning occurs without drive reduction.

## Skinner's radical behaviourism

The final major figure of behaviourist theory was Burrhus Frederic Skinner
(1904–90) of Harvard. Skinner noted that, despite the rejection of
introspectionism, Hull's neobehaviourism had ended up by trying to
establish the nature of internal entities: observable behaviour was explained as the output of the interactions of an internal system of
unobservable and entirely hypothetical entities (like drive and habit
strength). Skinner's goal was to restrict psychology entirely to visible
entities—stimuli, responses, and, most important of all, the consequences
of responses. Before discussing his approach, I should introduce Skinner's
distinction between two types of responses that were, he believed, objects
of two types of learning.

### Respondents and operants

The basic distinction that Skinner originally[15] drew between the two types
of response lay in whether or not they are elicited by the presence of a
specific environmental stimulus. Put two rats in a novel apparatus, and their
responses will differ: they may both show exploratory responding, but the
nature and sequencing of their responses will not be the same. In that sense,
their responses are spontaneous, and Skinner referred to these responses as
'operants'. But give two hungry dogs food, and both will salivate: the
salivation is not spontaneous, it is elicited by the food—it is a reflex in the
traditional sense, and Skinner refers to these responses as 'respondents'.

The typical classical conditioning experiment clearly involves a respondent: before conditioning can proceed, some stimulus (like food) must be
found that reliably elicits a response (like salivation). After pairing the
eliciting stimulus with some arbitrary stimulus (a bell, for example), the bell
acquires the power on its own to elicit salivation. Unlike Hull (but like
Watson), Skinner believed that the simple pairing of the arbitrary and the
eliciting stimulus was sufficient to obtain conditioning of a respondent. No
further principle of reinforcement was involved.

But Skinner did not believe that respondent conditioning was very important: it might *prepare* an animal for the arrival of food, but it did not contribute to the much more important process of actually *obtaining* the food. That is the province of operant conditioning.

Operant responses are so called because they operate on, and vary, the animal's environment, and Skinner came to define operants[16] according to their environmental effect. The press of a lever, for example, belongs to that class of movements (which will normally vary to some extent from one occasion to the next) that result in the downward movement of a lever. The probability of occurrence of an operant changes according to its consequence. Consequences that *increase* the subsequent rate of occurrence of an operant are known as 'reinforcers', which may be either positive or negative. The presentation of certain types of stimuli (which we could call rewards) increases the probability of occurrence of operants, and these are known as *positive reinforcers*; the removal of other types of stimuli (aversive or punishing) may similarly increase the rate of occurrence of an operant, and these removals are known as *negative reinforcers*. Thus if the press of a lever is followed by the presentation of food, the rate of lever pressing will increase; and if the press of a lever is followed by the removal of an aversive stimulus (bright light, for example), the rate will similarly increase. Both of these events—presentation of a reward and removal of a punishing event—are said to reinforce the strength of the operant (the former, as a positive reinforcer; the latter, as a negative reinforcer).

The strength of an operant may be *decreased* either by punishing it, or by ceasing the delivery of a reinforcer previously contingent upon the occurrence of the operant (extinction). In punishment procedures, the rate of occurrence of an operant will decrease if it is followed by the presentation of an aversive event (bright light, for example) or the removal of a reward (a dish of food, for example). In an extinction procedure, the rate of occurrence of an operant is reduced by the non-presentation of a reinforcer that had previously been contingent upon the occurrence of the operant; thus if the press of a lever is no longer followed by a food reward, the rate of lever pressing will decline.

My account thus far has shown only one, relatively minor, difference between the position of Skinner and Hull: Skinner believed that classical conditioning obeyed different laws from instrumental (operant) conditioning. But the major difference between Hull and Skinner—the one that led to Skinner's approach being known as 'radical' behaviourism—is that Skinner rigorously avoided the use of any terms that referred to processes or states that existed 'inside' the animal (in its mind, or its head, or its brain, or whatever). So, for example, he did not accept Hull's concept of 'drive' as an internal variable that might affect learning. He preferred to refer to deprivation (an external and visible process) as a procedure that altered the effectiveness of reinforcers. And, what is more relevant here, he did not suppose that S–R bonds or associations existed—instead, the probability of an operant changed as a consequence of the occurrence of a reinforcer. The denial of association formation has little bearing on the central implication of radical behaviourism: like previous versions of behaviour- ism, the claim is that learning consists only in altering the probability of occurrence of a *response*, and organisms—human or animal—do not learn about relationships between stimuli.

Skinner's programme was to uncover the events (the reinforcers) that modified the probability of operants, and to explain behaviour—operant behaviour—in terms of the organism's history of reinforcement. In effect, Skinner's claim was that all important behaviour (human and non-human) could be entirely accounted for by the strengthening and weakening of voluntary responses as a result of rewards and punishments.

*Private events as operants*

Skinner was just as concerned as the other behaviourists that we should eliminate mental entities ('explanatory fictions') from psychology: he contended that 'my toothache is just as physical as my typewriter'[17]. But he did distinguish between two classes of physical entity—public and private. There *are* such things as private stimuli: these are stimuli that are not observable by other members of the community. Commonly, their occurrence may be inferred by the community both from external circumstances (a sharp blow, for example) and from the collateral responses (groans and so on) that private stimuli may elicit. Given such an inference, then, the community may reinforce verbal responses such as 'that hurts' and so teach a child the art of self-description.

Skinner's next step is to claim that human consciousness consists simply in the use of verbal responses to private stimuli. So, non-human (non-verbal) animals may be conscious in the sense that they are awake and use their senses, but they are not conscious in the sense of being *aware* that they are seeing anything, or doing anything. Does this mean that Skinner believes that non-verbal organisms are not self-conscious but may be feeling-conscious? Although he makes a number of remarks that are, to say the least, ambiguous, it is unlikely that he did accept feeling-consciousness: first, because of the parallel he draws between a typewriter and a toothache; and second, because of an odd remark made about the preverbal child: 'We have reason to believe that the child will not discriminate among colors—

that he will not see two colors as different—until exposed to such contingencies'[18] (meaning differential reinforcement by the verbal community contingent upon properties of different colors). This remark is hard to reconcile with the common sense notion that lights of different wavelength result in different visual *experiences*—whether or not those experiences have been differentially reinforced.

Stimuli were not the only private events that Skinner envisaged. Like Watson and Hull, he acknowledged that (operant) responses might be incipient and unobserved: his analysis of our silent thought processes is in principle no different from theirs.

## Overview: major dogmas of behaviourism

### Learning about responses

Because behaviourists rejected mentalistic terms as relics of dualism, much of their theoretical writing consisted in the effort to translate such terms into acceptable terminology—a terminology that regarded learning as necessarily constituting changes in the probability of responses. For Hull, all learning consisted in changes in the strengths of S–R bonds; for Skinner, all (important) learning consisted in changes in the probability of operant responses. The strength of conviction behind their writing might lead one to suppose that there is a stark choice between dualism and behaviourism, and that behaviourism is the *only* alternative to dualism. But to insist that the existence and properties of any proposed learning device must be tested against the responses made by an animal is not to assume that the device should concern itself solely with learning about responses. It is easy to see how odd the notion is.

Consider, for example, the effects on a hungry dog of pairing a bell with food. The dog comes to salivate when the bell alone is presented. Both Hull and Skinner (Pavlov too, for that matter) believed that this came about because of some kind of link between the bell and the salivation response. They would have regarded it as mentalistic to suggest that the bell led the dog to expect food, and that that expectation induced salivation. But what of the proposal that the bell does activate some internal correlate of the food—a correlate that has much in common with the events that occur when real food is presented, so much so that the salivary reflex is elicited by it? Although introspectionism may be a dangerous pastime, it is perhaps worth observing that the idea that expectation of food plays some role does have a powerful intuitive plausibility.

The point here is that being scientific does not require that we believe that learning consists only in modifying the probability of responses; responding could alter as a by-product of a process of learning that does not critically involve responses. An organism *could* learn that a bell signals the imminent arrival of food. Whether organisms *do* learn in that way is a question of fact, not of dogma—a question capable of experimental determination.

### The role of reward and punishment

Both Hull and Skinner believed that no learning occurred in the absence of reward (or punishment). Intuitively, this seems an even more remarkable claim. Where were the rewards that created the memory for something read in a book? Do infants learn *nothing* about language by observing adults talking to each other? Of course, the behaviourists came up with invisible, unnoticed rewards for such instances, and such questions were not genuinely testable. But it is clearly an odd hypothesis, and it is not at all clear that it could provide an efficient learning system.

A further consequence of the role ascribed to reinforcers is that common sense accounts of the simplest examples of animal behaviour must be rejected, not simply because they are in 'mentalistic' terms, but because, when translated into acceptable 'behaviouristic' terms, they would still be wrong. Consider a hungry rat in a testing chamber with a lever present. Things are arranged so that if the rat presses the lever, food is delivered. Not surprisingly, the rat eventually learns to press the lever. Now *why* is the rat pressing the lever? The unsophisticated observer might suggest that the rat is pressing the lever 'to obtain the food'. But Hull and Skinner would allow only that the lever-press response has increased in probability as a consequence of the reinforcing effect of food. No 'trace' representing food exists in the rat's brain. In pressing the lever, the rat does not 'expect' the food—it 'knows' nothing of the existence of the food, and has no notion whatever of *why* it is pressing the lever. The function of the food is simply to increase the probability of a press of the lever.

Perhaps the behaviourists are right; perhaps the rat's brain contains absolutely no information about the food at all. But it is, again, a question of fact: *do* animals in any sense 'know' anything about the rewards that they (apparently) are working for? In fact, modern research has shown clearly that animals *do* learn about rewards, and that a common sense, intuitive account of what animals do know does have at least some validity. Before looking at those animal experiments, we should briefly consider work on human cognition, because it was this that began the overthrow of behaviourism.

## The fall of behaviourism

The beginning of the end of behaviourism as a driving force in contemporary psychology can be seen in two publications that appeared in the 1950s. Both were concerned with pivotal issues of human psychology, and their appearance signalled a split between animal and human psychology. The major figures of behaviourism had written freely about both humans and animals, seeing no need to draw any limits on the generality of their claims across different species. Contemporary human psychologists largely ignore work on animals, and contemporary animal psychologists rarely consider, at least in writing, the implications of their work for human thought. The first of the two publications was the monograph *Perception and communication*, published in 1958 by the English psychologist Donald Broadbent (1926–93); this book was the first important statement of cognitive psychology.

### Cognitive psychology

What is now known as cognitive psychology began with efforts to account for well-known effects seen in humans with which behaviourists were in general not concerned, and for which they could provide no convincing theoretical explanation. We can briefly consider here two of those phenomena—selective attention and short-term memory.

It is a common experience that in a buzz of conversation from several sources, we may listen to one voice at the exclusion of others without changing the nature of the physical input (without, for example, moving so as to be closer to the person whose conversation is of interest). This phenomenon has come to be known as the 'cocktail party' effect. We can attend selectively to one voice, and can readily shift that attention to another voice. Traditional behaviourism did not conceive of any internal device that could accept some sensory inputs and reject others—information from all the senses poured in all the time, and formed the set of stimuli that could become associated with responses.

The second phenomenon concerns different types of memory. Most of us can readily repeat a six-digit number that is read out to us at normal speed. But few of us can do the same with a twelve-digit number. Why should that be? It cannot be the case that our memory is in any sense full since we can, given sufficient repetitions, accurately learn many different twelve-digit numbers. Why, then, can we learn six-digit numbers in a single presentation, but twelve-digit numbers only after repetitions—and why do repetitions help? Behaviourism had nothing to say about this problem, and in fact little to say about memory in general. For behaviourists, memory was no more than the system that preserved the current state of S–R bonds, and the notion of studying memory independently of learning made no sense.

In contrast to the behaviourist approach, cognitive psychologists view the mind as an information-processing device; they are concerned to track the flow of information through the system and to characterize the ways in which the information is transformed at different stages of its flow. Their most characteristic method of explanation consists of a flow diagram with boxes symbolizing devices or mechanisms having various properties, linked by arrows that show the flow of information between the boxes.

Selective attention and memory were two of the central topics in *Perception and communication*. Broadbent proposed that incoming sensory information was processed by a filter that passed information from high-priority sources in preference to information from low-priority sources. Information that passed through the filter entered a short-term memory store (STM), and when it was rehearsed sufficiently in the STM it passed on to a long-term store (LTM). The concept of rehearsal incorporates the introspective notion that we do actively repeat new items to ourselves—telephone numbers, for example—when given them to remember.

Two important differences between STM and LTM were, first, that STM had a limited capacity of about seven items, compared to the unlimited capacity of LTM, and, second, that information in STM was subject to rapid decay whereas information held in LTM was permanent. This cognitive account of memory provides a ready explanation of why we can readily recall six- but not twelve-digit numbers: the latter exceeds the capacity of STM. It explains also why repetition helps us retain longer numbers: with each repetition, more rehearsal in STM is possible for those items, so that more and more of the digits in the number may be transferred to LTM (with its unlimited capacity). We can best gain a clear idea of the contrast between the cognitive and behaviourist approaches by seeing how they apply to a related problem in memory.

*Cognitive versus behaviourist accounts of serial learning*

If we give someone a long list of new items and immediately after presentation ask the person to recall as many of those items as possible, recall is best for items at the beginning and end of the list, poorest for items in the middle of the list. The superiority of the early items is known as the 'primacy' effect, and the inferiority of the late items, as the 'recency' effect. How should these effects be explained?

Hull proposed in 1935[19] an account in terms of S–R bonds. He argued that correct performance reflected the formation of associations between each item in the list and (the response to) the item that succeeded it. Hull referred to this correct association as the 'immediate forward excitatory tendency' of an item. But each item, according to his account, also gives rise to a 'trace' that persists, gradually weakening, for the duration of the remainder of the list. The trace of each item would become associated with (the responses to) all the items that succeed the 'correct' item. So, the recall of an item would evoke not only the correct response (that is, the utterance of the next item on the list), but also a tendency to utter each of the succeeding items on the list (that tendency being weaker the greater the distance between the items on the list). Hull refers to these distant, 'incorrect' associations as 'remote forward excitatory tendencies'. For somewhat complex reasons that need not concern us here, Hull postulated that when a remote excitatory tendency 'spanned' an item on a list, its effect was to inhibit the production of the correct response. Figure 4.1 shows that whilst neither the first nor the last item on a list would suffer any inhibition from spanning tendencies, the central items would suffer the most. His account can, therefore, explain both the primacy and the recency effect.

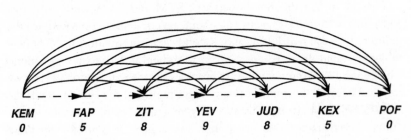

| KEM | FAP | ZIT | YEV | JUD | KEX | POF |
|-----|-----|-----|-----|-----|-----|-----|
| 0   | 5   | 8   | 9   | 8   | 5   | 0   |

**Fig. 4.1** Hull's diagrammatic representation of the immediate and remote forward excitatory tendencies that he assumed to be operative in learning a series of 'nonsense syllables'. The straight broken arrows represent immediate excitatory tendencies and the curved solid arrows, remote excitatory tendencies. The number of remote excitatory tendencies spanning a given syllable, such as YEV, is given by the formula $(n - 1)(N - n)$, where $N$ is the total number of syllables in the series and $n$ is the ordinal number of the syllable whose span value is under consideration. Thus in the above example $N = 7$ and the $n$ for YEV = 4. Accordingly, $n - 1 = 3$ and $N - n = 3$. Consequently, YEV should have $3 \times 3$ or 9 remote excitatory tendencies spanning it. The number of remote excitatory tendencies spanning a syllable is given beneath each syllable; the larger that number, the greater the inhibition and the poorer the recall for the syllable. (From Hull (1935), with permission.)

The cognitive two-memory store account of the same effects is considerably simpler to follow. The first few items presented enter STM and are rehearsed there until STM is fully occupied; this rehearsal will allow these items to be transferred successfully to LTM. Later items will enter a full STM and enjoy relatively poor opportunity for rehearsal and hence for successful transfer to LTM. So, when only two or three items have been presented, they may be rehearsed while awaiting the arrival of the next item, but when seven or eight items (or more) have been presented, it is not possible to rehearse all the items effectively. The primacy effect can therefore be explained by supposing that the early items in a list are better represented in LTM than are the later items. At the end of the presentation of the list of items, the last few items only will be in STM, since its limited capacity prevents all the items of a long list from co-existing in STM. If recall follows immediately after list presentation, the last few items can, therefore, be retrieved from STM—giving rise to the recency effect. In essence this cognitive account supposes that both STM and LTM are used in learning a list: the superiority of the early items in a list is due to their successful transfer to LTM, and the superiority of the late items is due to their continuing representation in STM.

How can we decide between these accounts? One interesting contrast between them is that whereas the behaviourist account supposes that both effects have the same cause—maximal inhibition of the central list items, the cognitive account supposes quite different causes of the two effects. If the cognitive account is correct, it should be possible to manipulate procedures so as to affect one of the effects but not the other; independence of the primacy and the recency effects would argue strongly against the behaviourist account. There have in fact been a number of experiments that have successfully operated on one effect without affecting the other.

The cognitive account of the primacy effect supposes that it is a consequence of rehearsal. Time for rehearsal will be greater if the items are presented at a slow rate; similarly, opportunities for rehearsal will be minimized at a fast presentation rate. So, if rehearsal is responsible for the primacy effect, then the primacy effect should be enhanced by a slow presentation rate, and reduced by a fast presentation rate: this is exactly what is found experimentally[20]; moreover, presentation rate, as would be expected from two-memory account, does not affect the recency effect.

If the recency effect is due to the existence in STM of the late items of a list, then manipulations that reduce the effectiveness of STM should reduce the recency effect. Another experiment explored the effect of introducing a delay between list presentation and recall; during the delay, subjects were asked to count out loud (a manipulation designed to prevent rehearsal). Items in STM are supposed to show rapid decay unless there is an opportunity for rehearsal, so that the ultimate effect of a delay in which rehearsal is not possible should be to eliminate items from STM. The experimenters expected that their introduction of a delay between presentation and recall would reduce the recency effect, and this is what they found; the delay, as anticipated, did not affect the primacy effect[21].

It is not my intention to give a detailed account of the contest between behaviourist and cognitive positions across the whole range of attention and memory. I hope that, although I have simplified the arguments, I have outlined the basic differences between their approaches, and have shown that these differences can be tackled experimentally. Cognitive theory has advanced considerably since 1958: the belief now is that there are several relatively independent memory stores, and it is no longer supposed that information necessarily enters LTM through STM[22]. New ideas on the organization of memory owe nothing, however, to behaviourist theory. Contemporary ways of looking at memory processes show a clear continuity with the approach introduced by Broadbent and other early cognitive psychologists. The idea that there is more than one memory store, and that active rehearsal plays a role in memory, still lie at the centre of contemporary theorizing.

The rapidly declining influence of behaviourism can be clearly traced in the literature of cognitive psychology. In 1958 Broadbent saw Hull's behaviourist approach as the obvious alternative to his own—as a serious theoretical rival worthy of respect. There were, accordingly, 21 references to Hull in the index to *Perception and communication*. The next major monograph to appear was *Cognitive psychology*[23], written by the Cornell University psychologist Ulric Neisser. Although that book was published only nine years later, in 1967, Neisser cites Hull only once, and does not discuss his theories at any point in the book. And Broadbent himself mentions Hull only once in his 1971 book, *Decision and stress*[24]. As far as psychologists interested in human cognitive processes were concerned, behaviourism was decisively rejected some thirty years ago.

## The acquisition of language

A second nail in the coffin of behaviourism was provided by the Harvard psycholinguist Noam Chomsky's lengthy review[25], in 1959, of Skinner's 1957 monograph *Verbal behavior*[26]. That book purported to give a scientific account of the acquisition and use of language. Much of the scientific gloss was achieved by translations of conventional terms into different terms with a more scientific 'ring'. 'Verbal behaviour', for example, simply means using language; Skinner also introduced 'textual behaviour', to refer to reading; 'mands', to refer to questions, commands—anything used to evoke a response in another human; 'tacts', to refer to objects or events; 'echoic operants', to refer to imitations of speech. But the real core of Skinner's argument was the claim that human speech utterances are operants and that, like any other operants, they are strengthened by reinforcing consequences. Children learn to talk by the reinforcement of the use of appropriate words, and the non-reinforcement of the misuse of words.

Chomsky's attack on Skinner had two main strands. First, he argued that no coherent account of language emerged even if Skinner's overall theoretical stance was adopted. Chomsky criticized Skinner's failure to use basic terms such as stimulus, response, and reinforcement in accordance with the strict definitions that were given for them. That rather technical argument was already causing widespread unease among scientists working on animal learning; it was the second strand of Chomsky's argument that carried most persuasive force.

Chomsky argued that any sensible attempt to relate the stimulation we receive to our overt behaviour would have to incorporate assumptions about our internal structure. Most of us believe that we human beings are immensely complex organisms; but Skinner in fact assumes an internal structure so simple that all our behaviour can be accounted for in terms of changes in one parameter—operant strength—brought about by rein- forcement. He assumes that this simple structure is common to all humans and indeed, presumably to all animals—certainly to the rats, pigeons, and monkeys used in laboratory experiments. According to Skinner, the major determinant of language acquisition is environmental feedback, in the form of reinforcement.

The alternative approach, favoured by Chomsky, is to suppose that humans do possess a complex internal structure, and that, in consequence, we make a substantial 'independent contribution' to the acquisition of language. Which of these two views is correct can only be decided by appealing to the facts of language acquisition. At that time, few systematic findings were available—Skinner had relied entirely on anecdotal and hypothetical examples rather than on experimental data, and Chomsky did likewise in his review. But merely by appealing to what all of us know about language, Chomsky was able to show the remarkable implausibility of Skinner's account. We all know, for example, that language is peculiar to humans; other animals, to be sure, have systems of communication that may be remarkably effective, but are different and much less flexible than language. But if all animals learn in the same way, why is it that only humans acquire language?

Skinner's account of language acquisition supposes a dominant role for feedback (in the form of reinforcement) from adult language users. But in fact, Chomsky argued, it is obvious that children learn a great deal (and not only about language) 'by casual observation and imitation of adults and other children'[27]. Similarly, it simply is not the case that adults do provide endless correction when children make their first efforts at talking.

Chomsky's final remarks returned to another aspect of the importance of structure. Once a language has been learned, the speaker regularly produces strings of words that form grammatically correct sentences; moreover, the speaker can readily identify an entirely new string of words as being either grammatical or not. In other words, speakers impose a grammatical structure on their speech, and they can detect the presence or absence of grammatical structure in the speech of others (and this is, of course, crucial to successful language acquisition, since the meaning of sentences depends not only on the words that they contain, but upon such factors as the order in which they occur). In that sense, speakers acquire—whether or not they can articulate them—the rules of grammar.

In order to understand language acquisition we should, then, have to explain how grammar is acquired; but to do that, we first have to characterize successfully the grammar of a language—to state unequivocally the set of rules that determine for all word strings whether or not they form grammatical sentences. This is a task that has so far defied the efforts of linguists—a fact that again points to the implausibility of Skinner's claim that language is readily acquired by an organism having a simple internal structure.

Given that we cannot yet adequately describe the grammar of any human language, it is hardly surprising that no account of human language acquisition has yet achieved universal support. Chomsky himself supposes that humans have a substantial amount of innate language competence. All children readily acquire the rules of the grammar of their own language, at roughly the same rate, and more or less independent of how intelligent they appear to be. These facts suggested to Chomsky 'that human beings are somehow specially designed to do this, with data-handling or 'hypothesis-formulating' ability of unknown character and complexity'[28].

We shall return to Chomsky's notions of an innate human capacity for language acquisition when we consider work on language acquisition by non-humans. Whatever the virtues of that proposal, Chomsky's review did succeed in persuading the majority of the scientific community that language is indeed too complex to be accounted for using the few simple principles advocated by Skinner, and that Skinner's attempt to do so without recourse to any serious analysis of linguistics should be rejected. We can surely agree with Chomsky that 'what is necessary . . . is research, not dogmatic and perfectly arbitrary claims, based on analogies to that small part of the experimental literature in which one happens to be interested'[29].

## Behaviourism and animal learning

Psychologists in general are well aware that behaviourism no longer figures as a major force in theorizing about human thought processes; but in fact behaviourism has also been widely rejected by animal psychologists. There still remains a widespread belief that psychologists that work with animals—with rats or pigeons in particular—are, almost by definition, behaviourists. It is of course true that animal psychologists interested in the intelligence and memory of animals study their behaviour: but this does not make them behaviourists any more than those who study human behaviour are *ipso facto* behaviourists. A behaviourist is a psychologist who adheres to the school of thought to which Watson, Hull, and Skinner belonged, and that is an approach long since abandoned by the great majority of animal psychologists.

There were, throughout its history, many experimental studies that caused severe difficulties for behaviourism—reports, for example, that strongly suggested the formation of associations between one stimulus and another (rather than between a stimulus and a response—the only legitimate association for a behaviourist), or that cast doubt on the notion that reward was necessary for learning (as both neobehaviourists and radical behaviourists believed).

Behaviourists proved remarkably adept at concocting theoretical accounts (increasingly convoluted) of discordant findings and it was, perhaps, the cumulative effect of such findings, rather than any particular result, that finally demonstrated its bankruptcy as an explanatory system. I have selected two topics which show why behaviourism has been rejected and also give some feel for the contemporary theory of animal learning that has replaced it. The first topic provides a striking demonstration of S–S learning and the second, an insight into the role of reward in learning and performance.

*Stimulus–stimulus learning: the phenomenon of autoshaping*

The pigeon's 'key peck' was for Skinner a prototypical example of an operant. The essence of an operant was that it was a response that was controlled by its consequences: in conventional terms, operants are voluntary responses that are strengthened by reward and weakened by punishment. But a surprising experimental finding, first reported in 1968[30], showed that the 'key peck' is no ordinary operant. The experiment was very simple. A hungry pigeon was placed in a testing chamber, and from time to time (once a minute, on average) a response key in the front wall was illuminated from behind with white light. Eight seconds later, the light went off, and food was made available (for four seconds) in a food tray under the key. The sequence of events was wholly independent of the pigeon's responding: whether it pecked or not, the food was delivered. It turned out that the pigeons in fact pecked the key—a phenomenon now known as 'autoshaping' (the pigeons themselves 'shaped' the behaviour of pecking the key).

Why should pigeons peck keys that precede the arrival of food? The obvious Skinnerian interpretation is that the birds' pecks are in fact followed by food, so that the key peck operant is strengthened, as usual, by reward. Skinner referred to this type of responding as 'super-stitious' since, in fact, the key peck plays no role in obtaining the food. But further experiments have shown that this is not a tenable explanation. The most convincing disproof was provided in 1969[31] by another very simple experiment that used the same training procedure except that now, if a pigeon pecked the illuminated key, no food was delivered when the light went off (a procedure known as 'omission training'). Once again, the pigeons began to peck the key and continued to do so after extended training, despite the fact that *every time the key was pecked, no food was delivered*. This finding shows clearly that autoshaping is *not* the result of key pecks being followed by reward; no key peck was ever followed by reward. In fact, the reverse was true—the pecks prevented reward.

What is the correct explanation of autoshaping? It is clear that the essential condition for the emergence of autoshaping is simply that the light is followed by food, and contemporary accounts accept what is so clearly implied—namely, that the animal forms an association between the light and the food (an association between two *stimuli*). The light makes the animal expect food (or, as most psychologists would prefer to say, evokes an 'internal representation' of food). But why should the fact that the animal expects food make it peck the signal for food? The notion is that the idea of food (its internal representation) produces some of the same effects as perceiving real food (so, thinking about food when we are hungry makes us salivate). The lit key, in other words, substitutes for food: pigeons peck at food, so pigeons peck at the key. It is easy to see that this is an intuitively satisfying account: consider Pavlov's dogs—the bell makes them think of food, they are hungry, so thinking of food makes them salivate. Further work with pigeons has found direct evidence for this explanation. Pigeons drink in relatively long gulps, so that their beaks open for much longer when drinking than when pecking at food. Thirsty pigeons can be autoshaped to peck at illuminated keys that signal the arrival of water, but photographic analysis shows that those pecks are of longer duration than pecks autoshaped for food reward[32]. In other words, it seems that pigeons 'drink' signals for water and 'eat' signals for food.

This S–S account of autoshaping is further strengthened by direct evidence, from the phenomenon of sensory preconditioning, that animals can in fact associate two neutral stimuli, neither of which initially elicits any overt response. A typical sensory preconditioning experiment consists of three stages. In the first stage, animals experience a series of pairings of two neutral stimuli (S1 and S2)—a light (S1) followed by a tone (S2), for example. In the second stage, S2 is paired with a stimulus of motivational significance (a reward or a punishment)—so, for example, the tone might now be followed by a food reward; at the end of this stage, S2 elicits a conditioned response (salivation, for example). In the third stage, S1 is presented alone, and it is routinely found that it now produces the same conditioned response that had developed to S2 in the second stage—the light, a stimulus that has never been paired with food, now elicits salivation. Sensory preconditioning is readily explained by the notion that animals form S–S associations. In the first stage, the animals learn to associate the light with the tone; in the second stage, they come to associate the tone with the food; so that in the third stage, presentation of the light elicits a representation of the tone, which in turn elicits a representation of the food, which ultimately elicits the appropriate response—salivation. The outcome of the omission training experiments and the phenomenon of sensory preconditioning, taken together, show, first, that neither a reward nor the occurrence of a response is necessary for learning to occur, and second, that S–S associations *are* formed by animals.

It might, incidentally, seem that the fact that hungry pigeons continue to peck food signals despite the fact that pecking prevents the arrival of food would suggest that pigeons are unintelligent. Why else would they fail to learn to stop pecking? We can empathize with the pigeon's problem if we consider a comparable human problem. Suppose an experimenter made you hungry and consistently rang a bell a few seconds before giving you some highly desired morsel of food. You would, naturally, salivate on hearing the bell. Now, suppose we introduce the rule that you will only be given the food if you do *not* salivate—would that be easy? Intuitively, we might expect not (and in fact dogs find it very difficult to stop salivating in such conditions, just as pigeons find it difficult to stop pecking). The problem does not, then, seem to be one of intelligence, but rather something to do with what might be called the 'reflexiveness'; just as we find it difficult to stop salivating at will, so pigeons find it difficult to stop pecking.

Exploration of the autoshaping phenomenon has shown that animals *do* form S–S associations, and it is not therefore true that all learning consists in learning about *responses*. These results also show that it is no easy matter to decide which responses should be regarded as 'operants' and which, as 'respondents': the pigeon's key peck certainly *looks* like a 'voluntary' response—but it is in fact surprisingly reflexive, and resistant to modification by its consequences.

*Response–stimulus learning: the effect of reward devaluation*

It is now clear that animals do form associations between stimuli, so that the occurrence of one stimulus leads to an expectation of another. The next question to be explored is one raised earlier—namely, what is the function of reward in learning, when learning involves responding in an arbitrary way? *Do* animals learn about the consequences of their own responses? *Do* they, for example, learn that their actions are followed by reward?

Consider again the example of a rat that has been trained to press a lever for food reward. We have seen that Hull and Skinner agree that the effect of the reward is solely to increase the probability of the lever-press response in the presence of the stimuli. The information or the 'knowledge' used by the animal in responding does not include anything about the reward that is obtained. The rat is not working in order to obtain food: it 'knows' nothing about the food. The food has served only to reinforce the likelihood, given the situational stimuli, of the lever-press response— *that* is all that the animal 'knows'. This account of what was supposed to be the cause of the rat's action seems wildly implausible, particularly since it was supposed to apply to humans as well. But behaviourism's history has shown, if nothing else, that however implausible and contrary to common sense an idea may be (and however ineffective in predicting any new finding), it may nevertheless, in the hands of skilled propagandists, be remarkably difficult to overthrow. Appeals to common sense alone will not do: experimental disproof is needed.

Many studies have suggested that animals *do* learn about the rewards that they work for (or appear to be working for). But that conclusion was not universally accepted until relatively recently. One particularly forceful study used, again, a very simple design[33]. Hungry rats were trained to press a lever for a sugar reward. They then experienced, in a different apparatus, a single delivery of sugar immediately followed by an injection of an aversive solution (lithium chloride) that made them mildly ill. The effect of a pairing of this kind is to make the taste of the previously attractive food less rewarding or even actually unacceptable. (A similar effect will be known to those of us who have developed a life-long aversion to a particular type of alcoholic drink after an unfortunate, if self-inflicted, excess in our youth.) After recovering from the illness, the rats returned to the lever press apparatus. The question of interest was, would the rats press as eagerly for a reward that was no longer attractive? Clearly, the behaviourist prediction is that the devaluation of the reward should have no effect on performance—it could not have affected the strength of any Hullian S–R association involved in the response (associations can only be affected by manipulations that involve the *occurrence* of the response; similarly, Skinnerian operant strength can only be modified by procedures in which the response actually occurs). In case lever pressing was influenced by the arrival of now-devalued 'rewards', no sugar was delivered in this test, and the experimenters counted the number of responses made before the animals abandoned lever pressing. They found that reducing the value of the reward dramatically reduced the number of responses made in the test (compared with animals that had been made ill in the same way, except that the lithium chloride was not delivered in association with the sugar reward which, accordingly, did not become less rewarding).

The implications of the experiment are clear. Animals do not simply emit responses blindly as a result of S–R associations (or of strengthened operants): animals that *appear* to be working for a reward *are* doing just that. If we change the value of the reward, their performance changes accordingly. The animals 'know' that their responses will result in a certain consequence. As Anthony Dickinson, a Cambridge University psychologist and one of the authors of the experiment, has noted, this is a conclusion that 'will surprise few people. What might be more surprising is that the issue was not properly settled long ago'.[34]

## Contemporary animal learning theory

Although contemporary theorists have rejected the neobehaviourist claim that all learning consisted in the formation of S–R associations, they have not rejected the idea that association formation plays a major role in learning[35]. We have seen that autoshaping is now taken to be an example of S–S learning. Similarly, the force of the experiments on the effect of devaluation on responding is to show that what is learned is, not an S–R association, but an R–S association, where the response (R) is the lever press and the stimulus (S) is the reward.

The central core of contemporary animal learning theory remains associationist, but now theorists see animals as forming associations between *events*, be they stimuli or responses. Animals may form S–S associations (in classical conditioning paradigms), R–S associations (in instrumental learning), and even S–R associations (in what some have called 'habit formation')[36]. There is no supposition that these different associations are in any important sense different *types* of learning. The consensus is, rather, that when animals experience real dependencies between the events that they perceive, they form associations between those events.

It looks as though, after their long struggle with behaviourism, animal learning theorists have simply returned to the beliefs held before behaviourism emerged. William James, after all, believed in the formation of both S–S and R–S associations—although, of course, his terminology was very different: 'Objects once experienced together tend to become associated in the imagination, so that when any one of them is thought of, the others are likely to be thought of also . . .'[37]; 'Volition is the association of ideas of muscular motion with the ideas of those pleasures which the motion produces'[38].

The difference between contemporary animal learning theory and traditional associationism is that we now have the concepts and the techniques necessary to *prove* the existence of associations of specific types. Contemporary theorists use these techniques to answer such basic questions as: what are the necessary conditions for the formation of an association—for example, does rehearsal play a role? What is the nature and content of the internal representations of events—for example, which aspects of a stimulus are represented?

Although its current concerns have persuaded many that animal learning theory is more 'cognitive' in its approach, it is not clear that contemporary associationism has direct implications for the consciousness or otherwise of animals. We may now speak readily enough of the 'expectations' of animals, but what is meant is simply the formation of S–S or R–S associations. When we say, for example, that hearing a bell leads to a dog's expectation of food, we mean that the activation of the internal representation of a bell leads to the activation of the internal representation of food. It is not clear that the ability to form S–S and R–S associations as well as S–R associations means that animals are any more likely to be conscious. Animals possess devices that detect dependencies between events in their worlds, and form associations between internal representations of those events. But do 'internal representations' necessarily imply a mind? This is a question in which contemporary associationists have shown little interest, at least in public. They do not share the behaviourists' strident concern with the existence (or non-existence) of consciousness. Similarly, they see no reason to dispense with introspection as a technique that may yield insights (with the reservation that an insight is valuable only if leads to testable predictions: if a prediction is not confirmed, then the introspection will be rejected). They accept that behaviour is the only test for a theory but, unlike behaviourists, they have used behavioural findings to help develop their theories, and have not clung dogmatically to a theory for which there never was sound experimental support.

Behaviourism—the central concern of this chapter—was a theory that was intended to apply equally to humans and non-humans. Behaviourists did not conceive of any fundamental distinction between human and non-human intelligence, nor did they suppose that there were any marked intellectual differences amongst non-humans (at least, not amongst mammals). Hull, for example, although believing that there are 'innate' differences between species, argued that they were a consequence solely of differences in constants in basic behavioural equations that applied equally to all species: 'the natural-science theory of behavior being developed by the present author and his associates assumes that all behavior of the individuals of a given species, and that of all species of mammals, including man, occurs according to the same set of primary laws'[39]. We have seen that psychologists working with humans were able to throw off behaviourism some years before animal learning theorists did so. In fact, animal psychology, or at least the psychology of animal learning, has proceeded in the last four decades largely independently of human psychology. We should now ask whether there are major differences between the cognition of humans (who are conscious) and non-humans (whose consciousness is the issue), and, in particular, whether there are any contrasts in cognition that might suggest a difference in consciousness. Since there is a widespread view that some animals are more conscious than others (who may not be conscious at all), these are questions that can hardly be tackled without first discussing whether there are any cognitive differences among animals. Such questions are the province of comparative psychology, and in fact comparative psychologists have been ready to make claims about consciousness in animals. Chapter 5 will, accordingly, focus on the comparative psychology of intelligence with a view to preparing the ground for seeking links between cognition and consciousness.

## Notes and references

1. For a highly readable account of the beginnings of animal psychology, see Boakes (1984).
2. Thorndike (1911/1970), p. 24.
3. Morgan (1894), p. 53.
4. There is a possible ambiguity in the use of the term 'association'. It may be used to refer either to an association—in the sense of a real dependence or contingency—between events in the outside world, or to an association 'in the mind' between what can neutrally be called 'internal correlates' of events in the external world. In this book, 'association' will be used in the latter sense, to refer to an internal connection—mental, neural, or whatever— between internal entities. So, when I speak of an association between a stimulus and a response, I mean an internal connection between internal correlates of an external stimulus and an external response.
5. Thorndike (1911/1970), p 123.
6. Watson (1913/1994).
7. Ibid., p. 250.
8. Ibid.
9. Ibid., p. 249.
10. Watson (1930), p. 2.
11. Ibid., p. 238.
12. Hull's major theoretical papers are reprinted, with a useful introduction, in Amsel and Rashotte (1984).
13. Hull (1930) (reprinted in Amsel and Rashotte (1984)).
14. Hull (1937) (reprinted in Amsel and Rashotte (1984)).
15. Skinner (1938).
16. Skinner (1953).
17. Skinner (1961), p. 285.
18. Skinner (1969), p. 229.
19. Hull (1935) (reprinted in Amsel and Rashotte (1984)).

20. Glanzer and Cunitz (1966).
21. Ibid.
22. See Anderson (1995) for an introduction to contemporary cognitive approaches to memory; Anderson's book is noteworthy for the fact that he does discuss animal memory alongside human memory.
23. Neisser (1967).
24. Broadbent (1971).
25. Chomsky (1959).
26. Skinner (1957).
27. Chomsky (1959), p. 42.
28. Chomsky (1959), p. 57.
29. Chomsky (1959), p. 43.
30. Brown and Jenkins (1968).
31. Williams and Williams (1969).
32. Jenkins and Moore (1973).
33. Adams and Dickinson (1981).
34. Dickinson (1985) p. 72.
35. For clear accounts of modern learning theory, see Dickinson (1980) or Mackintosh (1983).
36. Dickinson (1985); see also the discussion of an 'intentional' account of instrumental conditioning in Chapter 8.
37. James (1950), p. 561.
38. Ibid., p. 599.
39. Hull (1945), p. 56 (reprinted in Amsel and Rashotte (1984)).

# 5

## Of mice and men

### Comparing intelligences

#### Intelligence testing for animals

The rejection of behaviourism means that it is once again legitimate—and interesting—to ask whether different species vary in their intelligence. From our point of view, this might provide a way of determining which animals are conscious and which are not, or some sort of scale of consciousness (if, as William James (and others) believed, consciousness is a state that varies in degree between animals of different species).

The first question that arises is: how we should go about assessing the intelligence of animals? Insistence on reliability and objectivity means that we cannot simply rely upon anecdotal accounts of apparently intelligent animal behaviour—we must devise tests. How should we set about designing tests? The answer is basically the same as for designing tests to be used with humans: we have to rely on hunches for tests that demand intelligence for their solution. When the tests are actually used, we can decide whether or not they seem to provide valid measures of intelligence. Human intelligence testing has encountered severe difficulty with the issue of validity—how do we decide whether a high intelligence test score *does* reflect high intelligence? 'Objective' measures such as performance in school and university exams, subsequent career success, and so on, have been used—and good performance in intelligence tests does correlate with such measures. But it is possible to argue that the same non-cognitive factors that influence test performance—motivation, for example—impair performance in the 'objective' sphere, and bring about a correlation that has in reality nothing to do with intelligence. We need not concern ourselves here with the validity of human intelligence tests, but it should caution us that devising valid tests is not easy.

The most obvious problem when testing animals is that of ensuring that differences in test performance are not due to inter-species differences in such things as sensory capacities and motor skills. The fact that rats learn colour discriminations less rapidly than monkeys (if at all) need not mean that rats are less intelligent—they have, after all, very poor colour vision. And the fact that goldfish cannot pile boxes on top of one another, as chimps can, reflects, not necessarily a difference in intelligence, but the absence of limbs in goldfish. These sensory and motor factors—along with other relevant non-cognitive factors such as motivation and type of reward—have been called 'contextual variables' by Jeff Bitterman of the University of Hawaii (one of the most influential comparative psychologists of recent decades). Ruling out the influence of contextual variables is a problem that arises when one species performs more poorly on a test than some other species. But if two species show comparable performance (if both, for example, successfully solve a given problem after a similar number of trials) there is no need to concern ourselves with the potential influence of contextual variables. This is, therefore, only a relevant issue when claims are made that a given test *does* provide evidence of intellectual differences between species.

A decade or so ago, I began a survey of all the experimental work that I could find on comparisons of cognitive capacities among the various classes of vertebrate animals—fish, amphibians, reptiles, birds, and mammals. I included all tests of learning, whether 'simple' or 'complex'. Although some workers believe that only complex tests make demands on intelligence, it did not seem justified to rule out in advance the possibility that similar mechanisms were involved in both simple and complex tasks—even if complex tasks seem more likely to involve 'extra' mechanisms. The results of my survey[1] were not as I had anticipated.

## 'Simple' learning

My first overall conclusion—and one that has not been too controversial—was that, as far as simple tasks are concerned, there is no evidence that any one group of vertebrates (excluding humans) performs any more or less efficiently than any other group.

The simplest examples of learning that I investigated did not even use association formation, but instead tasks such as habituation—in which some unlearned response, like a 'startle' movement declines over trials as a consequence simply of the repeated presentation of an initially novel stimulus. It is not, perhaps, surprising that all vertebrates show habituation, nor that this simple learning process is equally efficient in all vertebrates. Most of the examples of 'simple' learning that I considered did, however, involve association formation, and it may be a little more surprising that I could find no evidence here either of species differences. Animals drawn from all the major groups of vertebrates can form associations, and there is no evidence that any one species forms associations more or less rapidly than any other group.

There is basic evidence for at least one species from each of the four classes of vertebrate to support the claim that all species form associations equally rapidly and that associations may be formed in a single trial. Two examples, drawn from fish and amphibians (commonly regarded as the two 'lowest' classes of vertebrate) will illustrate the point. In the first report, goldfish were placed in a tube of moving water with a still-water area at one end; they spontaneously swam against the current, into the still area. But after receiving a single shock in the still area, they swam very much more slowly on the succeeding trial. In the second report, toads were offered bumble-bees on the ends of strings held in front of them. After a single attack, they then refused to attack the bumble-bees (but they continued to attack edible prey such as dragonflies); other toads given bumble-bees whose stings had been removed, continued to attack the stingless bees. If a single trial is enough to establish an association in fish and amphibians, it makes little sense to suppose that their association formation is less efficient than in 'higher' vertebrates—and this is generally accepted by comparative psychologists.

There is, moreover, no compelling evidence that any vertebrate is restricted in the *type* of association that can be formed—for example, to only S—R, or only R—S, or only S—S associations. At the time that my review was published (in 1982) there had been wide acceptance for some years of the claim (by Bitterman[2]) that fish could not form S—S associations, and it is worth following the fate of that assertion.

### The Crespi effect

The basic evidence for claiming that fish could not form S–S associations came from experiments that investigated the effects of changing reward. In one such experiment, goldfish that had been accustomed to swimming down a swimway for a large food reward (40 worms) were suddenly shifted to swimming for a much smaller reward (one worm). With the reduced reward size, the goldfish showed no change in swim speed (despite the fact that fish trained throughout with a one-worm reward swam much more slowly). When a comparable procedure (involving a shift in the number of food pellets) is carried out with rats, then, typically, there is an abrupt fall in running speeds—a fall so sharp that the rats in fact run more slowly than rats that have been, from the beginning, accustomed to running for the small reward. (This effect is known as the Crespi effect, after the name of its discoverer.)

Bitterman suggested that rats form S-S associations—in this case, between the runway and the food reward—so that in effect they learn to 'expect' the reward. The Crespi effect occurs, then, because the rats 'expect' a large reward, and the contrast between the expectation and the actual reward severely disrupts the rats' performance. This explanation has considerable intuitive appeal. The failure of goldfish to react to a reduction in reward size could, therefore, be understood if goldfish did not form expectations. And if we interpret expectations as S–S associations, we could accept Bitterman's conclusion that fish can form S–R but not S–S associations.

In 1982, I resisted the notion that fish cannot form expectancies by pointing to a potential role for contextual variables. For example, rats do not always show a Crespi effect—the effect depends upon the reward used, and it is not clear which reward for a rat should be equated with a given goldfish reward. My sceptical position has been justified since then by Bitterman himself, who has reported experiments which make it quite clear that fish *do* form S–S associations[3]. In this work, goldfish were rewarded for responding to 'compound' stimuli that consisted of two independent elements—for example, a horizontal white line on a green background, or a vertical white line on a red background. Bitterman found that as a consequence of this exposure the goldfish (like mammals) formed within-compound associations—that they learned to associate, say, the horizontal line with green. It is not necessary here to describe the somewhat complicated paradigm that was used; what is important is that it is generally accepted (and accepted, in particular, by Bitterman) that within-compound associations are S–S associations. We are still not certain why the Crespi effect is so elusive in fish, but there is no longer any dispute concerning the ability of fish to form 'expectancies'. So, this specific proposal for a difference in association formation is universally rejected, not because of an appeal to the possible role of a contextual variable, but because there is now proof that the supposedly 'inferior' animal *can* achieve what at one time seemed impossible for it.

The fact that different vertebrate groups all form associations does not, of course, show that they all form them in the same way, by using comparable mechanisms. There is, however, no evidence that suggests any differences in mechanism, and I shall describe in a later section (concerned with the phenomenon of 'blocking') some findings that do support what is the natural conclusion—namely, that fish ('lower' vertebrates) form associations in the same way that mammals ('higher' vertebrates) do.

## 'Complex' learning

A large number of complex tests have been introduced as potential animal intelligence tests, and it is not easy to classify them. To bring some order to their diversity, I will divide them into two groups. The first group consists of tests that show—or are claimed to show—differences between species in the rate at which they are mastered: different animals successfully master these tests, but require varying amounts of training in order to do so. Differences of this kind suggest that the various subjects all solve the tests in the same way, but that some animals are simply faster learners than others—that the intellectual differences revealed are differences of degree, not of kind. The second group consists of tests that are claimed to reveal differences in kind of intelligence: problems, for example, that one species can solve, but another species cannot, however long the training.

The unexpected outcome of my survey was that I could not find convincing examples of differences between species revealed by complex tests—so that, given the similar outcome concerning simple tests, I had to conclude that there was no solid proof available that the different non-human vertebrate species do vary in intelligence. Before considering the implications of my conclusion, I will outline the kinds of tests used by discussing three specific examples, one, of a test that supposedly yielded evidence of differences in degree, and two, of tests showing differences in kind.

### Learning-set formation

This first test was introduced in the late 1940s by Harry Harlow (1905–81) of the University of Wisconsin, who used monkeys as subjects. The monkeys were trained, first, to choose one of two objects for a food reward. The objects were readily discriminable by differences in height, colour, shape, and so on—such things as blue pyramids, red cubes, or 'junk' objects such as cups, bottles, toys. Both objects were presented simultaneously to the monkeys, who learned after a few trials to choose the object that had food hidden under it in preference to the object that had no reward. Simple visual discriminations are, of course, readily acquired by all vertebrates with reasonable vision, and presumably simply reflect the formation of associations—a capacity which, as we have seen, is clearly present throughout vertebrates. What Harlow did next was to ask the monkeys to learn a second discrimination of the same kind, but using new objects—and then a third, a fourth, and so on, until literally hundreds of discriminations had been learned. The interesting feature of the monkeys' performance was that there was a dramatic improvement in the rate at which the monkeys solved the later discriminations—so much so that they eventually chose the correct object on the second trial of each new discrimination more than 80 per cent of the time. Since the later problems were (apart from the specific stimuli used) identical to the earlier problems, it seems that the monkeys had 'learned to learn'. This achievement is not readily accounted for in terms of association formation: why should the association of the correct object with food be so much stronger in late discriminations than in early discriminations, following a single trial? And—even more puzzling for an associationist account—why should a single experience of the incorrect object and no reward lead immediately to the choice of the other object in late, but not in early discriminations?

Harlow referred to the improvement in performance over a series of similar discriminations as 'learning-set formation', and suggested that it might provide an example of 'higher-order' learning. More specifically, it has been suggested that learning-set formation involves the adoption by the animal of a 'win, stay–lose, shift' strategy: the animal remembers the choice and outcome of the previous trial—if rewarded, it chooses the same object again (stays with its choice); if not, it avoids the object (shifts).

If learning-set formation does involve higher-order learning and, perhaps, the adoption of strategies, it clearly is a candidate for a useful intelligence test—animals less intelligent than monkeys may be efficient formers of associations, but less efficient at this more demanding task. The results of early studies of learning-set formation in various vertebrates supported this view: Fig. 5.1 summarizes results from experiments on monkeys, cats, rats, and squirrels. The best performance is that of the rhesus monkeys, old-world primates more closely related to humans than new-world primates like the squirrel monkeys and marmosets, who are less efficient than rhesus monkeys but more efficient than cats, who are in turn better than the rats and squirrels. This ranking of the species supported the idea that efficiency of learning-set formation might provide a good measure of intelligence, because it showed that the species most closely related to humans were the most efficient, and because it agreed pretty well with informal preconceptions of the likely relative intelligence of the various species.

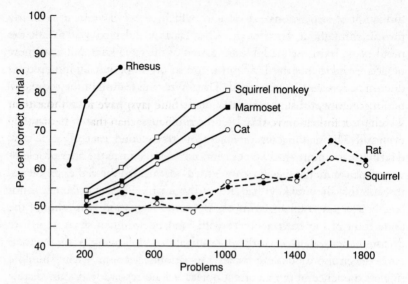

**Fig. 5.1** Learning-set formation in six mammalian species. (From Warren (1965), with permission.)

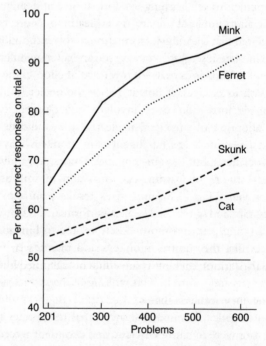

**Fig. 5.2** Learning-set formation in four species of carnivores. (From Doty, Jones, and Doty (1967), with permission; © 1967 American Association for the Advancement of Science.)

Later work has thrown up two problems for the idea that learning-set formation measures intelligence. First, although cats are generally poor performers, some of their close relatives, such as ferrets and mink, are extremely good—better (as comparison of Fig. 5.2 with Fig. 5.1 shows) than new-world monkeys, and about as good as rhesus monkeys. And other experiments using birds (American blue jays) have found that their learning-set formation is, similarly, more efficient than that of new-world primates. The ranking we now have does not, then, accord well with either degree of relatedness to humans or our preconceived notions. Birds, whose closest living relatives are the crocodilians, are very distantly related to humans (much more distantly than any mammalian species); and birds are widely supposed to be not very bright—a status reflected in the derogatory phrase 'birdbrain'.

The second problem with learning-set formation is that there is perfectly good evidence that performance is, as might be expected, heavily influenced by contextual variables. One experiment, for example, confirmed that the performance of rhesus monkeys was superior to that of new-world capuchin monkeys when the standard learning-set procedure was used; but when minor changes to that procedure were introduced— the most significant being the use of grey instead of coloured objects—the new-world capuchins outperformed the old-world rhesus monkeys. What this result shows is that there is no unique ranking of species to be obtained from learning-set studies—the ranking varies according to the procedure, and no one procedure has any special claim to validity. It is also worth further comment on the effect of removing colour. Capuchin monkeys do possess colour vision, but it differs from that of rhesus monkeys (which is very close to ours); it is hardly surprising that changing the sensory properties of the stimuli used affects the relative efficiency of species having different sensory capacities. It is perfectly plausible that the poor performance of rats in conventional learning-set tasks reflects, not low intelligence, but poor vision. This proposal has been directly supported by more recent work[4] showing efficient learning-set performance by rats in a procedure in which they had to discriminate between a large number of different spatial locations, each of which could be identified by a number of cues.

Learning-set formation does not, then, provide a convincing intelligence test for animals: the rankings can be changed simply by changing details of the testing procedure in ways that do not appear to have any relevance to cognitive activity, and the same animals that perform very poorly in some versions of the test perform extremely efficiently in others.

*Insight*

Probably the first claim that at least some animals are capable of insightful problem solving was made by Wolfgang Köhler (1887–1967)[5], who worked with chimpanzees during an enforced stay on the island of Tenerife during the First World War. In what became his best-known experiment, Köhler suspended a banana from the roof of a compound in which there were six chimpanzees. The banana was out of reach of the animals, but there was, on the floor nearby, a wooden crate. All six animals attempted to leap up to the banana, but failed. After about five minutes, one chimpanzee (Sultan), after pacing back and forth between the crate and the part of the floor immediately beneath the banana, suddenly took hold of the crate, moved it beneath the banana, climbed up on to it, and then seized the banana. The apparent suddenness of the solution and its smooth, co-ordinated performance suggested that this was not an example of trial-and-error (associative) learning, but involved an additional process—'insight'.

Not surprisingly, many of those who agreed that the crate problem (and other similar problems) did require insight also supposed that there were animals, less intelligent than chimpanzees, who would not be capable of insight. The suggestion here was not simply that chimp intelligence is superior, but that it differs in kind—the process responsible for insight is simply not present in 'lower' beings.

It is of course difficult to carry out the obvious direct test of this notion by giving the same problem to different animals—we have already mentioned the difficulty goldfish would have. But, with some ingenuity, a similar problem has been given to pigeons (who do not like bananas, can fly, and cannot move wooden crates around). What the Harvard psychologist Robert Epstein and his colleagues did was to devise an analogue for pigeons[6]. In the training stage of their experiment, pigeons were given two types of session. In one type, the birds were trained to climb on to a small cardboard box and to peck a toy banana (suspended from the roof), for which they received a food (grain) reward. In these sessions, the box was fixed in place below the banana, and the birds were not rewarded if they flew at the banana instead of climbing on to the box. In the other type of session, the banana was not present, and the cardboard box, now unfixed, was placed at various locations within the apparatus. In these sessions, there was a green spot visible somewhere on the wall of the apparatus (in different places in different sessions) and the pigeons were trained, with food reward, to move the box (with their beaks) towards the green spot.

The pigeons in this experiment were, then, trained to do two different things: first, to climb on to the box and peck the banana; second, to move the box towards the green spot. In the crucial test session, the box was free to move, there was no green spot, and the banana was present—although the box was not beneath the banana. Would the pigeons now move the box so that it ended up beneath the banana? The answer is that the birds *did* move the box so that they could climb on to it and peck the banana. What's more, they, like Sultan, appeared to look back and forth between the box and the banana before suddenly performing the solution. Did these pigeons, therefore, achieve 'insight'?

Before claiming a major intellectual breakthrough for the lowly pigeon, some reservations are, obviously, needed. The procedure did, after all, differ in important ways from that that Köhler employed—most importantly that the pigeons received training that was specific to the solution. That said, the fact remains that the pigeons *did* succeed in solving a problem that was as close an analogue as has yet been devised. We cannot conclude with any confidence that pigeons are not capable of insight until they actually *fail* some relevant problem—some analogue that is not clearly impossible because of some such trivial factor as the pigeon not being strong enough to move a crate.

What may be more telling for the pigeon/chimpanzee comparison is, moreover, the finding made some decades after Köhler's original research, that chimpanzees do *not* solve problems of the 'insight' kind unless they have had extensive previous experience with the objects involved. Chimpanzees, of course, spontaneously play with and move objects; pigeons do not. This example, then, has two 'take-home' messages: first, pigeons have not (yet) failed a fair test of 'insight'—in fact, they have passed the only test they have been set; second, the fact that chimpanzees require extensive previous experience suggests that their 'insight' may not be as dramatic as it originally seemed—perhaps they do rely in these tasks on 'trial-and-error' learning (on associations, in other words). My final example provides further striking evidence of an apparently complex achievement—reasoning—that turns out in fact to be an example of association formation.

*Inference*

In 1977, Brendan McGonigle and Margaret Chalmers, of the University of Edinburgh, reported an ingenious experiment on reasoning in monkeys[7]. The logic of the experiment can be summarized as follows: if a monkey knows that A is better than B, and that B is better than C, will he be able to infer that A is therefore better than C? For reasons that will become apparent, what the monkey actually learned was: A is better than B, B is better than C, C is better than D, and D is better than E. And what they were 'asked' was: is B better than D?

In the first stage of this study, monkeys were trained to choose between four different pairings of coloured cylinders (each of a different colour), drawn from a set of five which we can label A, B, C, D, and E. The animals learned the following discriminations: A+ vs. B−, B+ vs. C−, C+ vs. D−, D+ vs. E− (where '+' indicates that the choice of that cylinder was rewarded (with food), and '−', that the choice was not rewarded). After a series of discrimination sessions, the monkeys responded appropriately whenever any one of those pairs was presented to them. They had learned, therefore, to prefer cylinder A to cylinder B, cylinder B to cylinder C, cylinder C to cylinder D, and cylinder D to cylinder E. An important feature of this stage of training is that choice of cylinder A was always rewarded, and choice of cylinder E, never. Cylinders B, C, and D, however, have each been accompanied, in equal measure, by reward and non-reward, so that the association of each of those cylinders with food would be expected to be equally strong. Pairings B vs. C and C vs. D were presented in training, and the interesting question is, what preference will the monkeys show given a choice between B vs. D—a pairing they have never previously seen? If choice is based simply on associations, then they should choose B and D equally often; but if monkeys can infer, they could reason that since B is preferred over C, and C is preferred over D, they should prefer B to D. (Notice that if they had learned only A vs. B and B vs. C, and been tested on A vs. C, both associations and reasoning would predict the same outcome, since A would always have been rewarded, and C, never.) In fact, when tested on B vs. D, the monkeys showed a very strong preference for cylinder B, supporting the idea that they can indeed infer.

Unfortunately, although it may not at first seem particularly plausible, there is an alternative associative account of the monkeys' performance. On half of the training trials in which cylinder B was seen, it was seen alongside cylinder A. It could therefore have formed an association with A and indirectly acquired a stronger association with food (since A was always rewarded). But in half of the trials in which cylinder D was seen, it was seen alongside cylinder E. It could therefore have formed an association with E and indirectly reduced its association with food (since E was never rewarded). It now seems clear that this is in fact the correct account. First, a precisely analogous experiment has been carried out with pigeons (using small illuminated shapes instead of cylinders), and pigeons, like monkeys, show the same strong preference for B when given the B vs. D pairing[8]. Rightly or wrongly, most of us find it intuitively unlikely that pigeons can reason, even if we think it possible that monkeys might. Second, analytical experiments on pigeons have shown that associations *are* formed between the separate members of a pair of stimuli in a discrimination, and that those associations *do* cause, as suggested in the associative account of the 'inference' test, changes in the overall associative strength of the stimuli[9].

The work on inference finds, therefore, no difference between monkeys and pigeons, and clear evidence that an apparently complex test is in fact 'solved' using associations alone.

## Conclusions

My argument is that there has so far been no conclusive evidence for differences in intelligence between non-human vertebrates. It is certainly true that most comparative psychologists believe that I am wrong and that there *are* tests that do demonstrate differences. Unfortunately, these eminently sensible psychologists cannot agree among themselves over which test does succeed; whilst it is not controversial that there is no consensus on a test or tests that demonstrate intellectual differences.

Two possible conclusions are either that psychologists have simply not been ingenious enough in devising intelligence tests for animals; or that in fact there are no differences to be found—goldfish *are* as intelligent as chimpanzees. Elsewhere[10], I have favoured the latter response, but have probably had little success in persuading others of the possible validity of a conclusion that seems so counter-intuitive—and I shall not insist on it here. What I shall do is to emphasize the positive aspects of work on the comparative psychology of intelligence.

One of the striking features of work on supposedly 'lower' and 'less intelligent' species has been the repeated finding that they are in fact more successful at mastering tests than might have been anticipated. The specific examples that I introduced have concentrated on birds, and we have seen that blue jays show learning-set performance comparable to that of some monkeys, and that pigeons succeed in tests of both 'insight' and 'inference'. More generally, *specific* proposals (of which there have been surprisingly few) of intellectual differences between species have been rejected, not because of some 'contextual' variable that might explain away the poor performance of a species, but because careful testing has found that species originally believed incapable of successfully mastering some test are in fact capable. So, supposedly unintelligent animals have turned out to be intelligent.

A second important conclusion to emerge has been that not only is association formation equally efficient in all vertebrates, but associations clearly play a central role in many (if not all) complex tasks. We have seen evidence of this in tests for both 'insight' and 'inference', and many other examples are available (there is, for example, an account available of learning-set formation in terms of association formation[11]). Psychologists have found it very difficult to establish that learning processes other than the 'simple' processes such as habituation and conditioning are involved in complex learning.

My goal here, therefore, is not to settle controversial issues such as whether there are any intellectual differences between species, or whether what might be called 'supra-associative' learning processes exist. It will be sufficient to conclude that association formation is ubiquitous in vertebrates, and that it forms the core of learning in all vertebrate species. Whether or not some vertebrates have evolved, in addition, more sophisticated processes, is an issue that we can leave open.

## Language and intelligence

There may be disagreement over the question of whether some animals are more intelligent than others (and there certainly is over the question of specifically how animals differ), but there is, of course, no dispute that we humans are more intelligent than any other species. So, where does our superior intelligence come from—do we, for example, differ from animals in degree, in kind, or both? As soon as we ask this question, we are confronted with the role of language in human intelligence. It is clear that much of our problem solving relies heavily on language—either directly, when we 'talk to ourselves' in trying to find solutions; or indirectly, when we use solutions given to us through education (formal or informal) by other members of our language-using community.

Why, then, do animals not talk? Before tackling this question, we should acknowledge that animals do, of course, communicate with each other in many ways; and some of their communication systems are referred to as 'languages'—the language of bees, for example. But none of their systems have anything approaching the flexibility of human language: none create anything analogous to sentences, which allow us to attribute any of a large (essentially infinite) variety of properties to an equally large number of possible things; and none use such words as 'and', 'not', 'some', 'all'— words that allow us to form logical arguments, and so give us our power of reason to solve problems.

Two possible reactions to the absence of language in animals are: first, that they are simply less intelligent than us, and that the level of intelligence they reach is inadequate for learning something as complex as a language; or second, that humans (and only humans) have evolved a mechanism specifically for learning language—a language-acquisition device—and that, in the absence of this device, learning a language is not possible. The first alternative could reflect simply a difference in degree between animal and human intelligence, but the second implies a difference in kind—an extra process (and human intelligence might otherwise be no different from animal intelligence). Given that language confers on us a huge advantage in problem solving, and so, in intelligence, these alternatives could be rephrased as: do animals fail to learn language because they are less intelligent than us, or are we more intelligent because we learn to talk? Is there any evidence that might allow us to decide between these alternatives?

## Intelligence of non-linguistic humans

It might seem that we should look into those many cases of 'wild' children who have grown up without learning a language, to see how intelligent they are. If they are clearly more intelligent than any animal species, then we might decide that the failure of animals to talk was due to their inferior intelligence. In fact, in almost all reported cases, these children appear to be not very intelligent; but, of course, most effort by those caring for them goes into trying to teach them to talk (usually with little success). Moreover, we do not know why they were abandoned by their parents—perhaps they appeared subnormal at an early age.

A second approach might be to explore the intelligence of children who have not learned language because they were born deaf. We now take great care to test hearing in infants, and if deafness is detected, then care is taken to ensure that language—spoken or signed—is acquired. But in the last century, deaf children remained mute and were commonly sent to institutions for mentally subnormal people, and the phrase 'deaf and dumb' became a term of abuse. While this might suggest that children of perfectly normal intelligence appear to be pathologically unintelligent if they do not learn a language, the fact remains that we have no solid evidence on what is a fascinating question—in what ways, if any, would the intelligence of a non-linguistic (but otherwise normal) human differ from that of, say, a chimpanzee?

## Teaching language to animals

Since we cannot decide on whether humans with no language would be more intelligent than animals, perhaps we should look at animals instead. If language is absent in animals because they are simply less intelligent, then possibly, with careful training, animals could learn at least the rudiments of language; but if language requires some process that is wholly absent in animals, then no amount of training would be successful. This provides a rationale for looking at the many efforts to teach animals to talk.

Modern explorations of language learning by animals have, naturally, concentrated on our closest relatives, the great apes, and, in particular, on chimpanzees[12]. One early study attempted to teach a chimpanzee, Viki, to talk. Viki was brought up from an early age in the experimenter's home, and treated like a human child. The results were not impressive: Viki learned to say only a few words, and did not produce sequences of words as sentences. A problem with trying to get chimpanzees to talk is that the physical characteristics of their vocal tracts make it impossible for them to make many of our speech sounds. Subsequent studies have accordingly used a variety of artificial languages that do not require actual speech. One chimpanzee, Sarah, learned to produce and to respond to plastic symbols (representing words) held by magnets on to a board; another chimpanzee, Lana, learned to press in sequence illuminated symbols shown on a large display; and chimpanzees Washoe and Nim, and Koko the gorilla, were taught American Sign Language (ASL)—a language for the deaf in which each sign represents a word.

### Can apes learn the meanings of words?

All of these modern studies agree that apes can acquire an extensive vocabulary of symbols that they can both respond to and produce appropriately. Washoe, for example, learned to sign correctly on being shown photographs of a large number of different objects. Does this show, therefore, that apes are capable of learning the meanings of words, and so, capable of learning at least a minimal language? Most commentators, myself included, think not, since there is a more economical explanation. In most of these studies, the symbols are learned with some system of reward— typically something to eat or drink, or some 'social' reward (a hug, for example). So, the ape learns to produce the appropriate response to some object as a consequence of the reward that follows. But this can be seen as a case of associative learning, like a pigeon learning to perform one response to a green light, and another, to a red light (and we would not say that the pigeon understands the *meanings* of the colours).

## Can apes form sentences?

So, what do we need as minimal evidence of true language? There is a reasonable consensus that it would be sufficient to show that apes can form sentences—however short. For this, it is not enough simply to produce more than one sign in an utterance. The key requirement is that the animals must demonstrate an appreciation of the importance of grammar and, in particular, word order. They must discriminate between the meanings of sentences like 'Me tickle Mary' and 'Mary tickle me'. (No effort has been made to see whether chimpanzees could use another grammatical feature—case (the difference, for example, between 'I' and 'me').) There has been considerable controversy over this issue. The studies that have used artificial symbols may appear to have demonstrated sensitivity to order, since only 'correct' sequences obtained reward. But that is exactly the problem—the sequences were restricted and could be learned largely by rote, without any general appreciation of grammar. This criticism has been widely endorsed by psychologists, including psychologists who believe that apes are capable of language.

The apes that learned ASL—Washoe, Koko, and Nim—all produced multi-sign utterances (usually of two signs), and these utterances were also reported to show appropriate ordering (for example, subject before action, object following action). But these findings were severely undermined by a detailed analysis by the Columbia University psychologist, Herbert Terrace, and his colleagues, in 1979[13]. They found that although most two-sign utterances did show appropriate order, the data did not force the conclusion that grammar had been learned. One problem, for example, was that the utterances frequently contained a sign that only appeared in one of the two possible locations—first or last; a specific example, from Nim's output, was the sign for 'more', which only occurred as the first of two signs. Nim could, therefore, have learned that the sign for 'more', followed by some other sign, frequently led to reward, and no grammar is needed for that. (Indeed, pigeons can readily learn to respond in the appropriate order to a series of simultaneously lit, coloured lights.) But the most harmful aspect of the Terrace report was the evidence, from close analysis of videotapes of Washoe's performance, that her appropriate word order was largely due to unconscious prompting by the experimenters—a latter-day 'clever Hans' effect[14]. Since 1979 there has been widespread agreement amongst experimental psychologists that there is as yet no support for the view that apes can form sentences.

*Can apes understand sentences?*

The foregoing conclusion has not surprisingly discouraged research into ape language, but one current project[15] has explored the interesting possibility that although apes cannot produce sentences, they can understand them. This study has concentrated on comprehension of spoken language by Kanzi, a bonobo (pygmy chimpanzee). Kanzi's understanding (at the age of eight) of spoken sentences was compared to that of a child (tested when she was between 18 and 24 months old). Typical sentences were, for example: 'Put the rock in the water'; 'Hide the rubber band'; 'Give the potato to Kelly'. There was very little difference between the bonobo and the child in responding to these sentences. Three points can be made about this study. First, it raises the basic question of whether it is plausible to suppose that apes might possess the cognitive apparatus for *understanding* the rules of grammar while being unable to *use* those rules to construct sentences. Second, the data will not convince everyone: relatively few actions are involved, and in most cases, the object that occurs first in the sentence is one that should be picked up first. Third, it emphasizes the fact that whether or not apes are capable of even rudimentary language remains an open question (although I shall assume that they are not).

*Language in a bird?*

Given my scepticism over intellectual differences between animals, I cannot resist a brief digression to attempt to raise the birdbrain somewhat above its traditionally low status. Although most of these language-learning studies have used apes, other animals have been used—and not only other mammals (such as sea lions and dolphins), but a bird (Alex, an African grey parrot). The advantage of using a parrot is, of course, that it can mimic the sounds of human speech. Traditionally, parrots have been trained to 'talk' simply by continually repeating words or phrases to them, and rewarding them if and when the sounds are correctly repeated back. It is hardly surprising that, when trained in this way, parrots show no sign of 'understanding' what they are saying.

   Irene Pepperberg, whilst at Purdue University, devised a new training protocol which she hoped might lead to the meaningful use of language by her parrot[16]. Alex was shown objects in which he was interested while two trainers talked to each other about the object. One trainer acted as an instructor; the other, as a 'model' for the parrot. So, the instructor (holding up a piece of wood) might say to the model: 'What is this?', to which the other trainer might answer: 'wood', and receive in reply: 'yes, good' (accompanied by other signs of approval). If Alex at any stage interrupted the proceedings (as he frequently did) and said 'wood', he was given the wood to play with. One idea behind this system of training is that it should have encouraged Alex to realize that a given word referred to a particular object.

Alex rapidly learned to use the appropriate word when shown a range of different objects, and learned also to use words for the colours and shapes of the objects. This allowed him to demonstrate some appreciation of concepts—he can respond, when shown a green square piece of cloth with either: 'green' (when asked 'what colour is this?') or 'square' (when asked 'what shape is this?'). Although Alex's vocabulary is not (at least not yet) as extensive as those reported in some of the ape studies, he can respond appropriately to more than one hundred different objects—so his achievement is not dramatically different from that of apes. He cannot produce sentences—but then neither can apes. Whether he 'understands' the words or not remains open to doubt. Alex is rewarded (by being given an object of interest) for making a specific response to a specific stimulus, and the fact that he learns to make that response is no more proof that he understands a word than is the production of a manual sign by a chimpanzee. The most economical conclusion remains, that animals cannot master even the rudiments of human language.

## Is grammar in our genes?

The idea that animals cannot learn to talk is, of course, not new—philosophers over the centuries have debated the issue, arguing for one side or the other—but only in the modern era have these arguments been supported by evidence drawn from experiments using animals. And the same conclusion has been reached in our era by using a quite different type of evidence. We saw in Chapter 4 that the inadequacy of Skinner's attempt to explain language acquisition in terms of a simple and unitary reinforcement process was brilliantly exposed by Noam Chomsky in his review of Skinner's *Verbal Behavior*. We can consider now the positive aspect of that attack—Chomsky's own account of the genesis of language.

Part of Chomsky's genius lies in his drawing our attention to facts, many of which are relatively simple and widely known, and making us think about their significance. Chomsky has pointed out that the course of acquisition of language by infants follows the same stages—from babbling, through one-word utterances, to two-word utterances, and finally to sentences—and the same general time course in all cultures (so, children from all over the world learn to talk properly somewhere between their second and third birthdays). Although children do, of course, make many mistakes as they learn to talk, they very rarely make mistakes of grammar. And some of the mistakes that they do make are very telling. Children, for example, frequently form past tenses of irregular verbs incorrectly: they will say 'goed' instead of 'went', 'drawed' instead of 'drew', and so on. What is interesting about this type of mistake (over-regularizing) is that it shows that the child has extracted a rule about how to form past tenses—a rule that the child applies despite never having heard the resulting word before.

The remarkable accuracy of children's grammar indicates that they have learned the correct rules, and this despite the fact that there are thousands of rules that might conceivably account for the regularities in the relatively restricted body of language that they have actually heard. Some have supposed that children settle on the correct rules because their parents systematically correct them when they do make grammatical errors. But investigations of mother–infant interactions in Western societies have given little support to this idea—and there are societies in which the adults apparently speak very little to young children, but in which language acquisition proceeds, of course, at exactly the same rate as in other societies.

The speed and accuracy with which children acquire the rules of language suggested to Chomsky that there are innate constraints upon the rules that children deduce from their linguistic input—that, as it were, the hypotheses that children try out are limited to those that are most likely to succeed. Human infants, whatever the language of their natural parents, are equally capable of acquiring any of the thousands of human languages—it is not our genes but our upbringing that predisposes us to learn, say, English, rather than Japanese. Chomsky argues, therefore, that the innate constraint on the learning of grammar constitutes an innate universal grammar—a template for the grammar of all human languages.

The notion that there is a universal human grammar gains support from two rather less well-known facts, drawn from examination of the grammars of different human languages. First, there are striking similarities between the grammars of all natural languages. Second, the complexity of the grammar of all languages is comparable—although there are marked

differences between languages in the number of words in their vocabul-
aries, no human language is, in terms of grammar, more primitive or more
sophisticated than any other.

We need not go any further here into Chomsky's linguistic theories[17]. I
hope that I have shown that there is good support from both animal studies
and work on humans for the view that there is a real qualitative difference
between humans and animals—a difference that consists in humans posses-
sing an innate capacity for the acquisition of language. One clear consequence
of this conclusion is that the marked gap between the intellectual achievements of animals and humans may very reasonably be put down to the fact that
animals cannot master language. It may even be that this is the *only* substantial
gap between our minds and theirs. In later chapters I shall explore some
possible unexpected consequences of language for humans.

## Associations revisited

The arguments thus far in this chapter can be readily summarized: first, all
vertebrate animals form associations, and it has been very difficult to show that
there are other, perhaps more sophisticated, differences between their
intellects; second, the one demonstrable difference between the human
and the animal intellect is that humans can acquire language. We humans
could, therefore, be regarded as (association-forming) animals with language.

The final sections in this chapter have two somewhat opposing goals.
The first is to emphasize the value of an association-forming intellect—we
should not necessarily disparage an intellect on the grounds that it can *only*
form associations. The second, however, is to prepare the ground for what
will be the major thrust of the final chapters of the book—the notion that
the acquisition of language does indeed mark a dramatic change in the
evolution of the mind.

## Ecology and intelligence

We can begin to think about the significance of association formation by
considering one obvious objection to the idea that there may be few (if
any) differences in intelligence between different groups of animals. This
objection derives much force from the fact that it appears to follow on
naturally from Darwin's theory of evolution by natural selection. Different
animals live in different environments; different environments will pose
different problems; so, we should expect that different environments

would favour the evolution of processes tailored specifically to solve different problems. In other words, the problem-solving capacities of animals would be expected to correlate with their ecological niches.

Despite the appeal of this ecological argument, it has been surprisingly difficult to come up with specific examples of learning that proceeds more efficiently in one species than in some other species for whom the learning appears less ecologically relevant. The search for examples continues, however, and it is worth introducing an example of one current proposal, if only for its considerable intrinsic interest. Once again, the example concerns birds—but before we look at birds, we have to review a little mammalian neurology.

### Spatial learning and the hippocampus in mammals and birds

One of the 'hottest' areas of neuroscience over recent decades has been the mammalian hippocampus, and the search for an understanding of its role in learning and memory. The hippocampus—so-called because its shape somewhat resembles that of a sea horse (whose scientific name is *Hippocampus*)—is tucked away in the human cerebral hemispheres. In origin, however, it is a surface structure, and so known as 'cortex'; but, unlike the neocortex, which has six layers and comprises all the visible surface of our hemispheres, the hippocampus has only three layers, and has been pushed inwards from the surface by the expansion of the neocortex. (Figure 5.3 shows the general appearance of mammalian neocortex and hippocampus.) Although interest in the hippocampus was sparked by the discovery (to be discussed further in Chapter 6) that damage to it causes dramatic recent memory impairment, work on the role of the hippo-campus in non-human mammals has pointed to a role in spatial learning.

Birds too have a hippocampus, although its appearance is very different from that of the mammalian hippocampus. In fact the bird brain in general looks very different—it resembles the reptilian model much more than the mammalian. There is, for example, no multilayered surface structure in either reptilian or avian brain hemispheres—so, the avian hippocampus is not three-layered, and there is no six-layered neocortex. (Figure 5.3 also shows the general appearance of an avian hemisphere.) But before deciding that this surely proves a difference between intellects, two other facts should be considered. First, although there are striking anatomical differences, there are equally striking functional parallels between compar-able brain areas (comparable in such aspects as general location in the brain and connections to other parts of the nervous system) in birds and mammals. The example that we shall shortly be considering rests precisely on the comparability of function of the avian and mammalian hippocampus.

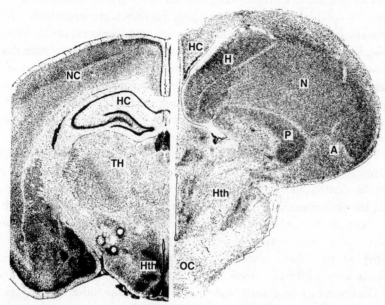

**Fig. 5.3** Shown on the left is a section through the hemisphere of a rat brain, and on the right, a section through a pigeon hemisphere. Both sections are cut in the frontal plane—they are, that is, seen as they would be from the front of the animal. The tissue has been stained with a stain that selectively highlights cell bodies, and does not show up fibres. Note the layering of cells in the neocortex and hippocampus of the rat, and the absence of layering in the pigeon brain. Key: A, archistriatum; H, hyperstriatum; HC, hippocampus; Hth, hypothalamus; N, neostriatum; NC, neocortex; OC, optic chiasma; P, paleostriatum; TH, thalamus. (Rat brain section from Paxinos and Watson, 1986, with permission; Prigeon brain section from Karten and Hodos, 1967, with permission.)

A second fact to consider—and one that is remarkably little known—is that although bird brains are indeed small, this reflects primarily the fact that birds are small. Brain size varies with body size, and, in general, the bigger the animal, the bigger the brain (so, elephants and whales have bigger brains than humans)[18]. And the size of a bird's brain is roughly the same as that of a mammal of comparable body weight—for example, a pigeon's brain is about the same size as a rat's brain. The bird brain may look very different from the mammalian brain, but—after taking body size into account—it is about the same size, and seems to be organized in a similar way.

Guided by the notion that the hippocampus is involved in spatial learning, recent work has looked at the size of the hippocampus in corvids (crows and their relatives), parids (the various species of tits), and sittids (nuthatches). These avian families were chosen because some (but not all) corvids, some tits, and some sittids hide food in caches from which it is later retrieved. Perhaps the most spectacular example is provided by Clark's nutcracker—a North American corvid. These nutcrackers collect pine seeds in the autumn, bury them in the ground in communal caching areas, and recover them some months later, when little other food is available. An individual bird might store some 30 000 seeds, in about 8000 caches; and it is reckoned that, to survive, the bird must recover about 3000 of those caches. Observations of the birds in the wild have suggested that they do use their memories to find the hidden seeds (rather than rely on some strategy such as hiding them next to some large object and then simply searching at random near all large objects). Laboratory experiments have provided additional proof that they can use memory to recover hidden food—although the numbers of sites involved in the laboratory tests have been substantially smaller.

If different ways of life encourage the evolution of different learning mechanisms, it would be reasonable to expect that food-storing birds should develop better spatial memory than non-storers. And given the notion that the hippocampus plays a role in spatial learning, it makes sense to ask whether the hippocampus in storers is bigger than the hippocampus in non-storers. Neuroanatomical work shows that indeed it is: there is no difference in overall brain size, but there is a reliable difference between them in hippocampal size[19]. The marsh tit, for example, stores food, and is a small bird, weighing about 11 gm; the great tit does not store food, and weighs about 20 gm. The marsh tit's brain is, as we would expect, smaller than that of the great tit (by about 20 per cent); but the marsh tit's hippocampus is 30 per cent *larger* than the great tit's.

The fact that the hippocampus is bigger in food-storing birds than in closely related birds that do not store food has interesting implications.

First, it suggests that demands on spatial memory have indeed encouraged the enlargement of a device that plays a critical role in the processing of spatial information. Second, it provides a nice example of an avian brain structure that—despite its different appearance (absence of layers)—seems to play a similar functional role to the corresponding mammalian structure.

*Storers versus non-storers in the radial maze*

However convincing the data are on hippocampal size in storing birds, we have not yet established that there *is* a difference in spatial memory between the storer and the non-storer. Non-storers, to be sure, do not recover large numbers of hidden food caches—but then, they do not hide food either, and so have no reason to look for hidden stores. If the storer spatial memory is better than the non-storer memory, then storers should, presumably, excel at *any* task that makes demands on spatial memory. Since non-storers do not spontaneously hide food, this is a proposition that has to be tested in the laboratory—and at present, the results from laboratory studies are not unequivocally in favour of the storers having a general superiority. We can consider here two reports that used the same rationale and comparable procedures, but that point to different conclusions.

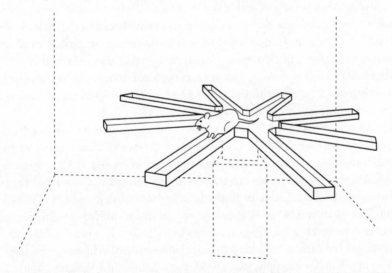

**Fig. 5.4** The radial maze. Each trial begins with the placing of the rat at the centre of the maze. Food is available at the end of each of the radiating arms, and perfect performance consists in the rat running down each arm once only—and not, in other words, revisiting any arm from which the food has already been removed on a previous run. (From Kolb, Sutherland, and Whishaw (1983), Fig. 1., with permission)

Both studies used apparatus designed to serve as an avian analogue of the radial maze—an apparatus (shown in Fig. 5.4) that has recently become popular for exploring spatial memory in rats. The typical rat apparatus consists of a central start box from which eight alleys radiate, each ending in a goal box. At the start of each trial, food is available in all the goal boxes, and the optimal strategy is for the rat to visit each box once, and once only, in its first eight choices. Rats are remarkably efficient in the radial maze, and control studies have shown that their performance relies upon their remembering which boxes they have visited, rather than adopting some non-memory strategy (such as turning left and choosing the adjacent alley after each choice). The radial maze does, then, provide a good example of a task that depends upon memory for spatial locations—and rats with hippocampal damage perform very poorly in the radial maze.

One study[20] compared two non-storing species of tits (great tits and blue tits) with two storing species (coal tits and marsh tits) in an avian radial maze task, and found no differences between the storing and the non-storing species—even when the task was made more difficult by introducing a delay between the first four and the second four choices. On the other hand, a second study[21], using four corvid species, found that two species that stored intensively (Clark's nutcrackers and pinyon jays) did outper-form two species that stored less (scrub jays and Mexican jays). We clearly cannot yet conclude that there is a real difference in spatial memory between storing and non-storing birds: the jury is, then, still out on this, the most promising example yet available of a difference between species in learning that can be attributed to a difference in ecological niche (and to a correlated difference in neuroanatomy).

Our exploration of the storer/non-storer contrast has allowed two points to be made. The first is that there is less difference between the bird brain and the mammalian brain—whether in size or in functional organization—than might have been supposed; and the second is that it has proved very difficult to find any concrete examples of differences in intellect that might be explicable in terms of differences in natural environment.

## Associations and causally linked events

We have looked at one side of the ecological coin, and asked whether different ecologies lead to different intellects. Given limited success in answering that question, we can look now at the other side of the coin, and ask whether relatively small variations in intellect could be reconciled with large differences in lifestyle. This can best be done by looking again at associations.

The associations explored by psychologists typically involve the arbitrary pairings of events—the sounding of a bell followed by the delivery of food, for example. But in what circumstances would two events be 'paired' in the wild? As soon as we think about it, the answer is obvious: events reliably co-occur in the real world when (and only when) there is a causal link between them. So, any animal that forms associations will detect the occurrence of causally linked events. The ability to form associations will allow an animal to uncover what Antony Dickinson has called 'the general causal structure of its world'. This simple but powerful idea also makes sense of some non-obvious features of association formation. One nice example is provided in the phenomenon of 'blocking'.

*Blocking*

The examples of conditioning that we have looked at have typically involved the pairing of one event—a stimulus or a response—with another. But what happens if two simultaneous events regularly precede another? Suppose, for example, a bell and a light *both* signal food? Does the animal learn to expect food on hearing the bell, the light, or the compound (light plus bell) stimulus? This was not an issue of any interest to behaviourists; they discarded the very possibility of any such ('mental') process as attention, and the co-occurrence of other stimuli was irrelevant to the learning of a given stimulus. But in fact analysis of the effects of presenting compound stimuli has been highly influential in the development of contemporary theories of learning.

The case of conditioning with a compound stimulus that I now consider differs slightly from my simple introductory example. Rather than asking what happens when a compound stimulus is used from the outset of training, this example asks what happens when a compound stimulus is introduced following training with one of its constituent stimuli. Table 5.1 summarizes an experiment on rats in which there were, for the experimental group, three stages: in Stage 1, a light was followed by a mild aversive shock to the feet; in Stage 2, a compound stimulus of the light and a tone was followed by shock; and in Stage 3, the tone was presented alone, and its fear-inducing effect was assessed. The procedure for the control group was identical, except that Stage 1 was omitted. The table shows that although the tone elicited fear in the control group, it did not do so in the experimental group: learning about the tone was, for the experimental animals, 'blocked' by the prior learning about the light. What is striking and thought provoking about this result is that the number of tone–shock pairings is identical in the two groups—and yet one group learns, the other does not. It is one demonstration (among many now known) of the fact that simply pairing events does not guarantee the formation of an association between them.

**Table 5.1** The design and results of a blocking study.

| Group | Stage 1 | Stage 2 | Stage 3 |
|---|---|---|---|
| Experimental | L→Shock | L+T→Shock | T→No fear |
| Control | | L+T→Shock | T→Fear |

Key: L = light; T = tone; → = consistently followed by.

In a typical experiment, the light and tone stimuli might be of 30 seconds duration, and there might be some eight pairings of the stimuli with mild foot shock in Stages 1 and 2. Fear would be measured by the reduction in ongoing rate of bar-pressing for a reward when either stimulus is presented. In practice, other control conditions are required to control for the experimental animals' increased exposure to shock, for their previous experience of the light stimulus, and for their previous experience of a predicted shock—none of these factors affect the outcome of the experiment.

Now *why* should an animal that has learned that a light leads to shock fail subsequently to learn that a tone co-presented with that light leads to shock? It is clearly not because the tone is inaudible, nor that the tone cannot be detected if the light is on—because the control group learn about the tone perfectly well. There is, in fact, more than one way of answering the question. Consider, first, two alternative and specific theoretical answers. The first relies on the notion of *attention* and supposes that the training in Stage 1 results in the animal attending to the light, to the exclusion of other stimuli: so, in Stage 2, the tone is not attended to, and, as a result, not learned about. A second theoretical account relies on the notion of *surprise*: according to this account, animals do not alter the associative values of stimuli—do not learn about them, in other words—unless something unexpected occurs. In Stage 1 the shock is initially, at least, surprising, so the (experimental) animal modifies the associative strength of the light until it comes to expect the shock; there is, however, no surprise in Stage 2 because the animal, given the light, expects the shock—the associative value of the tone will not, therefore, alter, and the animal will not expect the shock on the basis of the tone alone. The control animals, of course, do experience a surprise when the compound is followed by shock, and do modify the associative values of the constituent stimuli. This view has considerable intuitive appeal—if an animal is successfully predicting events, there is little sense in its altering associative values (and so, future predictions)[22].

But a more general answer to the question of why blocking occurs goes, as it were, over the head of the specific attention or surprise accounts, and appeals to the *function* of blocking. Suppose that the function of association formation—the evolutionary advantage conferred by it—is the detection of causes; and now suppose that you had learned that a light caused a shock, and then encountered a light–tone compound followed by a shock. You would, of course, attribute the shock to the light—you would not imagine that the *tone* caused the shock.

Hume argued that we humans associate events whenever we experience a 'constant conjunction' (a series of pairings) of those events. As a result of the discovery of such phenomena as blocking, we have at last advanced a little on Hume's analysis, and can show that a constant conjunction is not always sufficient to obtain an association. But we can also see that failure to obtain association formation following constant conjunction can best be interpreted as the result of a process that is designed to detect the most likely cause of an event. And this in turn strengthens the idea that the role of association formation is indeed to uncover causal relationships.

Armed with the idea that associations formed in the real world will most likely represent causal links, we can see one good reason why at least this process should be common to all vertebrates: causal relationships are common to all environments, and the ability to detect them allows accurate predictions to be made, whatever an animal's ecological niche. Since in fact the *only* way to predict the future is to uncover causal relationships, we can see also that the ability to detect associations should be regarded not as a 'simple' form of learning, but as an immeasurably valuable skill.

One final remark: in case it might be thought that perhaps association formation in mammals is a development of some much simpler system—a system that, for example, simply reacted to pairings of events, ignoring such complications as the previous history of the animal, or of the co-occurrence of other stimuli—it is interesting to know that blocking has been observed in birds, in fish, and even in slugs[23]. And although we have concentrated here on blocking, there are other examples of phenomena that similarly demonstrate that pairings of events do not necessarily guarantee associations—and these also are seen in all animals that have been tested. All vertebrates (and who knows, perhaps all invertebrates) not only form associations, they form them in the same way—a way that suggests that the role of association formation is to take advantage of the causal nature of the universe so as to predict events that have not yet occurred.

## Language and thought

Food caching is one of those complex activities that have so impressed Donald Griffin that he believes they require us to suppose consciousness in animals. He argues that food-storing birds 'not only hide large numbers of seeds, but while doing so look closely at the hiding places, suggesting that they are thinking about returning later to find the food they are hiding'[24]. Whether animals *think* or not depends, of course, on what we mean by thinking. It is perfectly reasonable to suppose that there are modes of thought that do not use language, and so, that at least some types of thought are available to animals. But whether those non-verbal types of thinking imply the existence of *consciousness* is quite another question, and one that cannot, I believe, be resolved simply by piling up examples of animal 'cleverness'. The basic reason for this scepticism is, of course, that it is possible to imagine computers that have been programmed to perform in a way that is just as 'clever' (and flexible) as some instance of animal cleverness, but still doubt whether the installation of cleverness alone is sufficient to guarantee consciousness.

Part of the rationale for this chapter was that exploration of animal cognition might give some insight into such questions as whether some animals might be conscious, and some not, and whether some animals might be more conscious than others. My conclusions have not been very helpful. We have seen that associative processes are ubiquitous in animals, and have been unable to find evidence for a significant 'leap' in cognition between one animal species and another—with one exception. We have found, in the evolution of language, a leap between non-human animals and the human animal. If there is a strong link between consciousness and cognition, this suggests a difference in consciousness between animals and humans. But we do not know whether cognition *is* related to consciousness. Is language merely a cognitive leap, or is it the Rubicon between unconsciousness and consciousness? This is the central question that we shall explore in the remaining chapters of this book.

In Chapter 1, I rejected the idea that the ability to learn could be used as a criterion for consciousness, partly because of the existence of learning in apparently 'simple' invertebrates whose consciousness we might be inclined to question, and partly because learning can also be demonstrated in the isolated spinal cord. We have seen now that, although animals cannot master language, they are capable of relatively sophisticated learning—albeit learning mediated primarily by associative processes. Chapter 6 will explore two questions of pressing concern. First, do humans—despite the evolution of language—still use the non-verbal modes of learning (or thought) used by animals? Second—a question whose meaning will become clearer as Chapter 6 progresses—if we do, do we use them 'unconsciously'?

## Notes and references

1. Macphail (1982), in which can be found details of and references for many of the experiments described here. Where an experiment is not described in the main text, references will be given in the footnotes.
2. Bitterman (1975).
3. For a description of this experiment, see Macphail (1987).
4. Zeldin and Olton (1986).
5. Köhler (1925/1957).
6. Epstein, Kirschnit, Lanza, and Rubin (1984).
7. McGonigle and Chalmers (1977).
8. Von Fersen, Wynne, Delius, and Staddon (1991).
9. Zentall and Sherburne (1994).
10. In Macphail (1982), for example.
11. Reese (1964).
12. See Macphail (1982) for further details of these studies.
13. Terrace, Pettito, Sanders, and Bever (1979).
14. Clever Hans was a horse who in the early 1900s convinced numerous experts that he could read, spell, and do arithmetic (answering questions by tapping his hoof a certain number of times, or by pointing his head at appropriate objects or cards). It was eventually shown that his performance was a result of his responding to involuntary and scarcely perceptible visual cues given by his questioners. See Boakes (1984) for an account of this fascinating episode.
15. Savage-Rumbaugh et al. (1993).
16. For details of Pepperberg's procedures, and for her further exploration of parrot cognition, see Pepperberg (1981, 1983, 1994); Pepperberg, Garcia, Jackson, and Marconi (1995); Pepperberg and Kozak (1986).
17. For a readable introduction, see Chomsky (1972) or Pinker (1994).
18. For facts and theories about brain size, see Jerison's classic book (1973).
19. Krebs, Sherry, Healy, Perry, and Vaccarino (1989).
20. Hilton and Krebs (1990).
21. Kamil, Balda, and Olson (1994).
22. See Mackintosh (1983), pp. 236–9, for a formal exposition of these two alternative accounts of blocking.
23. For studies of blocking in fish and birds, see Macphail (1982); for blocking in a slug, see Sahley, Rudy, and Gelperin (1981).
24. Griffin (1984), p. 71.

# 6

## Unconscious minds

### Unconscious learning

I argued in Chapter 5 that a key distinction between the animal and the human mind is that whereas humans use language, animals do not, but rely instead upon a cognitive system, the central core of which operates to form associations. This chapter will begin by focusing on the question of whether the cognitive achievements of animals lead to the conclusion that they are conscious. Paradoxically, in order to approach that question, I shall rely largely on human data—data that show that we at least can carry out sophisticated information processing at a non-conscious level. I shall begin by asking whether we humans have retained an associative system that operates alongside our linguistic system.

### The problem

It might seem natural to assume that humans have simply added a linguistic capacity to their ancestors' animal system and that, when called upon, we too could employ that same associative system. But, of course, it is possible that humans have not added language to the associative system, but have replaced it altogether. This chapter will show that it has not been simple to decide whether humans form associations in the way that animals do, and exploring this question will take us into areas that have surprising implications for the evolution of consciousness.

#### 'Conditioning' without association formation?

If you devise an experiment in which you present people with pairings of events like those used in studies of animal conditioning, then they, like animals, show what appear to be conditioned responses. If, for example, you pair a buzzer with a puff of air to the eyeball, a human subject will soon come to blink to the sound of the buzzer alone. But there is a problem with concluding from that finding that humans condition as animals do. The difficulty is well expressed in a provocative article[1] published in 1974 by William Brewer, an experimental psychologist at the University of Illinois. His article has received much less attention than it deserved, perhaps because of the unwelcome implication that the study of animal learning might be irrelevant to human psychology.

Brewer advocated an alternative 'cognitive' account, namely, that the 'conditioned' responses seen in humans are a consequence of higher mental processes—such as the development of conscious hypotheses about the relationship between the paired events. A person might form the hypothesis that the buzzer signals an airpuff, so that the sound of the buzzer leads to a conscious expectation of the airpuff, which in turn elicits a blink. This process, relying as it does on explicit hypotheses, would not be possible in non-linguistic organisms. Given that both the 'associative' and the 'cognitive' accounts expect the same outcome from a standard experiment, what differential predictions could be used to tease them apart?

Brewer made a number of proposals. First, if the cognitive account is correct, then no conditioned responses should be produced by anyone who has not consciously detected the relationship between the paired events. Second, it should be possible to obtain conditioned responses simply by telling the subject that there is a relationship—that the buzzer will be followed by an airpuff; similarly, it should be possible to abolish the response by telling the subject that the relationship no longer holds. These predictions contrast with the expectations of the associative account, which has nothing to say about awareness, and assumes a gradual growth in the strength of associations—a growth that can occur *only* with actual pairings of the relevant events.

Brewer's review of the literature then available found that all the predictions of the cognitive account were supported: humans who show conditioned responses invariably know—and can articulate—the relationship between the paired events, and 'conditioned' responses can be induced or eliminated by informing them that a relationship does or does not exist. Brewer concluded that there was no convincing evidence for conditioning in humans.

In an article published some 15 years later[2], Robert Boakes, then at the University of Sussex, stated that Brewer's conclusion remained valid, but went on to suggest that perhaps the conscious awareness of a relationship between two events was a *consequence* of a 'preattentive' process dedicated to detecting temporal relationships between events (in other words, of an associative process). It is difficult to see how this proposal might be tested: how could we decide whether, on the one hand, we 'spontaneously' generate plausible hypotheses or whether, on the other hand, those hypotheses emerge in response to the output of an associative process?

It has, then, proved difficult to demonstrate that anything beyond Brewer's higher mental processes need be invoked to explain human performance in tasks that use fairly conventional conditioning procedures (in which one event is consistently paired with another). One interesting exception to this generalization was a report which merits description here, because it helps to clarify the distinction being drawn between the unconscious, incremental process of association formation and the conscious process of forming expectancies.

In this study[3], a dissociation was found between reported expectancy and conditioned responses. Subjects (undergraduates at the University of Paris) took part in a series of trials in which, on 50 per cent of occasions, a 1-second tone was followed by an airpuff to the eyeball. The pairings were organized according to a quasi-random sequence, with the constraint that there were no more than four consecutive tone-alone trials, and no more than four consecutive tone–airpuff trials. The subjects were told that half the tones would be followed randomly by airpuffs, and asked, before each trial, to rate their expectancy of an airpuff (on a scale of 0—'airpuff not expected', to 7—'airpuff expected'). Eyelid closures that occurred before the end of the tone (and before the arrival of the airpuff) were recorded, and scored as conditioned responses.

The basic rationale of the experiment was as follows: as a run of tone-alone (or tone–airpuff) trials continued, the subjects' *expectation* of the other type of trial—a tone–airpuff (or tone-alone) trial—was expected to increase (since the trials were organized randomly, this would be an instance of the 'gambler's fallacy'). So, if conditioned eyeblinks were closely linked to expectancies, the probability of their occurrence should *increase* as a run of tone-alone trials proceeded, and *decrease* as a run of tone–airpuff trials proceeded. If, on the other hand, the conditioned eyeblinks were the outcome of an automatic process that increased the strength of an association with each tone–airpuff pairing and decreased it with each tone-alone presentation, then the probability of a conditioned eyeblink should *decrease* as a run of tone-alone trials proceeded, and *increase* across a run of tone–airpuff trials. The results are summarized in Fig. 6.1. As anticipated, this shows that as a run of one type of trial progressed, subjects' expectancy of the other type of trial increased. The critical finding, however, is that conditioned responding showed the opposite pattern—as expectancy of the airpuff *increased*, the probability of a conditioned eyeblink *decreased*. These results provide, therefore, support for the notion that there is in humans an incremental associative process that runs in parallel with, and independently of, explicit hypothesis-forming processes that give rise to conscious expectancies.

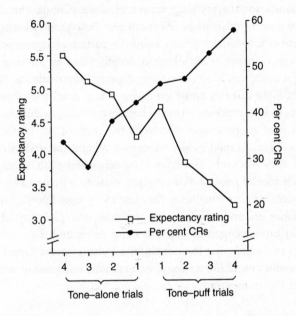

**Fig. 6.1** Mean subjective expectancy (left axis, full scale: 0–7) and conditioned eyeblink responses (right axis, as per cent) as a function of the length (1–4 trials) and nature (tone–airpuff/tone alone) of the preceding run. (Adapted from Perruchet (1985), Figs 2 and 3., with permission)

Perhaps surprisingly, the strongest evidence for the survival in humans of associative mechanisms can be found using tasks that are considerably more complex in design. Two to consider are, first, causality judgements, and second, 'implicit' learning of complex rules. In each case, we shall find evidence that human behaviour is influenced by 'knowledge' that cannot be expressed in words—knowledge of which people appear to be unaware. It is, of course, not *necessary* that humans should be unaware of the operations of an associative system inherited from animal ancestors—but when we can find evidence of learning of which people are unaware, we can at least dismiss the possibility that explicit hypothesis testing is involved in their performance.

## Causality judgements

The idea (introduced in Chapter 5) that the function of association formation might be to detect causal relations makes it sensible to ask whether we humans use the associative system in deciding whether events are causally related.

Experiments on causality judgement typically ask humans to decide, on the basis of a series of pairings of actions and outcomes, whether—or to what extent—a specified action causes a particular outcome. So, for example, a person might be asked to decide whether pressing a button made a light come on. Now, of course, if every press made the light come on, and the light did not come on at any other time, the person would rapidly conclude that pressing caused light onset. This finding *could* be the consequence of an association (between the press of the button and the onset of the light) formed by the associative system, the strength of which was consciously accessible. But it could equally well be the consequence of some higher mental process. For example, if asked why he had to come to his conclusion, a person might say: 'because every time I pressed the button the light came on, and it never came on otherwise'; he may, then, have relied upon higher cognitive capacities and integrated the two pieces of knowledge to deduce that the press of the button caused light onset. But the task becomes more interesting if we make the relationship between the two events less transparent.

## Contingency variation

One method of clouding the relationship between actions and outcomes is to vary the probability of the outcome (for example, light onset) given the action (for example, a press of a button)—so that, say, the action produces the outcome on only 75 per cent of occasions. But we could also vary the probability of the outcome occurring in the *absence* of any action—if such a probability is the same as that of its occurrence given the action, the action is not causally effective. If a light comes on just as frequently when you do not press a button as when you do, then the press of the button is not causally related to light onset.

The probabilities of an outcome given an action and given no action can be varied independently to cover an entire range of effectiveness—from the action having no effect, to the action having complete effectiveness. The causal effectiveness of an action—the real contingency between it and an outcome—can be thought of as varying between 0 (when the outcome is just as likely whether the action has occurred or not) and 1 (where the outcome occurs only when the action has occurred); technically, it is defined as the difference between the probability of the outcome given the action and the probability of the outcome in the absence of the action.

We can, therefore, ask whether humans are sensitive to the real contingency between actions and outcomes: do we take into account both the frequency of an outcome in the presence of an action and its frequency in the absence of the action?

It is, perhaps, not surprising that experiments in which humans are asked to rate the contingency between actions and outcomes agree that humans *are* sensitive to the real contingency between events (although we do make some interesting mistakes about the absolute value of the contingency). The question is, do we achieve these judgements by using higher mental processes, or do we use an associative system akin to that used by animals? Do people, for example, integrate pieces of knowledge like: 'the light comes on quite frequently whether I press the button or not, but it does come on somewhat more frequently when I do press the button'?; or do they access the output of a relatively autonomous incremental associative system—in which case we might not expect them to be articulate about the sources of their judgements? There are good reasons for supposing that in fact we use an associative system.

## Animals detect contingency

An important preliminary observation is that animals too are sensitive to real contingencies in conditioning experiments If, for example, the ongoing rate of occurrence of an event is no different in the presence of some potential conditioned stimulus than in its absence, animals do not—despite regular pairings—form an association between the stimulus and the event[4]. The sensitivity of animals to real contingency provides another illustration (like blocking) of the fact that the simple pairing of events does not in itself guarantee the formation of an association between them. The associative system of animals is not simple, and it has so evolved that it is well suited to forming associations between events that are genuinely causally linked.

## A cognitive hypothesis rejected

The most obvious 'higher' cognitive technique that would allow us to calculate the real contingency would be to estimate the two relevant probabilities—the probability of the outcome given the action, and the probability of the outcome in the absence of the action—and to derive the contingency from those probabilities. But when experimenters have asked subjects not only to rate the contingency between the action and the outcome, but also to estimate both the probability of the outcome given the action and the probability of the outcome in the absence of the action, it has turned out that their ratings of the contingency are strikingly more accurate than would be the ratings derived from the two probability estimates.

In one study[5], for example, the actual probability of the outcome given the action was 0.75, and of the outcome in the absence of the action, 0.25: the real contingency associated with the action was, then, 0.5. The average of the subjects' estimates of the effectiveness of the action was (on a scale of 0 to 1) 0.43—a fairly good estimate of the real contingency. But their estimate of the probability of the outcome given the action was 0.65, and of the outcome in the absence of the action, 0.38. Had they derived estimates of the contingency by using the difference between those probabilities, the effectiveness rating should have been 0.27 (0.65 − 0.38). It seems, then, that we do not deduce contingencies from our consciously available knowledge—or, at least, not from the knowledge that is most relevant. The most plausible candidate for a high-level process for estimating contingency can be ruled out. By a process of elimination, support for the alternative proposal—that we use the incremental associative system—is strengthened[6].

### Blocking

Further evidence is provided by a demonstration that the phenomenon of blocking, of such interest to contemporary animal learning theorists, is seen also in causality judgements.

In a blocking experiment (see Chapter 5), experimental animals experience two stages of conditioning. In the first stage of a typical experiment, rats might learn that a light predicts a shock; in the second stage, a tone is presented in compound with the light, and is followed by the shock. These animals are not alarmed by the tone when presented alone, although control animals who have experienced only the second stage of training *are* alarmed. Both groups have encountered the same number of tone–shock pairings, but the prior experience of the light predicting the shock has blocked learning about the tone. If human conditioning (as assessed by causality judgements) uses the associative system of animals, then we too should show blocking.

An ingenious analogue of this design for exploring causality judgements involved a computer game in which the subjects had to rate the effectiveness of shells at blowing up tanks[7]. Each trial consisted of a 'tank' moving rapidly across a 'minefield' on the computer screen. Pressing the space bar constituted 'firing a shell', and the bar had to be pressed when the tank was in a specific region of the screen to register a 'hit'. When a hit occurred, a 'blip' occurred on the screen. It was arranged so that it was quite difficult to achieve a hit; in fact, there was a successful hit on only about 50 per cent of the trials. In other words, on half the trials the 'action' occurred and on the other half, it did not. On some trials, the tank 'exploded', and the subjects were told that this might be the result either of a hit or of a mine.

An experimental group of subjects was first exposed to a series of trials on which the space bar was not in use, and they simply observed the tank crossing the minefield. The tank exploded in 75 per cent of these trials; these subjects should, then, have learned that the mines were pretty successful at blowing up the tanks. A control group received the same treatment, except that the mines caused explosions in only 5 per cent of trials; they would have concluded that mines are relatively ineffective. Both groups then experienced a second series of trials in which they now used the space bar to fire shells, and the probability of a hit exploding the tank was set at 0.75; the probability of the tank exploding in trials in which there was no hit was now 0.25—so that in fact there was a real contingency (of 0.5) between hits and explosions.

The judged effectiveness of the hits in the experimental group was lower (0.32) than that in the control group (0.73). So, the expectation that the mines alone would be effective in exploding tanks markedly reduced the perceived effectiveness of shell hits. Or—if we adopt the language of associationism, and assume that causality judgements are based on the output of an associative process—the prior association of the context (the minefield) with the outcome (explosions) effectively blocked the formation of an association between the action (shell hit) and the outcome.

## Causality judgement and the associative system

There are clearly striking parallels between association formation in animals and causality judgement in humans: both are sensitive to contingency, both show the blocking phenomenon. It is also the case that estimates of contingency in causality judgements gradually improve with practice, and the implication is that the same incremental associative system is at work in both. This conclusion clearly supports Robert Boakes' contention that we become aware of associations between events as a result of what he called the 'preattentive' process of association formation—a process that can be distinguished from higher mental processes that seem to be firmly under conscious control.

Introspectively, the associative system does not seem to be open to conscious inspection. Although we can use the output of the system, we are unaware of any conscious process of incrementing or decrementing associative strengths—particularly not in such complex tasks as those in which effect of contingency are measured. This suggests that there may be a distinction between an 'unconscious' learning system (shared by animals and ourselves), and a conscious system (involving 'higher' mental processes). But we must acknowledge that Brewer's original objections to the associative account of human conditioning still stand: it is, of course, a necessary feature of causality judgement that the subject is aware of the relationship between the events; it is also true that if we are informed by someone of acknowledged authority that there is (or is not) a causal relationship between two events, then our estimate of a causal relationship can be instantly altered. These facts should caution us *either* that causality judgements do not invariably rely solely upon the associative strength established by an autonomous associative system *or* that associative strengths can be directly influenced by higher mental processes. For stronger evidence of the existence in humans of an associative system whose operation is not open to introspection, and whose behavioural consequences cannot be readily influenced by higher mental processes, we must turn to yet more complex tasks.

## Implicit learning of complex processes

There have been in recent years a number of reports of striking examples of people who show clear evidence of quite complex learning, but who are entirely unaware that they have learned anything. There are now some ten different paradigms that have been used successfully, and to give a flavour of this work, I shall discuss two examples here.

### Artificial grammars

The first of these complex procedures was described in 1967 by the Brooklyn College psychologist, Arthur Reber[8]. His test material consisted of a set of 'sentences' derived from a very limited 'vocabulary' (the letters P, S, T, V, and X) according to the rules of an artificial (finite-state) grammar. This grammar is best explained through its state diagram, as seen in Fig. 6.2. This shows that all grammatical sentences must begin with T or with P, that P cannot be immediately followed by P, that PS can only occur as the end of a sentence, and so on. Some examples of grammatical sentences are: PTTTVPS; TSXXTVPS; PTTVV; PVV; TXXTTVV. Examples of ungrammatical sentences are: PTTTVPVS; TTVV; PTTPS; TXTVPS.

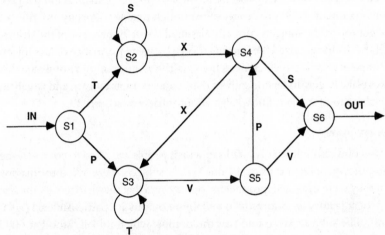

**Fig. 6.2** A state diagram showing how 'grammatical' sentences are generated. The process starts at S1, from which it can proceed to *either* S2 (in which case, it generates 'T') *or* S3 (in which case, it generates 'P'); all grammatical sentences must, therefore, begin with either T or P. If the process selects S2, it may then either move to S4 (in which case, it generates 'X'), or recycle to S2 (in which case, it generates 'S'). (There is no limit to the number of times that recycling may take place.) Permissible opening sequences therefore include: TX, TSX, TSSX, and so on. The process ends at S6, which may be reached from either S4 or S5. It can be seen that all grammatical sentences must, therefore, end with either S or V. (Redrawn from Reber (1993), Fig. 2.1., with permission)

In the first study using these materials, subjects were asked to memorize 34 strings of letters (using only letters drawn from the five-letter vocabulary). For one group, all the strings were constructed using the grammar, and for the other group, the letters in the strings were randomly ordered. Neither group of subjects was told anything about the way in which the strings had been constructed. All the subjects were told simply that they were taking part in an experiment on memory. But, after the first few strings had been learned, the subjects working with grammatical strings were learning substantially faster than those given non-grammatical strings. They were, therefore, in some sense exploiting the grammatical structure of the strings. However, if asked for any of the 'rules' of the grammar, none of the subjects (who were not conscious of any regularities in the strings) could suggest any—not even, for example, which letters could occur at the beginning or at the end of the strings.

A second experiment had even more striking results. Subjects were given 20 grammatical sentences to memorize. They were then told that the strings had been formed according to complex but rigorous grammatical rules, and asked to classify new strings as grammatical or non-grammatical (50 per cent were grammatical, 50 per cent not). Although unable to specify any rules of the grammar, the subjects correctly classified about 70 per cent of the strings. Reber has characterized the learning shown by the performance of his subjects as 'implicit learning', which he defines as: 'the acquisition of knowledge that takes place largely independently of conscious attempts to learn and largely in the absence of explicit knowledge about what was acquired'[9].

## Control processes

My second example involves tasks in which people are asked to control some computer-generated output. In one task[10], subjects were asked to imagine that they were in a sugar-producing country, and that they had to vary the size of a sugar factory workforce so as to stabilize output at a particular level (9000 tons). The subjects were told that the output, which initially stood at 6000 tons, could vary from 1000 to 12 000 (in increments of 1000); its current value was shown on a computer screen. The size of workforce (also shown on the screen) began at 600 workers, and could be varied by the subject (in steps of 100) to between 100 and 1200. In fact there was a simple arithmetic relationship between, on the one hand, the value of the workforce input by the subject and the current value of the output, and, on the other hand, the output resulting from the new workforce. Although the relationship was simple, it was nevertheless the case that the value of the output could not be predicted directly from the size of the workforce: the output depended upon both that value and the size of the preceding output. Table 6.1 illustrates the inputs and outputs of a series of seven trials, and gives the equation used.

The subjects of this experiment showed rapid improvement in control of the output: over the first 30 trials, subjects achieved the target level on approximately nine trials (responding at chance would have achieved about three successful trials); over the next 30 trials, the target level was hit on 16 trials. After completing either 30 or 60 trials, the subjects were asked to complete a questionnaire, the first part of which tested their ability to predict an output, given the value of a new input and the current state of both the workforce and the output. Performance on this part of the questionnaire was exactly the same after 30 trials as after 60 trials; what is more, it was no different from that of subjects who had simply been told what the task consisted of, and had no experience at all of controlling the output (and so, no knowledge whatever of the relationship between inputs and outputs). So, despite clearly having learned to control the output, the subjects appeared to have learned nothing consciously about the rules governing the system. This conclusion was reinforced by their responses to the second part of the questionnaire, which asked the subjects how they achieved control—many simply refused to answer, complaining that they could not put it into words.

**Table 6.1**   An illustrative series of inputs and outputs for the sugar production task.

| Workforce ($W \times 100$) | Sugar output ($P \times 1000$) |
|---|---|
| | 6,000 |
| 700 | |
| | 8,000 |
| 900 | |
| | 10,000 |
| 800 | |
| | 7,000 |
| 1,000 | |
| | 12,000 |
| 900 | |
| | 6,000 |
| 1,000 | |
| | 12,000 |
| 1,000 | |
| | 9,000 |

The equation used was: $P = 2W - P_1$, where $W$ = the number, between 1 and 12, typed in to represent the size of the workforce (divided by 100); $P_1$ = the number, between 1 and 12, representing the *previous* sugar output (divided by 1000); and $P$ = the number representing current output (divided by 1000). If the equation resulted in an output of less than 1000 tons, 1000 was displayed; if the equation resulted in an output of more than 12 000 tons, 12 000 was displayed. The relationship was slightly obscured by the fact that the computer occasionally added or subtracted 1000 from the output determined by this equation.
(Adapted from Berry and Broadbent (1984), Table 1.)

*Implicit versus explicit learning*

I have introduced procedures that demonstrate implicit learning in the context of determining the fate of the animal associative system in humans. We have seen that there is, of course, no dispute that humans can learn and solve problems by using processes that are under conscious control and that yield explicit, verbalizable information about how learning is proceeding— for example, what hypotheses have been explored, what knowledge has been gained. Many if not all of these cognitive processes are based on language or on a related symbolic system (as in mathematics). The question that we have been pursuing is: is there another system available to humans— a system that has at its centre, processes that lead to association formation?

The very fact that implicit learning yields knowledge that is not verbalizable suggests that there are at least two systems (implicit and explicit) for knowledge acquisition in humans. Further evidence of a real contrast between these two systems comes from studies on the effect of providing explicit information in the procedures just discussed.

There have been a number of reports that explicit information, although entirely accurate, may impair performance in complex procedures[11]. In one study, a group of subjects memorizing sentences derived from Reber's artificial grammar were told, before learning them, that the sentences did have a structure and were formed according to consistent rules. These subjects performed more poorly than subjects given no prior information about the sentences: they took longer to learn the sentences, and were less accurate subsequently at discriminating between grammatical and non-grammatical new letter strings. An analysis of the problems experienced by the informed subjects made good sense of the disruption of performance by what might have been expected to be useful information. It turned out that in many cases the subjects had hit upon rules that were in fact wrong—leading Reber to the conclusion that 'looking for rules won't work if you cannot find them'[12].

Similar studies using other complex procedures have also found that explicit information may actually make learning worse. There are, however, reports of improvements following explicit information. A reason for contrasting outcomes can be found by considering another version of the experiment just described. In this condition, not only were the informed subjects told that rules had been used, but the sentences were presented to them in groups according to their particular grammatical structures. This manipulation should, then, make the rules more salient, and in this version of the task, the informed subjects showed improved performance. A similar beneficial outcome from instructions that encourage subjects to look for underlying rules has been found in a number of studies in which the rules were in fact relatively salient. So—'looking for rules will work if you can find them'[13].

### What is learned?

It appears that humans use an implicit learning system when confronted by a structured stream of events whose underlying rules are far from obvious. It is as though the explicit system is well adapted to test hypotheses about relatively simple rules, involving cues that readily command attention. By contrast, the implicit system non-selectively stores information about all the cues present, and gradually builds up knowledge of the overall structure of the stream. What can we say of the way in which the implicit system uncovers the underlying rules?

There is good general agreement amongst those who have worked on implicit learning that the implicit system is sensitive to 'covariations or contingencies'[14] among events. This is, of course, precisely the business of the associative system in animals—a fact that has been emphasized by Reber himself, who has used principles of evolutionary theory to argue first, that the implicit system evolved before the explicit system, and second, that the implicit system should vary little from one species to another. We do not need to explore those arguments now: what is interesting here is that we have come to precisely the same conclusions by considering behavioural evidence.

It is clear that there is solid experimental support for the notion that there are in humans two systems for the acquisition of knowledge about the world, and that one of them is not open to introspection and has, to say the least, much in common with the associative learning system used by animals.

## Conscious versus unconscious

The account that I have given of implicit learning has been written in such a way as to persuade you that a conscious and an unconscious learning system run in parallel in humans. In some ways, I have taken a sledgehammer to crack a nut. There is, after all, no serious doubt that we can learn without being able explicitly to state what we have learned (imagine asking a child who had learned to ride a bicycle to articulate his new knowledge). But, as is no doubt inevitable in contemporary psychology, this is not an uncontroversial conclusion. Critics[15] have pointed to two principal difficulties in accepting the experimental work at face value. First, they argue that although subjects in these experiments cannot articulate correctly the rules used by the experimenter in scheduling the events, they may nevertheless have acquired some other (consciously available) information that would improve their performance above chance. Second, they argue that although the criterion for implicit learning may be exquisitely sensitive (a small decrease in response speed, for example), the criterion for explicit knowledge may be very demanding (subjects must, for example, acquire enough information to be able to articulate rules precisely).

Although these arguments are important, they seem to ask the impossible, in that they rely upon the notion that implicit knowledge must be *wholly* inaccessible to consciousness. The tactic of their proponents has been to seek evidence for any access whatever to potentially useful information following supposedly implicit learning: positive evidence is used to dismiss the implicit/explicit distinction. But there is no dispute that implicit knowledge *is* in some sense available to consciousness: decisions to push buttons are voluntary, conscious decisions. Similarly, causality judgements, if they do rely upon implicit processes, are examples of consciousness gaining access to unconscious processes. If implicit processes were wholly inaccessible to consciousness, then, presumably, only involuntary responses could be influenced by them. What we need to do here is to look for the most economical and plausible account of the experimental findings.

Experiments on conditioning in humans, and on causality judgements in particular, show a striking agreement between the properties of human conditioning and animal conditioning. And although our causality judgements are of course conscious, we have no insight into the processes that give rise to those judgements—processes that, again, parallel those seen in operation in animal conditioning. This is plausibly interpreted as supporting Boakes' proposal that, at least in some circumstances, it is the output of our conditioning system that is responsible for our conscious awareness of contingencies between events: the 'gambler's fallacy' study[16], however, suggests that the conditioning system need not always give rise to a conscious representation.

Finally, the protocols obtained from people after successful acquisition of an implicit learning task are surely compelling: subjects are, as often as not, surprised to learn that there was any regularity to be found in the procedure, and even more surprised to be told that they have uncovered the regularity. Something is, of course, available to the conscious process—or performance could not reflect it—but it is surely perverse to argue that it is knowledge that was entirely acquired and used consciously.

## Amnesia and two learning systems

The notion that there are in humans two different learning systems is supported by a further source of evidence—one that is directly relevant to the evolution of these systems.

In 1953 an operation was carried out on a patient, known as HM, in the hope of relieving his chronic epilepsy. The operation involved the surgical removal of a substantial part of both of his temporal lobes—regions which contained some neocortex, the amygdala, and, most significantly, the hippocampus. Following recovery from the operation, HM showed dramatic memory deficits[17]. He displayed reasonably good recall for events that had occurred before the operation, but virtually no recall for postoperative events: he could remember recent events for only a matter of seconds, or for as long as he was able to 'rehearse' them (for example, by repeating words over and over again to himself before being asked to recall them). HM is still alive today, and shows no alleviation of his problems; he still does not even recognize any of the psychologists who have been testing him, day in and day out, for many years.

There have been a number of other cases of similar memory deficits reported since 1953, most of them involving damage to the hippocampus or structures associated with it. Work on these amnesics has confirmed their total inability to lay down new memories that can be consciously accessed after anything longer than a few seconds. It has, however, also become clear that they *can* show long-term learning. They can, for example, learn new skills, such as drawing shapes when they can see the hand doing the drawing only in a mirror; and conditioning procedures are effective with them[18]. But reports of these successful tests have emphasized that the performance is independent of conscious recall: the amnesic subjects do not recall carrying out the task before, and do not recognize the apparatus or the experimenter.

The fact that amnesics can learn some things, but not others, has naturally led to the proposal that there are two long-term memory systems—one implicit (and available to amnesics), one explicit (and not available to amnesics for registration of new events). There are clear parallels between the amnesics' implicit system and the implicit system identified in the learning of, for example, artificial grammars—a system that, in its turn, appears to be like the system available to animals—associative in nature. There is, moreover, evidence that amnesics do show efficient learning in those complex tasks that involve implicit learning in unimpaired humans[19]. So, should we identify the implicit system of amnesics with an associative system available to animals? And is the explicit system a hippocampus-dependent system that exists only in humans? The answers are 'yes' and 'no': yes, the implicit system *is* preserved through animals and humans; but no, the explicit system of linguistic humans *does* have a forerunner in animals.

## A forerunner of the explicit system in animals

The evidence for the existence of a correlate of our explicit system in animals is straightforward. In non-human mammals, damage to the hippocampus and related structures (adjoining neocortical regions in particular) leads to disruptions in learning and memory that show broad parallels with the disruptions seen in human amnesics[20]. For example, hippocampal system[21] damage in animals does not affect learning and retention of either simple conditioning or of motor skills (processes that depend upon the implicit system). It does, however, affect a wide range of complex activities, including learning about places, and 'recognition' tasks in which they have to respond differentially to two objects (one entirely new, and one seen briefly on only one previous occasion). This should alert us to the fact that although associative learning forms the core of learning in animals, it is not a unitary system. This is, perhaps, hardly surprising given that, as we saw in Chapter 5, sophisticated achievements may be attained by associative processes. At least two neurological systems are involved, and the hippocampal system complements a basic associative system, contributing to the ways in which associations may be formed.

Unfortunately, it has proved extremely difficult to characterize the range of deficits that follow hippocampal-system damage. We saw in Chapter 5 the suggestion that the hippocampus might be involved particularly in spatial learning; but although there is no doubt that many spatial tasks are disrupted by hippocampal damage, many non-spatial tasks are disrupted also[22]. We need not attempt here to decide the controversial question of how hippocampal function should best be characterized. What is important is first, that in both humans and animals, relatively simple conditioning may proceed normally in the absence of hippocampal involvement, and second, that the hippocampal system becomes in humans, an explicit system. There is no conclusive evidence on whether the hippocampal system in animals is explicit or not, since the only certain criterion for a system being explicit is that its output can be talked about (which is why one way of characterizing the systems in humans has been to refer to the hippocampus-dependent system as 'declarative', and to the hippocampus-independent system as 'procedural'—'knowing that' versus 'knowing how').

## Learning and consciousness

If our unconscious learning system is in fact the human version of a basic associative learning system common to animals and humans, what is implied for animal consciousness?

The major implication is that, since the associative system works efficiently in humans without being subject to conscious monitoring, the fact that associative learning proceeds efficiently in animals can provide no evidence that animals are conscious. In other words, the obvious intelligence of animals does not imply that they are conscious. Hippocampal involvement may allow the basic associative system an increased sophistication, but there is no more reason for insisting that sophisticated associations must be conscious than there is for supposing that basic associations should be. It is perfectly conceivable, therefore, that the non-verbal thought of animals is not a conscious process. On the other hand, the fact that *we* are not conscious of the operation of our basic hippocampus-independent associative system does not prove that animals are not conscious of its operations in them. The evolution of our explicit system may have removed a formerly conscious system from consciousness. Similarly, the tasks for which animals employ their hippocampal system may or may not be conscious in them. It may be that this formerly unconscious system has become conscious in humans.

## Unconscious perception

I argued in Chapter 1 that the pain-like behaviour seen in animals in response to potentially dangerous stimuli does not provide unequivocal evidence of the conscious experience of pain. Our exploration of the fate in humans of the animal associative learning system points to the conclusion that animal cognition, although an efficient system, does not require consciousness for its successful operation. We shall now look briefly at a related question: whether it is plausible to suppose that another apparently high-level process—perception—can be achieved without consciousness.

Clearly, it makes no sense to suppose that we could be in pain without being conscious of the experience (and so, if we conclude that animals experience pain, we conclude that they are conscious). Does it make any more sense to suppose that we could see or hear without being aware of what we are seeing or hearing? We may query whether animals experience pain, but clearly they do have sensory systems—they *do* see and hear. Does perception imply consciousness? I shall introduce evidence of two quite different kinds to show that it does not.

### Blindsight

When humans suffer damage to the primary visual cortex—the part of the neocortex to which visual information is relayed from subcortical centres—they report that they have no visual experience of the part of the visual world with which the damaged region was originally concerned. So, if you show a patient with cortical damage something that would have caused cortical activity only in the now damaged region, the patient will report that he sees nothing. And if you ask him about some feature of the stimulus being shown, he will reply that, since he cannot see any stimulus, he cannot answer the question. But if you ask him to *guess* whether there is a stimulus there or not, he performs well above chance; he performs similarly if you ask him to guess and to point towards the stimulus; and if you ask whether, for example, the stimulus was an 'X' or an 'O', or whether a line is horizontal or vertical, he again performs very well— typically claiming that he sees nothing in any of the tests.

This phenomenon—the ability to make correct decisions about stimuli that are not consciously seen—has been labelled 'blindsight'[23]. It seems likely that blindsight is mediated by subcortical regions that receive visual information and (in the normal course of events) relay that information up to the visual neocortex[24]. In other words, when conscious access to the visual neocortex is denied, non-conscious access is still possible to subcortical visual areas, and visual perception (of a sort) may proceed.

Although patients with blindsight can make a remarkable number of correct decisions about visual stimuli, their vision, apart from being unconscious, is severely impaired. Their visual acuity—the capacity to discriminate fine visual detail—is much poorer. This is not surprising since it is precisely the visual cortex that is generally supposed to be the brain area specializing in detailed pattern vision. We can, however, turn to a very different type of evidence to show that high-level visual processing is possible without conscious experience.

## Reading 'unseen' words

There have been a number of reports demonstrating that people can read words which they are unaware of *seeing*, let alone reading. By way of illustration, I have selected examples using the 'lexical decision' task, in which subjects are shown a string of letters (for example, 'biology' or 'piology') and asked to say whether the string forms a word or not. Typically, very few mistakes are made, and the performance measure used is the time taken to make the decision—the reaction time.

Reaction times to words speed up when a target word is immediately preceded by a word with a related meaning. It takes a person less time to decide that 'tiger' is a word if he has just seen the word 'lion' rather than 'clock'. This is generally presumed to reflect some kind of 'priming' by words of related meaning—possibly by activation spreading automatically from the entry in the 'internal lexicon' for the word actually perceived, to entries for similar words.

Priming occurs even when the priming word is presented in such a way that the person is not aware of having seen *any* word presented before the test word. The procedure for doing this consists of showing the priming word for only a brief period—typically about 10 milliseconds—and by then exposing a brief patterned stimulus that effectively masks its trace. The duration of exposure is adjusted so that the subject performs at chance when asked after a trial whether there was a priming word present, or whether only the masking stimulus had been presented. But when asked to make a lexical decision about the target word—presented after the masking stimulus—the same subject nevertheless responds more rapidly when the (masked) priming word was related to the target word. So, although the subject is not aware that a word has even been presented, he has actually read the word and unconsciously retained its meaning.

An interesting insight into the nature of the unconscious activation of meaning is revealed by some experiments[25] which used ambiguous priming words—words like 'palm', for example. These experiments found that when the priming word was exposed for a time sufficient for it to be consciously seen and read, it would prime words related to only *one* of its meanings—'palm' would, for example, prime 'wrist' but not 'tree'. But when an ambiguous priming word was presented so that it was *not* consciously perceived, it successfully primed words related to *both* of its meanings. It appears, therefore, that an ambiguous word that is not consciously perceived allows *both* its meanings to be simultaneously activated, and speeds up reactions to words related to either of its meanings.

The main conclusion to be drawn from this work is, clearly, that unconscious perception can be so sufficiently sophisticated that words can be read, and their entries in our mental lexicons can be accessed. A critical difference between conscious and unconscious perception appears to be that when an ambiguous word is accessed *consciously*, we of necessity select *one* of its potential meanings. This makes good sense: intuitively it does seem that we cannot simultaneously entertain two meanings of a word. A secondary conclusion is, therefore, that we cannot select between alternative meanings without involving consciousness. We can unconsciously activate the lexicon, but we cannot achieve meaning unconsciously.

## 'Blindsight' in other senses

The two examples that I have used here to illustrate unconscious perception both involve vision, but there are many other examples referring to vision and other senses. One example concerning touch comes from a woman with damage to a region of the left neocortex which resulted in the disappearance of any feeling of sensation in her right hand. Nevertheless, when her neuropsychologist asked her to point (blindfolded) with her left hand to the region of her right hand that he was touching, she performed with remarkable accuracy. Her own comment says it all: 'But I don't understand that! You put something here. I don't feel anything and yet I go there with my finger. How does that happen?'[26].

There is a similar report on a patient with damage to the region of the cortex concerned with hearing. This man could not understand spoken language, nor recognize common environmental sounds. Although he could not repeat words spoken aloud to him (he could read aloud quite normally) he performed accurately in a test in which he was asked to guess which of two words had been spoken (despite his not being conscious of having heard words)[27]. A second example involving hearing is useful, if only for its intrinsic interest, since it shows that we access the meanings of words even when we are asleep. The evidence is quite simple: the threshold loudness for arousing a sleeping human is lower for the sleeper's own name than for other names[28]. This shows that, even when we are asleep, we 'hear' words and analyse them in at least enough detail to be able to decide whether or not our name is being spoken.

There is, of course, nothing in any of this to imply that animals when perceiving are *not* conscious—no suggestion, for example, of a non-conscious perceptual system, available to both humans and animals, acting alongside a conscious system, available only to humans. But what can be seen is that successful perception does not necessarily imply conscious perception.

## 'Blindsight' in monkeys?

We should not leave the topic of unconscious perception without discussing a report[29] of a phenomenon, similar to blindsight, observed in monkeys. Three rhesus monkeys had the primary visual cortex removed from the left hemisphere. As in humans, this region processes visual input from the right visual field, and damage to it would be expected to produce impairment in the right hemifield only. The monkeys faced a video monitor, and each trial began with the illumination of a 'starting light' in the centre of the touch-sensitive monitor screen. The monkeys were trained to touch this light; in doing so, they looked at the light and so centred it in their visual field, so that vision of the left half of the screen was now mediated by the right half of their brain, and the right half of the screen, by the left half of the brain. When the monkeys responded to the starting light, a visual stimulus appeared briefly in one of four possible positions on the monitor—two in the left hemifield, two in the right (see Fig. 6.3). The duration of the stimulus was so brief that it had disappeared before the monkeys could turn their eyes towards its position: in other words, this visual stimulus could be seen only by the contralateral side of the brain. The monkeys performed this task successfully with the stimulus in either hemifield, and the brightness of the stimulus was varied for each hemifield so that correct performance (touching the stimulus) was attained 90 per cent of the time. The brightness required to achieve this level of attainment was higher (but not dramatically so) for stimuli presented in the right hemifield—the hemifield 'seen' by the damaged side of the brain.

This phase of the experiment shows, therefore, that monkeys, like humans, can respond appropriately to visual stimuli in the absence of functional primary visual cortex. The question is, are they, like humans, not conscious of seeing these stimuli? Do the monkeys actually 'see' the stimuli? To test this question, a second test was introduced using, initially, only the left hemifield ('seen' by the intact hemisphere). Trials were started again by the monkeys touching the starting light. Now, when the light was touched, *either* a stimulus appeared briefly at one of five positions on the left side of the screen, *or* no stimulus was presented (see Fig. 6.4). If a stimulus was shown, the monkeys were rewarded for touching it; if no stimulus was shown, the monkeys were rewarded for touching a rectangle in the upper left part of the screen. The monkeys were trained, then, to respond to any stimulus that they saw, and to respond to the rectangle if they saw nothing. The question is: how will the monkeys react when stimuli are exposed in the right hemifield? We know (from the first phase of the experiment) that they *can* respond by touching them. But if they do not 'see' them, they may respond by touching the 'no-stimulus-seen' rectangle. The results were clear-cut: all three monkeys responded to stimuli shown in the right hemifield by pressing the rectangle—as though, in other words, they had not seen a stimulus. (And a control monkey, with no brain damage, responded, as would be expected, by touching the stimuli shown on the right hemifield.)

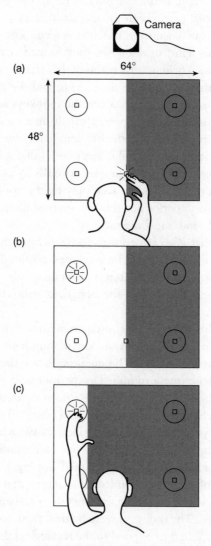

**Fig. 6.3** The procedure used to demonstrate functional vision in the right hemifield of monkeys with left primary visual cortex removed: (a) the monkeys press the starting light on the monitor whose right half then falls into the impaired right hemifield, indicated by the grey zone (eye movements are monitored with an infra-red sensitive camera); (b) triggered by the response to the starting light, a stimulus appears briefly at one of four possible positions; (c) the monkeys have to touch the position at which the stimulus appeared in order to obtain a reward. (From Stoerig and Cowey (1995), Fig. 2., with permission from Elsevier Science)

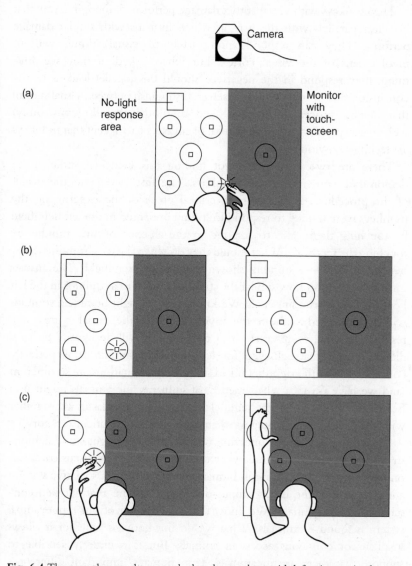

**Fig. 6.4** The procedure used to test whether the monkeys with left primary visual cortex removed treat suprathreshold stimuli in the right hemifield as stimuli or as blanks (no stimulus): (a) they start the trial by pressing the starting light; (b) the response to the starting light triggers either a stimulus or a blank (no stimulus) trial; (c) to obtain reward they respond to the stimulus by touching the position at which it appeared, and to a blank by touching the no-stimulus area in the (normal) left hemifield. (From Stoerig and Cowey (1995), Fig. 5., with permission from Elsevier Science)

The monkeys with visual cortex damage performed, then, in a way that has clear parallels with the way in which humans with similar damage perform. They can respond appropriately to visual stimuli without involvement of the visual cortex, but when 'asked' if they see anything, they respond in the negative. Should this parallel lead us to the conclusion that monkeys, like ourselves, distinguish between visual stimuli that they can process but not 'see', and stimuli that they do (consciously) see? To accept this conclusion would, of course, be to accept that monkeys *are* feeling-conscious.

There are two reasons for not finding this evidence sufficient to demonstrate consciousness in monkeys. The first[30] concerns the details of the procedure. In the second, critical phase of the experiment, the monkeys were trained to respond to stimuli presented in the left hemifield by touching them, and to respond to the absence of any stimulus by touching the rectangle. What should they do when shown a stimulus that is neither of those—a stimulus shown on the *right* hemifield? The answer must depend upon how similar the stimulus is to *either* a stimulus in the left hemifield *or* no stimulus at all. We know that the right hemifield stimulus will be processed without the involvement of the visual cortex: the resulting internal representation of the stimulus will necessarily be very different from that achieved for left hemifield stimuli. It is perfectly conceivable that the right hemifield stimuli representations are so different (and we have no idea what 'metric' of similarity the animals might use) from those achieved for left hemifield stimuli that they classify them rather with the 'no stimulus' category than with the left hemifield category.

The second reason for querying whether this blindsight study demonstrates consciousness in monkeys refers back to the work discussed earlier on two systems for learning in humans—one, a 'basic' associative system; and the second, the hippocampus-dependent system, that allowed conscious access in humans. We know that a forerunner of our hippocampal system is found in animals. What we do not know is whether it allows 'explicit' or conscious access in animals. But it is entirely sensible to suppose that there are in animals, as in humans, important differences between the two systems. Now suppose that information from the subcortical regions that are believed to mediate blindsight gains access to the basic system, but not to the hippocampal system; and suppose that the hippocampal system is involved, to at least some extent, in learned visual tasks—a view that readily explains the human data. Now since the monkeys' hippocampal system has indeed no information about stimuli presented to the 'blind' hemifield (to the extent that it is involved in a task), they will indeed respond as though no stimulus has been presented. In monkeys, as in humans, it requires careful training to overcome this hippocampal influence, and to devise tasks that can be mediated by the basic system alone.

The fact that blindsight can be demonstrated in humans can be used to prove that we can process visual input without being conscious of doing so—a conclusion that is strengthened by the other instances of unconscious perception previously discussed. But the fact that animals respond successfully to visual stimuli in some conditions, but behave as though they cannot see them in others, does not prove that they are conscious of seeing them in either condition: all that could be shown by dissociations of this kind is that more than one system is involved in determining the animals' choices—and that is not in dispute. The question is, and remains: are any of those systems conscious in animals?

## Origins of human consciousness

It is our ability to talk that wholly dispels any doubt about the existence of feelings in other human beings, and the principal difficulty facing anyone who wants to know whether animals are conscious (and, if so, which animals) is that animals do not talk. It may well be that non-human organisms do feel pleasure and pain, just as we do. But because they cannot talk, we are not as readily convinced as we are by other humans. There is, of course, one large group of humans who cannot talk—infants. Intuitively, it may seem obvious that babies have feelings. There has, nevertheless, been a long-running controversy over the question of whether infants do feel pain, and, if so, at what age—prenatal or postnatal—the capacity emerges.

### When do humans become conscious?

Until relatively recently, it was assumed by the medical profession in general that young babies felt little or no pain. Circumcision was (and still is) generally carried out without anaesthetic, and one survey found that, where babies were involved, doctors typically prescribed less than the recommended dosage for postoperative analgesia (and that nurses typically administered only about half of what had been prescribed)[31]. The assumption was that the neurological development of infants was not sufficiently advanced for the experience of pain. This attitude was supported by experimental reports which claimed that babies until a week or two old showed little response to such potentially painful stimuli as pinpricks.

Recent studies have, however, agreed that young babies do show many of the non-verbal components of the adult human response to painful stimuli. Babies less than two days old respond to a heel lance (used to obtain a blood sample) by showing facial expressions that adults readily characterize as indicating pain; they also cry and increase their heart rates[32]. Boys as young as six hours old respond to circumcision by showing an increase in the level of stress hormones (hormones typically released in adults by the cortex of the adrenal gland in response to stressful events)[33]. These perhaps unsurprising behavioural and physiological observations have persuaded most practitioners that babies do indeed feel pain, and the use of anaesthetics for surgical procedures on infants has become much more widespread. But this common sense view of infant sensitivity has not wholly solved the doctors' dilemma. If newborn babies feel pain, what of the unborn child? Surgical procedures on fetuses are now becoming relatively common, but there have been reports that levels of stress hormones are increased as a consequence of such surgical procedures as the insertion of a needle into the abdomen of an unborn child[34]. Does the foetus too feel pain—and, if so, at what stage of development?

I shall not recapitulate here the difficulties (outlined in Chapter 1) with the adoption of non-verbal behavioural or physiological responses as criteria for the existence of feeling-consciousness. Those arguments apply equally to infants as to animals: non-verbal responses are normal concomitants of pain in adults, but they do not *prove* the existence of pain, and they would serve the same purpose whether or not they were actually accompanied by pain. Given that infants develop into organisms that *do* feel pain, it may seem particularly implausible that they do not experience it. But there is inevitably, for any account, a very real difficulty in pronouncing on the stage at which feelings emerge. In what follows, I shall assume that it remains an open question, not to be resolved by appealing (for example) to the date on which the release of stress hormones is first observed.

Although babies do not talk, they develop into people who do talk. We could, then, ask people what was the nature of their experience when they were babies. But when we try to do that, we find that we cannot remember what it was like to be a baby. In fact, we cannot remember *anything* that happened when we were babies. When adults are asked for the earliest event that they can recall, it typically occurred when the person was some three to four years old[35]. This is in some ways very odd, given that the events of the first one or two years of life must surely have been significant and important—at the least, many of them must have been entirely novel! Why can we not recall any of those early episodes? Because our inability to recall events of our infancy constitutes an important block to our thinking about the conscious life of babies, we should look now for the cause of this peculiar amnesia: it is clearly possible that knowing the cause might itself throw light on the nature of non-verbal mental life.

## Infantile amnesia

Sigmund Freud (1856–1939) first drew attention to the riddle of infantile (or childhood) amnesia, and since then psychologists have tried many different ways to solve it. Some have proposed that infants do form stable memories, but that access to them is somehow blocked in adulthood—infant memories are repressed, for whatever reason. Others have argued that memories are formed, but that they are of a different kind from those formed by adults—memories, perhaps, but not comparable to the memories that we as adults consciously recall. Still others have believed that the infant brain was neurologically immature in such a way that stable memories could not be formed.

We can begin our exploration of infantile amnesia by dismissing the notion that babies simply cannot retain information over long periods: there have recently been a number of ingenious techniques developed that have allowed the exploration of memory in infants, and it has become quite clear that babies do show good long-term memory. I shall give a few examples here of the variety of memories that babies can store.

### Auditory and visual recognition

Before considering babies, it is worth mentioning that fetuses too can learn. In one particularly intriguing recent study[36], pregnant mothers read aloud a short (three-minute) children's story twice daily—the same one every day—for the last six weeks of their pregnancy. Within two days of birth, their babies were tested for recognition of the story. In the test, the babies were fitted with earphones through which they would hear either the same story or another story (read, again, by their mothers). The babies were also given a non-nutritive nipple to suck, and their spontaneous rate of sucking the nipple was recorded. The testing arrangement was that whenever a baby's rate of sucking increased or decreased from his or her spontaneous rate, a story was played. For eight babies, increases in rate obtained the familiar story, and decreases, a new story; for another eight babies, increases obtained the new story, and decreases, the familiar story. The babies altered their sucking rates—either increasing or decreasing them—so as to listen to the familiar story in preference to the new story. Fetuses can, then, acquire fairly subtle auditory information which is retained over at least the two or three days either side of their birth. Given that result, it is hardly surprising that newborn babies also show a preference for their mother's voice over those of strangers[37] (although, interestingly, they do not have any preference for their father's voice over other male voices[38]).

Visual memories can also be established in very young babies. One simple procedure, devised some 40 years ago, involves encouraging babies to look at two pictures displayed in front of them, and measuring how long their eyes fixate on each of the pictures. Babies prefer to look at new rather than familiar images, which shows that in some sense they recognize images which they have seen before. Using this technique, it was found about two decades ago that babies as young as five months old recognized abstract black and white pictures (originally seen for two minutes) up to 48 hours later; pictures of faces were recognized after a two-week delay[39]. More recently, it has been found that three-day-old babies prefer to look at new photographs (of female faces) to looking at photographs which they had been shown (once only, for about 40 seconds) some two minutes previously[40].

The immature brain can, then, in some sense recognize auditory and visual patterns, and over periods of up to at least two weeks. Other techniques have shown retention over much longer periods, and I shall describe two of those.

*Learning to do things*

Babies enjoy watching mobiles, and Carolyn Rovee-Collier, a developmental psychologist at Rutgers State University, has used this as a reward for kicking movements—a ribbon is attached to the baby's ankle, and tugs on the ribbon result in the movement of a mobile. This procedure is effective in babies once they are some four weeks old. The habit is usually learned within a few minutes and when re-tested some time later, babies as young as two months old show good evidence of retention over at least 24 hours. As the babies grow older, their memory improves, so that six-month-olds show good retention over two weeks. There is evidence, too, that retention may actually persist for longer periods. Babies can be given a 'reminder' before testing—which might consist simply of seeing the mobile in motion on the day preceding the memory test—and then three-month-old babies show good retention over four weeks[41].

## Deferred imitation

A technique known as 'deferred imitation' has been used successfully with older infants to demonstrate that they establish memories that persist as long as a year. In the training stage of these studies, the infants watch an adult performing an action using a particular toy or toys. The memory test consists of giving the child the toy to see whether he or she performs the action modelled by the adult. In one experiment[42], 11-month-old children watched an adult 'feeding' a teddy bear with a 'bottle' (actually a plastic cylinder with a plunger attached). When given the bear and the bottle to play with 12 months later, most of the children 'fed' the bear with the bottle (and few children who had not seen the original modelling did so— presumably because the 'bottle' did not resemble very closely the conventional feeding bottle).

Experiments using the deferred imitation technique have also shown that children as young as 11 months old can reproduce the correct order of two actions. In a typical test, infants were presented with a toy car and a hinged board that could be unfolded to make an incline. The experimenter modelled two actions: first, making the incline; second, placing the car on the board, so that it now ran down the incline. When the infants were given the car and the board immediately after the modelling, they performed the two actions—unfolding the board and placing the car—in the correct sequence. The correct order of three actions can be reproduced by 20-month-old babies, and 21-month-old babies show significant recall of order information over an eight-month delay[43].

## The transition to talking: toddlers' recall

We have seen perfectly good evidence that babies can retain memories for a variety of types of experience over relatively long periods. Why, then, do we not recall those experiences in adulthood? Is it possible that the development of language somehow makes these memories inaccessible? It seems not. One study[44] explored the memory of five 'highly verbal' toddlers approaching three years old for events that had occurred when they were between 6 and 40 weeks old. As babies, they had taken part in 15 to 19 sessions of laboratory testing involving such tasks as visual recognition and auditory localization (reaching for sound sources in the dark). The toddlers were re-tested in the same experimental room, and given essentially the same tests. Their performance in the tests clearly differed from that of toddlers who had not had the earlier laboratory experience (the difference consisting essentially in a much greater readiness to play with and reach for the objects used in the tests): these verbal toddlers did, then, show evidence of retention of their earlier, preverbal experience.

*Conscious recall?*

It is now beyond doubt that infants can store information about a wide variety of events, and that this information is not lost in the transition from preverbal to verbal life. But preverbal infants cannot show us in the conventional way that they have conscious recall of those events, since the conventional way involves using language—and it is the failure of adults to achieve conscious recall of infant experiences that is the issue in infantile amnesia. So, is there anything in the findings just presented that should encourage us to believe that infants show conscious recall? There is, inevitably, controversy on this question, and some have taken the view that if a simple associative account of some infant achievement is possible, then conscious recall is not demonstrated by that achievement. Given the evidence in this chapter for the unconscious operation of an associative system, this is the view that will be adopted here: an infant kicking to obtain the movement of a mobile is very likely an instance of associative conditioning, and so not proof of conscious recall.

Patricia Bauer, a developmental psychologist at the University of Minnesota, accepts the notion that recall is necessarily a conscious process, and argues that only one of the techniques that I have described provides evidence of true recall: the technique of delayed imitation of ordered actions. She regards this technique as a non-verbal analogue of recall because the child—like an adult achieving conscious recall—is retrieving a 'cognitive structure' for which there is no 'ongoing perceptual support'[45]. The stimuli present at the test (the toys, the general room cues) could, she argues, allow unconscious retrieval of specific responses to the cues—but there is nothing in the cues that provides information about the *ordering* of the events to be retrieved. This is an interesting but not a conclusive argument. It is not difficult to conceive associative accounts of ordered learning: the cues present at the beginning of the test might elicit the first response directly, and feedback from that response might provide the cues required to elicit the second response, and so on.

Not only is there no proof that any technique does demonstrate conscious recall, but there is at least some evidence that suggests that the memories retrieved by infants are unconscious. I have already described a study[46] in which it was noted that verbal toddlers had retained something of their experience of being tested when infants. But they were also asked questions about those previous visits, and their answers showed no evidence of conscious recall. All five children were asked whether they remembered the room, and none of them responded positively. This finding indicates a dissociation between what the toddlers had retained of their earlier experience and what was available to conscious recall.

Similarly compelling is a report on recall by babies suffering traumatic experiences[47]. These children were patients at the emergency room of a hospital, who were asked six months later what they remembered of their incident. One child, KB, 18 months old and not yet talking, caught a fish bone in her throat. Although it did not initially trouble her, her distress gradually increased until, when seen by her family doctor (who referred her to the emergency department), she was hysterical—and scored the maximum stress rating available on a scale given to the parents. The bone was rapidly removed at the hospital. Six months later, KB was talking, but could not recall in words anything about the incident. She did, on the other hand, pick out a photograph of the emergency-room doctor who removed the bone, and has refused to eat fish since the incident. Long-term retention of a sort occurred, but conscious access to a memory of the incident was not possible.

Another example suggests that it is not simply that memories originally available to consciousness are lost with the development of language, but that the memory of preverbal infants reflects the acquisition of information that even at the time is not consciously available. Eight-month-old infants were shown a puppet which had mittens[48]. When one of the mittens was removed, a treat appeared, and the infants grasped more or less immediately the idea of removing the mitten to obtain the treat. After extensive practice over a three-week period, the puppet was removed for some four months. When the infants were shown the puppet again, they displayed little interest in it. But when they did play with it, they touched almost exclusively the mitten that had concealed the treat, ignoring the other mitten. This generally resulted in the mitten falling off. However, when it did so, the infants did not look for the treat, and showed no surprise when there was in fact none. The infants had, then, remembered *something* about the appropriate mitten—something that led to their touching it, but they did not seem to know why they were touching it. They had, it seems, no conscious recall of their earlier experience.

## Memory after language develops

If we assume that infants do not consciously recall the events of their lives, we are led to ask the question: when *do* children start that process? What of conscious recall of everyday events by toddlers? Do children show evidence of recall as soon as they can talk? It is clear that they do. In the study already described[49], of children referred to a hospital emergency department, all of the children who were verbal at the age the incident occurred (from as young as 27 months old) showed clear evidence of conscious verbal recall six months later. Two recent studies point to the same conclusion. In one, conversations were recorded between Rachel and her mother[50]. In the other, the night-time 'presleep monologues' of Emily were recorded[51]. Both Rachel and Emily were 21 months old at the beginning of the recordings, and both children made frequent reference to clearly identifiable events (although these were invariably recent events—not events of preverbal infant life). As soon as language develops then, children show clear evidence of conscious recall.

### Language and recall

The evidence discussed here suggests that infants who have not learned to talk do not consciously recall the events of their lives, whereas children who can talk do, like adults, recall. If this account is valid, then infantile amnesia is not caused by a block or repression of infant memories, but by the failure to form conscious memories preverbally. Some interesting (if weak) support for the notion that language does play a critical role in infantile amnesia is provided by the fact that the earliest memories of female adults tend to be of events earlier in their lives than the earliest memories of males. This is suggestive because it is also the case that girls tend to start talking at a younger age than boys (but provides only weak evidence because there is in fact a range of perceptual and cognitive capacities which develop more rapidly in girls than in boys).

## The role of language in recall

It is one thing to conclude that language plays a critical role in the development of conscious recall, but quite another to understand how this comes about. That is the issue to which we should now turn. Two influential recent reviews of the source of infantile amnesia agree in supposing that the development of language brings about a qualitative change in the way in which memories are formed—a change that accounts for amnesia for the events of preverbal life. They propose, however, somewhat different roles for language.

### Two memory systems

In their 1989 review of childhood recall[52], David Pillemer of Wellesley

College, and Sheldon White of Harvard, proposed that there are in humans two memory systems. The first system operates throughout life, and cannot be accessed intentionally, but only by contextual cues. The second system is dependent upon language, and *can* be accessed intentionally. It is this latter system, then, that is used for conscious recall, and it is because the system does not develop until language develops that we cannot recall infant life.

### Development of the self-concept

In 1993, Mark Howe and Mary Courage, psychologists at the Memorial University of Newfoundland, rejected the notion of two memory systems, but proposed instead that autobiographical memory—the memory that allows conscious recall of specific episodes from one's past—develops as the concept of self develops[53]. In essence, their claim is that autobiographical memory is impossible in the absence of any notion of self—if I have no notion that 'I' am a particular (and special) person, how could I form memories about 'my' experiences? This proposal raises the question: when *does* the self-concept emerge?

Children begin to use the pronouns 'I' and 'me' just before the age of two, followed, a month or two later, by 'you'. These achievements can be taken as solid proof of the existence of a self-concept. If we assume, as seems likely, that the self-concept is one that develops over some time, then we have to look at preverbal evidence of its initial emergence. That evidence consists almost entirely of studies of visual self-recognition in babies, and points generally to the conclusion that the concept of self emerges at about 18 months of age. At that age, children can use mirrors to identify a coloured spot marked on their face and to touch it. At about the same age they begin to discriminate between video recordings of themselves and of other children of the same age.

There is controversy over the detailed time course of the development of the concept of self in children (and I shall cast doubt in Chapter 7 on the value of using mirrors to prove possession of a self-concept in animals). For present purposes, we need not go into details. If we accept that the self-concept is present at age two, and that it is likely to develop gradually, then we can accept the self-recognition findings as providing reasonable support for the conclusion that a concept of self emerges between the ages of approximately 18 and 24 months—roughly the period over which language begins to be used.

Although Howe and Courage emphasized the importance of the self-concept, they did not reject any role for language in the explanation of infantile amnesia. They suggested that it cannot simply be a coincidence that the offset of infantile amnesia occurs as language begins to be used as a matter of course in reflecting on current experience. According to their account, although the concept of the self begins its development independent of language, mastery of language allows for its refinement, and this in turn enhances autobiographical memory.

### Language, the self, and recall

Work discussed earlier suggests an account of the role of language in infantile amnesia that incorporates the central elements of both Howe and Courage's review and that by Pillemer and White. In Chapter 5 I argued that the major difference between the human and the non-human intellect is that non-humans cannot acquire language, and in the first part of this chapter I presented evidence to the effect that there are indeed two systems of learning available to humans. One, the implicit system, is not readily accessible to consciousness, and is the basic associative system available to humans and non-humans alike. The second, the hippocampus-dependent system is (in human adults) language-based, and open to conscious access; whether this system gives rise to conscious processes in animals remains an open question.

These conclusions lead to two proposals that accommodate the co-development of language, autobiographical memory, and the self-concept. The first incorporates Howe and Courage's notion that the concept of self is necessary for autobiographical memory, but supposes that there is a tight link between language and the self-concept. The proposal is that the self-concept is dependent on language, and that the emergence of language inevitably generates the self-concept—neither can exist without the other. So, language is necessary not simply for the refinement of the concept of self, but for its very existence. Thus, as non-humans and preverbal humans lack language, they also lack the concept of self. The second proposal incorporates the Pillemer and White notion that infants rely predominantly upon a different memory system from that used by adults for conscious recall. This proposal is that learning in both infants and animals is dominated by associative processes—processes that are not accessible to conscious inspection and that do not allow conscious recall of events.

We have seen that there is in animals the counterpart of the human conscious explicit system—the hippocampal system. Part of the evidence for this conclusion relates to tasks that intact animals can master that cannot be mastered either by animals with damage to the hippocampal system or by human amnesics. The implication is that animals do possess the forerunner of the system used by humans to gain conscious access to memories. There is evidence of a similar kind to show that human infants can also use the hippocampus-dependent system.

I described earlier a variety of techniques that have been introduced to show good long-term retention in infants, but have marshalled evidence that, nevertheless, conscious recall of the learning episodes was not possible. One of the techniques used was the 'deferred imitation' technique, in which the infants were shown some novel way of playing with a toy, and when tested later showed that they could imitate the method demonstrated. We can ask whether learning of this kind could rely solely upon the implicit hippocampus-independent system by testing adult amnesics on an analogous task. If amnesics can learn the task, then the implicit system is all that we need to suppose that infants use; but if amnesics cannot learn the task, we must conclude that the hippocampal system is necessary.

The results of testing amnesics are clear: they show no evidence of learning in the delayed imitation task[54], and we must conclude that infants do use the hippocampal system—the system that is explicit in adults. But given the conclusion that infants do not show conscious recall even for tasks in which (implicit) retention can be demonstrated, the appropriate conclusion here is that the hippocampal system is available to infants, but that it is not, at that stage of development, an explicit system. We may presume that in infants (as in animals) the hippocampal system complements the basic hippocampus-independent associative system (perhaps playing an important role in spatial learning), and note that operation of the hippocampal system is not necessarily accompanied by registration of conscious memories.

At what stage, then, does the hippocampal system become explicit? Since children seem to be capable of conscious recall as soon as they learn to talk, it seems that conscious access to the hippocampus-dependent system coincides with the development of language—which, of course, coincides with the development of the self-concept. Development of the self allows the child to obtain controlled access to the hippocampal (and now explicit) store, so that he or she may now deliberately recall, mull over, and 'daydream' about past episodes. Without that ability, 'memory' is a product of associative processes that give rise to no consciously accessible representations of events.

## Consciousness unproved

The general argument of this chapter has been that there is no conclusive proof, from cognitive or perceptual capacities, of consciousness in non-verbal organisms—be they animals or infants. The discussion of infantile amnesia concluded that self-consciousness develops alongside language, and suggested that there is a close causal relationship between language and the concept of self. Chapter 7 will consider this issue further by discussing experimental evidence that has been interpreted as demonstrating the existence of a self-concept in animals.

I introduced the question of consciousness in infants by asking at what stage of their development they first experience pain. But the subsequent discussion was entirely confined to cognitive issues such as infant memory, and the development of language and the self. This reflects the problem of getting to grips with any facts that have a real bearing on the question of whether any non-verbal organism has phenomenal experience. The second part of Chapter 7 will return to the problem of feeling-consciousness by considering the physiology of feelings, and Chapter 8 will ask whether there may be a causal link between self-consciousness (about which we can find testable things to say) and feeling-consciousness (which has so far not been tied down experimentally).

## Notes and references

1. Brewer (1974).
2. Boakes (1989).
3. Perruchet (1985). I am grateful to Tony Dickinson for drawing this study to my attention.
4. Rescorla (1968). The claim that animals detect real contingencies is an empirical generalization that makes no claim about *how* contingencies are detected; see Papini and Bitterman (1990) for a discussion of exceptions to the generalization.
5. See Shanks (1993) for a review, with details of this and other experiments on causality judgement.
6. The idea that animals might detect contingency by comparing probabilities calculated over relatively long time periods has, naturally, been a problem for the notion that animals detect real contingency. Some contemporary models of animal learning show how the performance of animals in studies in which contingencies have been varied may be accounted for by theories that rely

upon the pairing of events as the basic trigger for association formation (Mackintosh (1983); see also Papini and Bitterman (1990).)

7. Dickinson, Shanks, and Evenden (1984).

8. See Reber (1993) for details of his experiments on artificial grammars.

9. Reber (1993), p. 5.

10. Berry and Broadbent (1984).

11. See Reber (1993).

12. Ibid., p. 48.

13. Ibid., p. 49.

14. Ibid., p. 104.

15. See, for example, Shanks and St John (1994).

16. Perruchet (1985).

17. For details of HM's memory losses, see Corkin (1984); Scoville and Milner (1957).

18. See, for example, Corkin (1984); Weiskrantz and Warrington (1979).

19. Knowlton, Ramus, and Squire (1992).

20. See Macphail (1993) for a detailed account of hippocampal function in animals.

21. It is not yet certain which anatomical structures are critically involved in the human 'explicit' system—nor even whether the hippocampus itself, rather than the structures intimately associated with it, is involved. But I shall, for the sake of clarity, assume that the hippocampus is indeed crucial, and refer to the entire system as the 'hippocampal system', and to the explicit system of humans as a 'hippocampus-dependent' system.

22. Macphail (1993).

23. Weiskrantz (1986).

24. Stoerig and Cowey (1993).

25. Marcel (1980).

26. Paillard, Michel, and Stelmach (1983), p. 550.

27. Michel and Perronet (1990).

28. Oswald, Taylor, and Treisman (1960).

29. For a description of this experiment, and discussion of the implications of blindsight for consciousness, see: Stoerig and Cowey (1995).

30. I am grateful to Celia Heyes for suggesting this interpretation to me.

31. See Owens (1984) for an account of historical attitudes to pain in infancy.

32. Owens and Todt (1984).

33. Owens (1984).

34. Giannakoulopoulos, Sepulveda, Kourtis, Glover, and Fisk (1994 ).

35. Howe and Courage (1993).

36. DeCasper and Spence (1986).

37. DeCasper and Fifer (1980).

38. DeCasper and Prescott (1984).

39. Fagan (1973).

40. Pascalis and Deschonen (1994).
41. See Rovee-Collier and Shyi (1992) for a review of work using this technique.
42. McDonough and Mandler (1994).
43. Bauer (1996).
44. Myers, Clifton, and Clarkson (1987).
45. Bauer (1996), p. 30.
46. Myers *et al.* (1987).
47. Howe, Courage, and Peterson (1994).
48. Leichtman and Ceci (1993).
49. Howe *et al.* (1994).
50. Hudson (1990).
51. Nelson (1990).
52. Pillemer and White (1989).
53. Howe and Courage (1993).
54. McDonough, Mandler, McKee, and Squire (1995).

# 7

## Self and sensitivity

### Two final searches for evidence of non-verbal consciousness

The evidence discussed in earlier chapters has failed to provide unequivocal proof of consciousness in non-verbal organisms—animals or infant humans. In this chapter I shall consider two further possible sources of evidence: the first concerns experiments seeking proof of the existence of a self-concept in animals; the second, the physiological basis of feelings in humans and animals.

### Theory of mind

I argued in Chapter 6 that neither the learning capacity of animals nor their ability to perceive the world through their senses demonstrates that they are conscious. But there has been much interest over the last decade or so in the proposal, made in 1978 by the University of Pennsylvania psychologists David Premack and Guy Woodruff, that chimpanzees possess a 'theory of mind'. The essence of their notion is that an animal with a theory of mind 'imputes mental states to himself and to others (either to conspecifics or to other species as well)'[1]. Any animal having a theory of mind will necessarily possess a concept of self. One central function of a theory of mind is to enable an animal to predict what another animal will do, and so be able to manipulate the behaviour of other animals. This is, then, one specific version of the general idea that self-consciousness developed in response to social pressures.

As evidence for the existence of a theory of mind, Premack and Woodruff described some experiments in which their chimpanzee, Sarah (who had had extensive previous training in an artificial language programme) was shown a series of short videos of a person struggling with a problem (for example, trying to get out of a locked cage, or trying to make a radio work). After each video, she was asked to choose between two still photographs: one photograph illustrated a 'solution' to the video problem (a key, for example, or a plug and a socket); the other illustrated the solution to another problem. Sarah was remarkably successful at selecting the photograph that illustrated the appropriate solution, and Premack and Woodruff argued that this suggested that Sarah ascribed to the human actor in the video states of mind such as intention or purpose, and knowledge or belief.

Although the idea that chimpanzees might possess a theory of mind has taken firm root, the experiments that were originally used to illustrate the notion are not particularly persuasive. The problem is, as Premack and Woodruff acknowledged, that Sarah's success can be explained in terms of associative processes: had Sarah not seen keys in association with locks, for example, she would not have 'known' that keys were appropriate to locks. It was inevitable in those experiments that the correct solution was the item that one would expect to have been most firmly associated with the central feature of the problem.

Rather than go into further detail on Premack and Woodruff's experiments, I shall discuss here two quite different types of evidence that have been cited in support of the claim that apes have a theory of mind. The first concerns the idea that apes are self-conscious in the sense that they recognize themselves as individuals, and are aware of the difference between themselves and other organisms. The second explores the idea that apes manipulate the behaviour of others by intentionally deceiving them. Both pieces of evidence have been used to bolster the claim that a theory of mind is found only in the great apes—not in other primates (such as monkeys). We shall, therefore, be exploring here the question of whether there is a major qualitative difference between the mental lives of great apes (and humans) and those of all other animals.

## Touching the spot

### Using mirrors

In 1970 Gordon Gallup, a psychologist from the State University of New York at Albany, reported an intriguing experiment in which he explored chimpanzees' reactions to seeing themselves in a mirror[2]. Initially, when the chimpanzees saw their reflections, they responded as though they were seeing another chimpanzee, showing a variety of social responses (vocalizations, threatening gestures, and so on). After a few days, however, this behaviour disappeared, and the chimps appeared to use the mirror for such self-directed actions as grooming parts of their bodies that were normally invisible.

In order to see whether the chimps really did appreciate that it was their own bodies they were looking at, Gallup carried out a simple experiment. He administered a general anaesthetic to each chimp and, while it was under its influence, made a mark with an odourless and non-irritant red dye on a part of the body, like an eyebrow or an ear, that could not be seen directly by the chimp. After waiting a few hours for the chimpanzee to recover, Gallup measured how often, in the absence of the mirror, the chimps touched the marked area in a half-hour period. He then replaced the mirror, and counted touches made in the next half-hour. The basic finding was clear: the chimps touched the marked area more frequently when the mirror was present than when it was absent.

Similar experiments have been carried out using a wide range of species of monkeys, and with gibbons (primates that are apes, but not great apes). None of these experiments has found any evidence for the detection of body marks using mirrors. Orang-utans do, however, perform as chimpanzees, and Gallup has used these findings as evidence that chimpanzees and orang-utans are self-aware, and that no animal outside great apes and humans is similarly so[3].

### Does self-recognition imply self-awareness?

The results that I have cited so far might seem to fall into a neat pattern, with self-awareness emerging only in our closest relatives—the great apes. There is, however, a (large) fly in the ointment—the third great ape, the gorilla. Gorillas are more closely related to us than are orang-utans, but, with one exception (a gorilla called Koko)[4], several studies have reported failures by gorillas to show self-recognition in the mirror-guided mark tests[5]. Perhaps Koko is self-aware—although most gorillas are not (as Povinelli has suggested)[6]; or perhaps all gorillas are self-aware, but for some reason nevertheless fail the mark test (an argument that could, of course, equally well be applied to *any* of the species that fail this test). Perhaps unsurprisingly, not all chimpanzees pass the mark test: chimps younger than four and a half years old tend to fail. That could be taken to show that the self-concept needs some years to develop. But chimps older than 16 years of age also tend to fail the mark test[7]—surely they cannot have lost their concept of self? We just have to accept that whatever picture does emerge will not be as tidy as might have been hoped: gorillas may be self-aware, but fail the test; or maybe (most) gorillas are the exception amongst great apes, and are not self-aware. We still should look at the question—is any species that *passes* the mirror test necessarily self-aware?

One possibility is that a (self-aware) chimpanzee sees the mark on, say, his eyebrow, and, now knowing that the mark is on his body, moves his arm and fingers so as to touch the area. A second possibility differs only in that the chimpanzee might use the mirror to guide his arm towards the mark. But a third possibility is that the (non-self-aware) chimp sees the mark—a novel stimulus—and simply uses the mirror to guide his arm movements so that his finger contacts the novel stimulus. In this case, the chimp's experience with the mirror has taught him that reaching directly towards an object seen in a mirror will not succeed in achieving contact with the object; he has learned how to move his limbs so as to achieve a desired series of images in the mirror.

We know from other experiments that chimpanzees *can* use mirrors to guide their limbs towards things normally unseen—things that are not on their bodies[8]. But we also know that monkeys too can use mirrors to guide their movements[9], which raises the question: why do monkeys fail the mark test? Part of the answer may lie in two facts: first, the primate non-great ape species that fail the mark test show lower rates of spontaneous self-grooming than in chimpanzees[10]; second, pigeons too can use mirrors to guide their pecks toward a stimulus that cannot otherwise be seen. In one experiment[11], pigeons successfully obtained food rewards given for pecking a blue spot that was fixed to their bodies, out of sight under a ruff around their necks, and visible only with the use of a mirror. Now of course the pigeons had been trained to peck the blue spot, wherever it appeared; whereas the chimps require no training to touch the marks on their bodies. (The pigeons had also been given training in the use of mirrors to locate spots that were not on their bodies.) But the result clearly raises the question: what is special about using a mirror to locate something on the body surface as opposed to anywhere else?

The one remaining unique feature of the chimpanzee and orang-utan performance may be that they spontaneously touch marks on their bodies. But we do not know whether they would be just as keen to touch marks on other surfaces and, in particular, on the bodies of other individuals. If a chimpanzee did use a mirror to guide his hand to touch spontaneously a spot on some other chimp's body, we would have to conclude that chimps touch marks on chimps' bodies—whether their own bodies or not. We would have no reason to suppose that the chimp in any sense 'knew' that the mark in the standard test was on his *own* body.

At present, then, we cannot reach firm conclusions about the significance of the mirror-guided mark test. We shall have to look elsewhere for convincing evidence that great apes have mental concepts like the 'self'.

## Deception: the Machiavellian hypothesis

An animal that attributes knowledge and belief to other animals would know that one powerful way of manipulating the behaviour of others would be to manipulate what they believed. There has recently been a surge of interest in one particular version of the manipulation of beliefs— namely, the production of false beliefs as a consequence of intentional deception. Can animals deliberately behave in such a way as to mislead other animals into a state of false belief?

Intentional deception is, of course, a technique that could clearly be used to an animal's advantage, and it has been argued[12] that intelligence may have evolved in social species of primates precisely as a result of pressures of this kind. This account of the evolution of intelligence has been dubbed the 'Machiavellian intelligence hypothesis'[13]. We shall look here at support for that hypothesis drawn from both field and laboratory studies.

### Deceptive anecdotes

Researchers working with animals in their natural habitats have come up with a number of reports of behaviour that have appeared to them to involve deliberate deception. Many of these are described in an influential paper by the St Andrews psychologists, Andrew Whiten and Richard Byrne[14]. I shall take two typical examples here, both involving grooming and baboons.

The first example concerns a male Olive baboon who had killed an antelope, and was approached by a female who enjoyed meat. The female began by grooming the male; when the male lolled back under these attentions, she grabbed the meat and ran off with it. A plausible interpretation might be something like the following: the female knew that if she tried to seize the meat while the male was fully alert, he would strenuously and successfully resist; she therefore groomed him, deliberately deceiving him into believing that this was her intention in approaching him, and waited until, as she expected, the grooming succeeded in relaxing his attention.

My second example concerns a report (by Hans Kummer, an ethologist at the University of Zurich) of a female Hamadryas baboon who spent some 20 minutes gradually shifting herself, while maintaining a seated posture, a distance of some two metres. This brought her behind a rock, where she began to groom a young male baboon. This grooming would not have been tolerated by the male leader of the troop, had he been in a position to see it. From his position on the other side of the rock, he could see the female's head, but neither her hands nor the fact that she was grooming. An interpretation of this report is that the female understood what we might call the visual perspective of the male—she was able to envisage what the male would be able to see (and, more importantly, what he would *not* be able to see).

Although these interpretations are plausible enough, there are, obviously, simpler accounts available. It is possible, for example, that these observations are simply chance occurrences. Grooming is a very common activity among baboons: perhaps the female in the first example simply happened to be grooming the male when he relaxed, allowing her to grab the carcass; and perhaps the female in the second example simply happened to move slowly towards a male whom, naturally enough, she groomed. It is also likely that the females in these examples were displaying at least some results of learning from previous experiences. Female baboons surely learn that grabbing food from alert males does not succeed—indeed, is often punished—and that punishment for grooming weaker males is less likely when there is a major obstruction between them and a dominant male.

Arguments about the proper interpretation of anecdotal evidence can be interminable, as there does not seem to be any rational method for deciding between the seemingly infinite number of potential interpretations available. Although contemporary reports of apparently intentional deception in field studies are considerably more sophisticated than the nineteenth-century observations of Romanes, they are still open to the same objections that—as we saw in Chapter 4—gave rise originally to laboratory experiments on animals. What we need, then, are controlled studies, targeted at elements of the theory of mind, that are so designed that their interpretation is not open to doubt. I shall now turn, therefore, to some ingenious laboratory experiments, carried out by Daniel Povinelli and his colleagues, of Yale University's anthropology department, that asked whether chimpanzees and monkeys are in fact capable—as Hans Kummer's observation might suggest—of taking into account the visual perspective of another individual (a human, in this case).

## Ned Kelly and the chimpanzees

The goal of this first experiment[15] was to see whether chimpanzees could distinguish between a human who knew where a titbit was hidden, and one who could only guess. In each trial of the first stage of the experiment, one of two experimenters ('the knower') hid a food reward in one of four containers, while the other ('the guesser') left the room. (The same person was on some trials, the knower, on others, the guesser.) The chimpanzee could see the knower concealing the food, but could not see which container was chosen. Shortly afterwards the guesser re-entered the room. The knower now pointed at the container in which the food was concealed, and the guesser pointed at one of the other containers. The chimps were allowed to select a container, and two of the four chimpanzee subjects rapidly learned to choose the container pointed at by the knower.

Two interpretations of this result are possible. The first, derived from a theory of mind account, is that the chimpanzees understood that the guesser had not seen the containers being baited, and so could not know where the food was concealed; accordingly, the chimps appreciated that the guesser was deceiving them, and followed the pointing of the knower. The second interpretation, from a simpler associative account, regards the task as a fairly sophisticated discrimination: the food is associated with the container indicated by the person who remained in the room. To distinguish between these alternatives, a second (transfer) stage of training followed.

In the transfer stage, both the knower and the guesser remained in the room throughout, but the guesser had a paper bag over his head when the knower was hiding the food. The idea was, that if the chimpanzees could appreciate the visual perspective of other individuals, they would know that the guesser—although now in the room—could not see the food being hidden, and so could not know which container was baited. So, would the chimps perform just as well in this stage as at the end of the first stage? Would their understanding of the task result in immediate and perfect transfer to this new version? In fact, over 30 trials in this task, the chimps' accuracy was the same as that achieved over the last 50 trials of the first, training stage. This result did, then, support the notion that chimps do exhibit a theory of mind—a conclusion that would strongly argue the existence of self-consciousness in them.

A subsequent experiment used monkeys[16], but found that these subjects did not achieve good performance in the basic training stage. This outcome provides further support for the idea that chimpanzees used a theory of mind in the training stage of their study: monkeys are perfectly capable of discrimination learning, so that if discrimination learning had indeed been all that was involved in training, monkeys too would have performed well. The overall pattern of results can be explained by supposing that chimpanzees, but not monkeys, have a theory of mind.

Some have taken these findings, along with the mirror self-recognition findings, as evidence of a 'mental Rubicon' between the great apes and all other animals[17]. Although I shall go on to reject the notion that the knower–guesser experiments do demonstrate an important difference between chimpanzees and monkeys, it is worth noting here that many of the anecdotal field observations of 'deception' involved primates—like baboons—that are not great apes. If those observations are to be wholly dismissed, the evidence for deception in any species is thin indeed.

I have already argued that the mirror self-recognition data are of questionable significance, and Cecilia Heyes[18], a psychologist at University College London, has argued that there is good reason to doubt the knower–guesser studies also. In my account of the chimpanzee study, I reported that chimpanzees performed just as well in the transfer stage as in the training stage. But Povinelli, in response to Heyes' criticisms, has subsequently re-analysed the transfer data, finding in fact that the chimps' performance over the first two transfer trials was at chance, and barely above chance after five trials[19]. There was not, then, immediate transfer to the 'bagged-guesser' version of the task. This is critical, because since the rewards were still available for correct choices in this stage, the improvement seen over the last 25 transfer trials could be a consequence of learning a relatively new discrimination. The importance of this re-analysis is reflected in the fact that Povinelli himself now regards his experiment as evidence that chimpanzees *cannot* take account of the visual perspectives of other individuals[20]. (And it is worth mentioning here that Hans Kummer, the originator of the report of apparent perspective taking by baboons, also rejects the 'theory of mind' interpretation of his observation[21].)

If chimpanzees did not solve the training stage by relying upon a theory of mind—and by implication simply learned a discrimination—why did monkeys fail to master the training stage? The answer appears to be that, as Heyes has pointed out[22], the monkey study did not use precisely the same procedure as was used in the chimpanzee study. In the chimp study, the knower, after concealing the food, stood still and faced the chimp's cage until the guesser entered the room. In the monkey study, the knower moved across the room and knocked on the door of the room to which the guesser had retired, and both experimenters then walked together back to the apparatus. The monkey task clearly makes for a more difficult discrimination: the animal has to discriminate, not between a knower who stands still throughout and a guesser who walks back in, but between two experimenters, each of whom has recently returned to the apparatus.

In the end, these experiments support neither the idea that chimpanzees have a theory of mind, nor the supposition that there is a mental Rubicon between the great apes and other animals.

## Self-recognition without theory of mind

Both the mirror self-recognition findings and the data on deception from field and laboratory studies have been used to support the idea that chimpanzees are self-conscious. I have argued that neither set of findings allows a confident attribution of consciousness to apes. Before leaving this work, one intriguing finding from comparable work on children is worth mentioning.

If you ask a three-year-old child whether he knows what is inside a box, he will (correctly) say 'yes' if he has seen inside the box, and 'no', if he has not. But if you then ask the child whether some *other* child knows what is in the box, his answer does not take into account whether that other child has seen inside the box or not: either way, the child answers according to whether he himself has seen what is inside it. Above four years old, children answer the questions about the other child's knowledge correctly. They now take into account what the other child has seen in assessing what that child will know—they appreciate that other individuals have a different visual perspective from their own. Experiments of this kind are taken to demonstrate the gradual emergence of a theory of mind in children.

Autistic children perform very poorly on a variety of these and other similar tasks, so poorly that some now believe that the basic deficit in autism is precisely the failure to develop a theory of mind[23]. From our point of view, what is most interesting about autism is that autistic children show a normal development of the use of mirrors for self-inspection. So, children that show no evidence of comprehending the points of view, knowledge, or intentions of others can recognize themselves in mirrors. This in turn lends support to my earlier conclusion—namely, that even if it is eventually shown that apes can use mirrors to detect marks on their bodies, there is a large gap between that achievement and the development of sophisticated mental concepts.

## Self-consciousness: not proven

In this first part of the chapter I have explored and rejected the proposal that some primates possess a 'theory of mind'—a proposal that would imply at least self-consciousness in those animals. This conclusion agrees with the suggestion, made in Chapter 6, that self-consciousness is closely associated with the development of language and is thus absent in animals.

But, of course, to conclude that animals do not possess a concept of self does not necessarily imply that they are wholly unconscious. There is no immediately obvious link between cognitive capacities and the capacity to feel at all—the possession of feeling-consciousness. In the second part of this chapter, I return specifically to the issue of feeling-consciousness and ask whether, given the similarities between our nervous systems, it makes sense to suppose that humans are conscious and animals are not.

## The physiology of pain

A central claim of Chapter 1 was that behavioural similarities between non-human and human reactions to noxious stimulation are not sufficient to prove that non-humans experience feelings as humans do. But it is true that the basic sensory physiology of the pathways mediating detection of noxious stimulation is similar in humans and non-human mammals. Do parallels in physiological organization not provide support for the idea that there must be similarities in experience? I shall argue here that they do not, basing my conclusion on some striking peculiarities of the physiology of pain as compared to the physiology of sensations like vision and hearing.

The traditional view that there are five senses—smell, taste, vision, hearing, and touch—goes back to Aristotle. Helmholtz introduced the term 'modality' to refer to qualitatively different types of sensation, and we now recognize that there are many more than five distinct sensory modalities. The traditional global sensation of touch, for example, encompasses such distinct experiences as heat, cold, touch, and pressure; and there are other senses—the vestibular sense, which gives us our sense of balance; the joint position sense, which tells us the angles between our limbs so that we can sense their position in the absence of any external stimulation. One question that we can sensibly ask, therefore, is: when a sensory nerve is active, what determines the type of sensation that we experience? Why do nerves stimulated by light give rise to sensations of colour, while nerves stimulated by the movements of air molecules give rise to sensations of sounds?

### Specificity theory

Perhaps the most intuitively appealing answer is that given by Helmholtz's mentor, Johannes Müller, who proposed that the experience aroused by stimulation of a given sensory nerve was determined solely by the type of the nerve, and was independent of the type of stimulus that activated the nerve. So, a blow to the eye causes us to 'see stars'—a visual experience, not a tactile experience. Müller's 'law of specific nerve energies' (introduced briefly in Chapter 3) is the classical example of a version of specificity theory: the notion that there is, for each type of sensation, an unbroken series of cells, from the periphery to the cortex, each of which carries information about that sense alone; when, and only when, those cells are active, the appropriate sensation is experienced. Specificity theory has enjoyed general acceptance for four of the five traditional senses, but there has been controversy over its applicability to the sense of touch—here expanded to mean the skin senses in general.

The skin senses are now conventionally taken to include touch, pressure, heat, and cold; sensations like itch and tickle (for which we might not expect to find nerves that were active only when those sensations occurred) and, related to those and of particular interest here, the experience of pain.

Pain is specially associated with the skin senses because, although some smells, tastes, sights, and sounds may indeed be extremely unpleasant, we do not find them painful in the way in which a whole variety of skin-sense experiences may be. Not surprisingly, pain is commonly considered to be a further modality of skin sensation. There is, however, a school of thought which denies that pain is a sensation—beginning with Aristotle, who regarded pain and pleasure as emotions—and I shall explore here the physiology of pain without prejudging the question of whether it is or is not a sensation.

Müller was not certain whether the nature of the sensory experience caused by activity in a given nerve was the result of some property intrinsic to the nerve itself, or of the nature of the brain centre with which the nerve communicated. When the growth of electrophysiology established that all nerves operate according to the same principles, the idea that the cortical destination in some way determines the quality of a sensation gained support, and is now the dominant view. In other words, we now believe that if the optic nerve leading from the eye was somehow functionally attached, not to the visual cortex, but to the auditory region of neocortex, lights would cause us not to see colours, but to hear sounds.

If Müller's law applies to the skin senses (including pain), then we should expect to find separate sets of nerves specialized for touch, pressure, cold, heat, and pain. Not only should those nerves respond selectively to their appropriate type of stimulation, but also suprathreshold stimulation of a given type of nerve—say, a 'pain' nerve—should invariably cause pain, and no pain should be experienced unless a nerve of that type is stimulated.

This version of specificity theory was originally bolstered by some dubious psychophysics and anatomy, and a brief account of that early work may help to explain the notion of specificity theory.

## The 'punctate' theory of skin sensation

Towards the end of the nineteenth century, Max von Frey (1852–1932), Professor of Physiology at Leipzig, conducted research on sensory 'spots' in the skin. This work purported to show that when small probes (such as pins or horsehairs) were used, individual spots on the skin surface were peculiarly sensitive to stimuli of one of the four modalities of the skin senses. The skin was, then, a mosaic of hot spots, cold spots, touch spots, and pain spots. A hot spot, for example, was first, a localized region that was sensitive to a warm probe, but relatively insensitive to other types of probe; and second, a region in which no sensation other than warmth could be experienced.

Anatomists had at this time identified a number of structures in the skin associated with the terminals of sensory nerves. These structures were named after their discoverers and included Ruffini end-organs, Krause end-bulbs, and Meissner corpuscles. Most commonly, however, sensory terminals were simply branchings of the nerve, without any associated structure: these were known as free nerve endings. Von Frey proposed that each of these types of ending was a specialized receptor that served a different modality: free endings served pain; Meissner corpuscles, touch; Krause end-bulbs, cold; and Ruffini end-organs, warmth.

Von Frey's grounds for attributing modalities to structures were weak— for example, because pain spots were the most common, free nerve endings were supposed to be involved in pain. We now know that the entire enterprise was misguided. No anatomical investigation has succeeded in demonstrating a correlation between a given type of spot and any of the supposed specific receptors—and in any case, the area touched by even small punctate stimuli will cover more than 100 sensory nerve endings. There are areas of the skin—the ear lobes, for example—that show only free nerve endings, with no specialized receptors, but nevertheless give rise to all the modalities of skin sensation. Finally, successive determinations of spots on a given area of skin do not produce identical maps—spots appear to disappear, move, or coalesce.

## Properties of peripheral sensory nerves

Followers of von Frey generally supposed that the modality specific receptors were each associated with different sets of nerves, each of which transmitted information for one modality of stimulation via the spinal cord to the brain region exclusively concerned with that modality. The rejection of von Frey's claims for modality specific spots served by modality specific receptors does not rule out the possibility that the different modalities of skin sensation are nevertheless served by separate sets of sensory nerves. To explore that idea, we have to look directly at the properties of the nerves themselves.

Individual nerve fibres differ in their diameters; and the larger the diameter, the more rapidly activity is transmitted along its length. Skin sensory fibres, which run from the skin to the spinal cord, can be roughly categorized as being either large or small fibres. All large fibres are sheathed in myelin, a fatty substance that makes the fibres look white and further increases their transmission speed; some of the small fibres are myelinated, some unmyelinated. When we record from large and small fibres, we find that they show marked differences in the type of stimulation to which they are sensitive. The large fibres are sensitive to light touch or pressure—to mild mechanical stimulation. There is a wide variation in the types of stimuli to which the small fibres are sensitive. Some are sensitive to small decreases in temperature, others, to small increases; some small fibres respond to fairly intense heat stimuli, to heavy pressure, or to noxious chemicals (or to some combination of those stimuli).

The differential sensitivity of these peripheral fibres suggests that although von Frey was incorrect in his attributions of physiological properties to anatomical structures, he was correct in surmising that there are, in the skin, receptors that are specialized for different types of stimuli. We now know that free nerve endings, despite their similarity in gross appearance, do possess specific receptors embedded in their membranes. The notion that specific modalities of sensation are mediated by independent groups of fibres can, therefore, be maintained. So, light touch would be transmitted via the large fibres; cold by those small fibres that are sensitive to decreases in temperature; heat, by those small fibres that are sensitive to temperature increases; pressure, by small fibres; and pain, by the polymodal small fibres that respond to all types of intense stimulation.

### The central somatosensory system

Our primary interest is with conscious sensation, and we have good reason to suppose that conscious sensation requires the involvement of the neocortex (as we saw in Chapter 6, conscious visual experience requires intact visual cortex—although non-conscious access to visual information (blindsight) is possible using subcortical regions). None of the nerve cells whose fibres serve the skin project directly to the neocortex. Information about stimulation sensed on the skin surface is relayed to the cortex exclusively from cells in the thalamus—part of the so-called 'between-brain'. Those thalamic cells are in turn activated by cells whose fibres have ascended from subthalamic parts of the nervous system to terminate in the thalamus. Moreover, at least one other relay (and usually many more) is involved between a peripheral nerve fibre serving the skin and the thalamic cells.

There are at least seven different pathways[24] that may be used by cells carrying somatosensory information from the spinal cord to the thalamus, and no attempt to survey in detail all the types of specificity observed can be made here. In general, however, there are in most of these pathways—and, what is probably most relevant, in the thalamus—the following types of cell: cells that are, like the large peripheral fibres, peculiarly sensitive to light touch; cells that, like some peripheral small fibres, respond primarily, if not exclusively, to noxious stimuli; and thermosensitive cells that are generally sensitive to other types of stimulation also.

These data might be used to support specificity theory: there are major differences in the types of stimuli that best activate different groups of cells. But there are clearly problems also. One obvious one is the large number of polymodal cells—cells that respond to stimuli from different modalities (and, in particular, to both thermal and noxious stimuli). A second problem is that there are relatively few cells that are selectively responsive to noxious stimuli, either in the pathways that lead to the thalamus or in the thalamus itself.

There are further problems for specificity theory. First, the properties of cells in the spinal cord may be strikingly modified by inputs either from peripheral sensory cells or from regions in the brain. For example, spinal sensory cells are much more excitable in spinal animals, in which the brain cannot influence their activity; there is, in other words, a tonic inhibition of their activity by input from the brain. Other modifications include changes in the type of stimulation to which cells are maximally sensitive, and changes in the size of the area of skin surface to which the cell is responsive.

A second major problem is reflected in the fact that I have conspicuously omitted to mention cortical cells specialized for pain. This is of course because, as is fairly well known, such cells do not seem to exist. Cortical stimulation in conscious humans (used in some neurosurgical procedures to help check the location of an electrode) finds scant evidence of sites at which stimulation elicits reports of pain; and there is correspondingly little support for the idea that there are, in non-human mammals, cortical cells that respond selectively to noxious stimuli. It is easy to find sites at which stimulation evokes in humans reports of visual or auditory experiences, or of experiences of pressure; but despite the potential for pain of the entire body surface, no cortical region specialized for pain seems to exist. How can this conclusion be reconciled with the notion that we are conscious only of neocortical activity? I shall approach this difficult question in a somewhat oblique way, beginning with a discussion of an alternative to the specificity theory of pain perception.

## Gate control theory

In 1965, Ronald Melzack, a psychologist at McGill University, and Patrick Wall, a physiologist at University College London, published a seminal paper[25] that challenged the traditional specificity theories of pain perception, and proposed a radical new alternative theory. This theory immediately attracted controversy—in Ronald Melzack's words, it 'generated vigorous (sometimes vicious) debate', and 'the search for specific pain fibres and spinal-cells by our opponents now became almost frantic'[26]. Over the intervening three decades their theory has remained the subject both of widespread praise and condemnation. It accepts that there is a degree of specialization in the somatosensory system, but denies that there are cells whose activity is necessary and sufficient for the experience of pain. Instead, the theory emphasizes the role played by modulation of the peripheral inputs, and suggests that although the large peripheral fibres are selectively sensitive to weak mechanical stimulation, they nevertheless play an important role in pain perception.

There are two essential features of this theory: first, a gate control system; second, a central control system. Figure 7.1 summarizes the theory. Melzack and Wall posit a set of central transmission cells (T cells), located in the spinal cord, whose level of activity will trigger the behavioural systems associated with noxious stimulation. These T cells in turn are activated by input from both the large peripheral fibres (traditionally supposed to be involved only in the sensation of touch) and the small peripheral fibres (traditionally the exclusive carriers of pain sensations). But the activity of the T cells is inhibited by cells in part of the spinal cord known as the *substantia gelatinosa* (SG cells). The SG cells are excited by large peripheral fibres, but inhibited by small peripheral fibres. So, the effectiveness of the SG cells in inhibiting the T cells depends upon the balance between the activity of the large and the small peripheral fibres: the greater the activity of the large fibres relative to that of the small fibres, the more the SG cells will succeed in inhibiting the T cells. The SG cells operate, then, as a gate that modulates the effectiveness of peripheral fibre activity in obtaining T cell activity, and so, in causing pain.

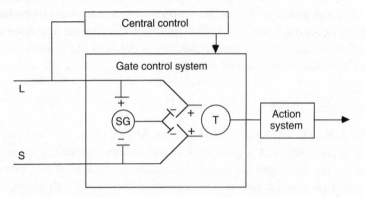

**Fig. 7.1** Schematic diagram of the Melzack and Wall theory of pain mechanisms. The large- (L) and small- (S) diameter fibres project to the *substantia gelatinosa* (SG) and first central transmission (T) cells .The inhibitory effect exerted by SG on the afferent fibre terminals is increased by activity in L fibres and decreased by activity in S fibres. The central control system is represented by a line running from the large-fibre system to the central control mechanisms; these mechanisms in turn project back to the gate control system. The T cells project to the action system—+, excitation; -, inhibition. (From Melzack (1993), Fig. 1.)

Operating in parallel with the gate control system of the spinal cord there is a central control system, which in turn may modulate the effectiveness of T cells in activating the noxious action system. The central control system receives its input from the fast, large peripheral fibres and makes decisions about the nature of the skin stimulus, using those decisions to modulate the effects of the much slower, small peripheral fibres. So, for example, if the central control system 'recognizes' some input and can classify it as *not* life threatening, it could inhibit the ability of the small-fibre component of the stimulus to activate the T cells.

The physiology of the skin senses is remarkably complex. Some of the cells involved are very small, which makes recording from them difficult; and the properties of cells can change according to such critical factors as the level and nature of anaesthetic used. It is fair to say that at present physiological findings on their own are inadequate to decide whether gate control theory is to be preferred to specificity theory. There clearly are mechanisms both in the spinal cord and the brain that can modulate peripheral input, but whether they operate in precisely the ways proposed by the theory cannot yet be determined. Instead of attempting to review the bewildering array of evidence on such issues as the true function of the (small) SG cells, I shall look instead at more general types of evidence. One of the major appeals of gate control theory is that it makes sense of a number of perplexing facts about the psychology and pathology of pain, and I shall concentrate on those whilst also introducing evidence from one relatively new and particularly relevant physiological technique—neuronography.

### The role of large-diameter fibres in pain

One of the most commonplace responses to a painful bruise is to rub the afflicted area. Since this is so common, it is perhaps difficult to see how very odd this is. Why should we want to increase the level of stimulation of a painful region? Specificity theory does not address this issue—but it is a clear prediction of gate control theory: rubbing a skin region will preferentially activate the large-diameter touch fibres, and these will close the gate to input from the small-diameter fibres activated by the bruise. The effectiveness of this type of action has been demonstrated in an experiment in which a vibrator was placed over an electrode on an arm. Vibration decreased the level of pain reported for mild electric shocks delivered through the electrode[27]. This principle, moreover, has found widespread application for people suffering from otherwise intractable pains—peripheral nerves can be stimulated directly by electrodes attached to the skin above them. Weak stimulation of the nerve selectively activates the low-threshold large-diameter fibres, and can be remarkably effective in counteracting pain. (This now common technique is known as transcutaneous electric nerve stimulation[28].)

Although one role of the large-diameter fibres is to close the gate, the theory states that they do also contribute to the firing of the T cells. There could, therefore, be instances when increases in large-diameter cell firing actually increase pain. One circumstance in which this seems to occur is the pathological condition known as causalgia, in which the slightest touch of an afflicted area may cause searing pain. A similarly painful effect of light mechanical stimulation was demonstrated also in the vibration experiment just described: whereas vibration decreased the pain reported for mild electric shocks, it increased the pain experienced with strong shocks.

There is then support for the notion of gate control by the balance between the activity of large- and small-diameter cells: the large-diameter cells do play a role in the perception of pain, and their activity may both decrease and increase the likelihood that pain will be experienced.

*Neuronography*

In 1968 reports appeared of a new technique—neuronography—in which microelectrodes were inserted by hand into human nerves, so allowing both recording from and stimulation of single-nerve fibres[29]. This is a particularly surprising achievement, as the size of the electrode tips is large relative to the size of nerve fibres; indeed it seems likely that the success of the procedure is mainly due to the fact that most of the fibres in the vicinity of the tip are actually blocked (and so, not functioning) as a result of the pressure engendered by the insertion of the electrode.

Since it seems that all of the unmyelinated small fibres in humans are high-threshold polymodal cells—responsive to intense heat, strong pressure, or noxious chemical stimulation—neuronography offers a way of deciding whether, as specificity theory would expect, the activity of these cells is directly reflected in sensations of pain. The effect of stimulating an unmyelinated fibre is, indeed, to cause a sensation of pain. But this is an outcome that would be expected both by specificity theory and by gate control theory (in which small-fibre activity both drives the T cells directly and opens the SG gate). So the question of interest is: does the level of activity recorded in unmyelinated fibres in response to noxious stimulation correlate directly (as specificity theory would expect) with the pain experienced? It seems clear that it does not.

When a volunteer's skin is subjected to strong pressure, or to intense heat, or to noxious chemical stimulation, neuronography finds that the unmyelinated fibres become active. But the threshold for the sensation of pain is not identical to the threshold for obtaining activity in the unmyelinated fibres: most unmyelinated fibres, for example, begin to 'fire' (that is, to generate nervous impulses that are transmitted along the fibre to the spinal cord) at levels of heat well below those that cause pain. Moreover, the time course of pain does not parallel that of unmyelinated fibre activity: when a painfully hot stimulus is applied to the skin, most unmyelinated fibres fire rapidly for about five seconds, and then show a sharp fall in rate; but the intensity of pain experienced continues to increase for some three seconds after the decline in firing of the unmyelinated fibres. Finally, different types of stimulation may vary in their painful effect, while producing similar levels of activity in unmyelinated fibres: pressure stimuli may obtain relatively rapid firing in unmyelinated fibres without causing any pain, while heat stimuli sufficient to obtain the same rates of firing are invariably experienced as painful. This particular finding is, of course, in line with the expectations of gate control theory: pressure stimuli, unlike heat stimuli, will activate the large touch-sensitive fibres and close the SG gate, so counteracting the activity of the unmyelinated fibres (just as rubbing does).

## Central factors in pain perception

Support for the second major feature of Melzack and Wall's theory—the notion of central control—comes from observations that may appear to be so commonplace as to be uninteresting. For example, sportsmen involved in contact sports simply shrug off all manner of bruises that in other circumstances would be extremely painful. Open denial that any pain is experienced is also found in more dramatic cases. One report on wounded soldiers entering combat hospitals in the Second World War found that most of the soldiers, despite severe wounds, either claimed to experience no pain at all, or pain so mild that no treatment for its alleviation was necessary[30]. A more systematic recent report found that more than a third of people visiting a hospital's emergency department experienced no pain, despite having a variety of serious injuries (such as amputated fingers, major skin lacerations, and broken bones). The people were not confused, spoke quite clearly of what had happened, and were not victims of shock. Absence of pain was reported also in people who had suffered relatively minor injuries, and who were certain that no pain occurred even at the moment of the injury (although the time course of their analgesia was limited—all these patients did within 24 hours experience at least some pain associated with their injuries).

A further good example of the weak relationship between the objective intensity of noxious events and the subjective reaction to them is provided by cross-cultural differences in pain thresholds. In one study, electric shocks were delivered to the skin of a group of Nepalese porters and of the Western climbers for whom they were to work[31]. Both groups showed comparable thresholds for detection of the shock: there was, then, no great difference in their general skin sensitivity. But the level of shock required to cause a report of pain in the porters was much higher than that for the climbers.

There is a classic example, too, of the way in which central factors can influence the responses of animals to noxious stimulation. Ivan Pavlov reported an experiment in which a hungry dog was given a series of trials in which a strong electric shock to the skin was followed by food. The dog initially showed the typical reaction to a localized noxious stimulus, but after a number of shock–food pairings, responded in a dramatically different way—it now showed no signs of distress, but instead smacked its lips, salivated, and moved towards the food dish. Similar experiments, using a variety of noxious stimuli, produced comparable results. Pavlov acknowledged that these experiments 'have been apt to upset very sensitive people', but argued that they were in error, since 'subjected to the very closest scrutiny, not even the tiniest and most subtle objective phenomenon usually exhibited by animals under the influence of strong injurious stimuli can be observed in these dogs'[32].

A final example may serve to bring home how odd our skin sensations really are. In this study, the experimenter touched the bare skin of the back of volunteer subjects with a metallic probe that had been heated so that it felt warm to the fingers. The subjects felt the warm stimulus, but when it was removed, reported a persisting sense of warmth that 'welled up into a distinct, pricking sting'[33]. On some trials, the experimenter used the metallic cap of a ball-point pen, kept at room temperature. The subjects frequently reported the same unpleasant stinging sensation. This occurred even when they were shown the cap, and told that they would be touched gently with it: now 'the subjects drew away sharply, and accused the experimenter of using a burning hot stimulus rather than the cool metallic cap that was shown to them before stimulation'[34].

What is interesting about these results is that we do not find them particularly surprising. We would find it odd if people could so easily be led to misreport sensations derived from the other senses, but we all know from our own experience that the skin senses, and pain in particular, are odd and peculiarly subject to such 'higher' influences as suggestion.

## No through road

This discussion of pain has shown that there is no direct through-line of fibres specific for pain from the periphery, via the spinal cord, to the thalamus, and finally to a pain-specific region in the cortex. Whether a given physical stimulus causes the experience of pain is dependent upon what can only vaguely be described as 'higher' nervous activity. I shall return to the significance of these facts for the overriding theme—the source of the conscious feeling of pain—after discussing the equally odd experience of pleasure.

## The physiology of pleasure

It is easier to discuss the physiology of pleasure than the physiology of pain, because so little is known about the former. Much of the complexity of the literature on pain derives from trying to establish the properties of the peripheral fibres that carry information about noxious stimulation; but no sensory physiologist has ever supposed that there are peripheral nerve fibres whose business it is to inform us that a stimulus is pleasant. No one supposes that there are, in addition to fibres that in some way code the warmth of stimuli, fibres that code the pleasantness of those warm stimuli; nor that there are, in addition to the fibres from the tongue that encode the taste of stimuli, fibres that code the pleasantness of tastes. There seems to be universal agreement that the pleasantness of stimuli is something that is settled by central processes alone. We can, therefore, dispense with any concern with peripheral processes, and consider what is known of central pleasure mechanisms.

## Self-stimulation

In 1954, James Olds and Peter Milner, physiological psychologists at McGill University, reported a bizarre serendipitous finding[35]. They had implanted, into the brains of rats, electrodes through which electrical stimulation could be delivered while the rats were moving around, relatively freely, in their cages. In one experiment, the rats could press a lever that resulted in brief stimulation of their own brains. To the experimenters' considerable surprise, the rats responded enthusiastically, and in many cases pressed the lever repeatedly for hours on end, day after day. Other experiments showed that brain-stimulation reward competed effectively with natural rewards, giving rise to the supposition that the cells stimulated might be involved in mediating the effects of rewarding natural stimulation. If there is an animal analogue of pleasure, these cells seem likely candidates to be involved.

Further work on this phenomenon—widely known as self-stimulation—has established its basic properties[36]. First, the areas of the brain in which stimulation acts effectively as a reward are widespread, and destruction of any one of those areas typically has little effect on self-stimulation of other areas. There is, then, no evidence of a localized 'pleasure centre'. Second, stimulation of the neocortex is generally ineffective as a reward, and this is particularly true of cortical areas involved in sensory processing. Third, the effective subcortical areas tend to show involvement in a general way with motivation, rather than with sensory processing. Stimulation of the parts of the thalamus that act as relay stations for sensory inputs en route to the neocortex, is not an effective reward; but stimulation of the lateral hypothalamic area (another part of the between-brain), which may result in such motivated behaviours as eating and drinking in satiated animals, is generally highly rewarding.

What limited work there has been on brain stimulation in humans confirms that cortical stimulation is typically neither rewarding nor (as we have seen) punishing. There is some evidence that certain subcortical stimulation is pleasurable—although most of the reports have involved psychologically disturbed individuals, whose testimony may not be reliable. Some indirect evidence of the importance of these systems to humans comes from pharmacological work. Animal research has found that brain systems of reward seem to rely heavily upon a specific neurotransmitter (a chemical involved in the transmission of activity from one nerve cell to another)—dopamine[37]. In humans, there is strong evidence that brain systems known to be critically involved in drug addiction—which is supposed to reflect a maladaptive hyperactivity of systems of reward—employ dopamine as their transmitter[38].

## The physiology of feeling

One rationale for this discussion of pleasure and pain was to look at the question of whether parallels in physiological organization between animals and humans should force the conclusion that animals experience pleasure and pain as we do. The physiological substrates involved in the perception of what may neutrally be called noxious and rewarding stimuli are clearly closely similar in other mammals at all subcortical levels. But, of course, we can say nothing about what happens in either humans or animals at the cortical level, because we have not found regions or cells that appear to be specifically involved in processing rewarding or aversive stimuli. We can begin to consider the significance of this fact in the context of another question raised earlier—namely, whether pain and pleasure are sensations.

### Are pain and pleasure sensations?

#### Reasons for action

There are at least three striking differences between pain and pleasure on the one hand, and the conventional sensations on the other. The first is, that characterizing an event as painful or pleasant gives an adequate reason for avoiding or seeking out that event. To say that we like something because it is, say, red, or dislike it because it is loud, is an explanation that can be adequate only if supplemented by some (perhaps unsaid) statement such as 'and I find red things pleasant' or 'and I find loud noise unpleasant'. Unlike descriptions based on conventional sensations, descriptions in terms of pleasantness or painfulness are not neutral accounts of what there is in the world.

## Ties with consciousness

The second difference is that pain and pleasure are much more closely tied to consciousness than conventional sensations. We can and do speak quite readily of the unconscious processing of visual sensations. The work on priming discussed in Chapter 6 showed that we can even read words without having been conscious of seeing them. But it makes no sense to suppose that there might be unconscious processing of either pain or pleasure.

We normally talk about seeing in such a way that it implies that anyone who sees something knows (is conscious of) what he is seeing. To say, for example, that someone saw a rabbit normally implies both that there was a rabbit in his view, and that he thought that it was a rabbit. If in fact there was only a hare present, or if there was a rabbit present but the observer reported seeing a hare, we would in each case qualify what was seen: we would say, for example, that he saw a hare but thought it was a rabbit, or that he thought he saw a rabbit (or a hare), and so on.

But the link between seeing and consciousness is not so strong that we cannot make good sense of the idea of unconscious seeing. The subjects in the priming experiments described in Chapter 6 did not know that they had seen any words (or, indeed, anything at all), but when it is shown that they had actually read the words, we are quite happy to agree that they must have seen them. By way of contrast, it makes no sense to suppose that there might be an experimental demonstration of the occurrence of pain or pleasure without the subject being aware of the experience. This is not to say that appropriate responses to noxious stimuli could not occur unconsciously—they can, of course (like the reflexes of spinal animals)—but those responses cannot have involved pain unless there was consciousness of pain. In summary, the notion of unconscious seeing is odd but acceptable; but we cannot make any sense of the notion of the unconscious feeling of pain or pleasure. So, an animal could sensibly be thought of as doing what we do when we see, but nevertheless not be conscious of doing so; but an animal could not do what we do when we experience pain or pleasure without being conscious.

## Cortical representation

The third difference between pain and pleasure and conventional sensations is that the former have no localized cortical representation: cells that respond selectively to painful and pleasant stimuli cannot be found in the neocortex. But consciousness is generally supposed (and with good reason) to be a state that is dependent upon and mediated by cortical activity. People without neocortical activity, for whatever reason, show no evidence of consciousness however lively their reflexes to stimuli might be. If we assume, as I do, that pain and pleasure are mediated by the neocortex, the implication of the absence of localized activity is that they are mediated by widespread activity—perhaps by global cortical action.

There are, then, important differences between pleasure and pain and the conventional sensations. We can either regard them as sensations with unusual characteristics, or as something other than sensations—feelings, perhaps. Nothing can be gained by attempting to legislate on the issue. What we should do is to ask what sense can be made of the differences that we have seen, and we can begin by asking why cortical representation differs.

## Role of the neocortex

The great majority of mammalian neocortex consists of regions that process information from a single sense—from vision, audition, the skin senses[39]. The function of these areas is to establish from those inputs the current state of both the external world and the organism's own body. It is clearly very much in the organism's interest to establish an accurate objective picture. But pleasure and pain serve quite a different purpose, and the same external input can yield quite different responses. We saw in Chapter 1 an example of the pleasantness of a taste being dramatically altered by manipulation of the hunger of the person tasting, and we have seen in this chapter a number of examples of the unreliable connection between noxious stimulation and painful experience.

So, an organism processes sensory information in order to construct an objective picture of its world. The next step is to interpret that picture, and to make decisions about appropriate action. Successful interpretation will require that the organism brings to bear its general knowledge about the world on the picture presented by its senses: so, Pavlov's dogs will decide the response most appropriate to shocks in the light of the knowledge that the shocks signal the imminent arrival of food; rugby players will respond to bruises in the light of the knowledge that they are to be expected, and that attention to them is less important than continuing to play the game effectively. This process of interpretation, in which all sources of knowledge are involved, would naturally be expected to involve global cortical activity.

The conclusion of this discussion is in effect an elaboration of the distinction drawn in Chapter 1 between the informative and the affective aspects of sensations. Processing of sensory information at peripheral, spinal, and subcortical levels is designed to enable the neocortex to achieve a reliable account of the objective state of the world. That objective account is then subjected to interpretation and judgement, leading to decisions about appropriate action. In humans, the experiences of pleasure and pain are the outcomes of that process of interpretation—a process that is in essence cognitive and informed by all potentially relevant available knowledge.

## Cognition and feelings

I have, throughout this discussion, referred primarily to the pleasure and pain to be derived from sensory experiences. But we use pleasant and painful to refer also to events that are not in any such simple sense merely sensations: we take pleasure in games, find disappointments painful, and so on. This account of the cognitive source of pleasure and pain readily accommodates the very general use of the terms. Mental life involves a constant process of interpretation, of the setting of desirable goals, of deciding what is undesirable.

It is important for animals and humans alike to achieve an accurate picture of their world, and there are strong parallels in the physiology of the sensory systems employed throughout mammals. But we know that there are major differences between the cognitive activity of animals and humans—differences, based on the human capacity for language, that clearly imply major distinctions in cortical activity and organization. Since the experiences of pleasure and pain are the outcomes of high-level cognitive activity, the similarities in the subcortical organization of sensory inputs do not force the conclusion that there must be similarities also in subjective experience. The argument of Chapter 6 was that, whereas humans are conscious of most of their cognitive activity, animals may not be conscious of any of theirs. Similarly, the conclusions reached here support the notion that animals *may* not experience pleasure and pain as humans do: pleasure and pain depend upon cognitive processes, and cognitive processes in humans are different from those in animals.

## A basis for speculation

This chapter has considered two types of data that might have led us to believe that we must attribute some form of consciousness to animals. The conclusions of the discussions have, however, reinforced the agnostic stand taken in previous chapters over the existence or otherwise of both self- and feeling-consciousness in animals—an agnosticism that was extended in Chapter 6 to include human infants. We have not, then, been able to find any definitive proof of consciousness in non-verbal organisms.

As this chapter is the last of those whose central purpose is to introduce experimental facts that seem to have a bearing on consciousness, we must of necessity return in Chapter 8 to philosophy and see where speculation might take us. Given the correlation between organisms that talk and organisms that we *know* are conscious, we should in the course of that speculation ponder whether there may not be a causal link between language and consciousness. One particular route that offers itself is that there may be, as suggested in Chapter 6, a direct link between language and self-consciousness; Chapter 8 will explore the possibility that there may, in turn, be a causal link between self-consciousness and feeling-consciousness.

## Notes and references

1. Premack and Woodruff (1978), p. 515.
2. Gallup (1970).
3. Gallup (1982).
4. Patterson and Cohn (1994).
5. Suarez and Gallup (1981); Ledbetter and Basen (1982); Povinelli (1994a).
6. Povinelli (1994a).
7. Povinelli, Rulf, Landau, and Bierschwale (1993).
8. Menzel, Savage-Rumbaugh, and Lawson (1985).
9. Anderson (1986).
10. Heyes (1994).
11. Epstein, Lanza, and Skinner (1981).
12. Humphrey (1976).
13. Byrne and Whiten (1988).
14. Whiten and Byrne (1988).
15. Povinelli, Nelson, and Boysen (1990).
16. Povinelli, Parks, and Novak (1991).
17. Byrne (1995).
18. Heyes (1993).
19. Povinelli (1994b).
20. Povinelli and Preuss (1995).
21. Kummer, Anzenberer, and Hemelrijk (1996).
22. Heyes (1993).

23. See Povinelli (1993) for a discussion of this and other dissociations between self-recognition and possession of a theory of mind in children.

24. For a readable introduction to the physiology of the skin senses, and for details on many topics associated with pain, see Melzack and Wall (1996).

25. Melzack and Wall (1965).

26. Melzack (1993), p. 619.

27. Melzack, Wall, and Weisz (1963).

28. For further details on this technique, see Melzack and Wall (1996).

29. For a discussion of microneuronography, giving details and references for the criticisms made here, see Wall and McMahon (1985).

30. For details of these and other cases in which unexpectedly little pain was experienced, see Melzack and Wall (1996).

31. Clark and Clark (1980).

32. Pavlov (1927), p. 30.

33. Melzack and Eisenberg (1968), p. 446.

34. Ibid.

35. Olds and Milner (1954).

36. See Milner (1991) for a review.

37. Wise and Rompre (1989).

38. Dichiara (1995).

39. Macphail (1993).

# 8

## Minds and machines

### Contemporary philosophy of mind

The main purpose of this final chapter is to draw together the strands of research discussed in earlier chapters in a sketch of the way in which consciousness might have evolved. But first I shall bring the account of the evolution of theories about the mind up to date, by giving a brief introduction to contemporary philosophical approaches to consciousness[1]. Discussing those approaches will serve also to provide a background against which to think about the proposals that I will advance.

### Decline of dualism

Our earlier exploration of philosophers' approaches to the problem of consciousness ended with Immanuel Kant and the transition to experimental psychology. At that time both philosophy and psychology were dominated by the dualist approach—the notion that mind and body were qualitatively different substances. Although there were materialists, there was no developed theory of how matter might have given rise to consciousness. The position now is entirely reversed: the great majority of both philosophers and psychologists reject the dual substance view—Cartesian dualism—and suppose that physical events are entirely responsible for mental events. Some of the principal reasons for this fundamental shift in opinion are to be found in advances made in three fields of research: cognitive psychology, computer simulation, and neuropsychology.

### New scientific approaches to the mind

We saw in Chapter 4 that cognitive psychology developed in opposition to behaviourism, and provided an intuitively more attractive approach to thought, language, and memory in humans. One of the central features of cognitive psychology is the treatment of cognition as being concerned with the processing of information—the 'black box' that accompanies each cognitive activity transforming input information in a systematic way.

The cognitive approach to human thought coincided with the development of computers, machines that are solely concerned with the systematic processing of information. The obvious parallels between cognitive models and computer function led naturally to the rapid development of computer programs designed to model specific cognitive processes—the enterprise of artificial intelligence. A major branch of contemporary artificial intelligence devises programs specifically to model the interaction of large numbers of units whose individual properties are based on the known properties of nerve cells. The success of these 'neural networks' in simulating a variety of human cognitive processes supports the now widespread view that human thought can perfectly plausibly be regarded as the product of nerve cells, whose actions conform to the laws of physics and are therefore causally determined.

Modern neuropsychology—principally concerned with interpreting the consequences of brain damage in humans—has had similar impact. Detailed analyses of damage-induced cognitive deficits have had three consequences. First, they have given broad support for the cognitive approach—the remarkable specificity of some deficits corroborates the idea that 'thinking' is not an indivisible unitary process, but best conceived as the interaction of a large number of relatively independent processes, each concerned with a specific type of information. Second, they have actually contributed to cognitive theory, since a new analysis of a cognitive deficit frequently involves identification of a process that has not previously been specified. And the third consequence is that they have provided more evidence for the close association (now universally accepted) of brain activity and mental activity: damage to specific cortical regions leads in a predictable way to specific disturbances of cognitive activity.

These modern disciplines have succeeded in making plausible materialist accounts of intellectual function, and so have provided some difficulties for traditional dualism; but they do not, of course, definitively rule out dualism, and I shall begin this contemporary review with a brief account of its current status.

## Current status of dualism

Although dualism has lost much of its hold on academic psychologists and philosophers, it is still probably the most widely held view amongst laymen—partly because it constitutes a key element of most religions.

The basic philosophical support for dualism comes from the difficulty that many see in conceiving *any* explanation of mental events in physical terms—recall (from Chapter 2) Leibniz' metaphor of the mill. The claim is that mental events are irreducible to physical events: that, for example, our experience of pain is simply *not* the same as the activity of a set of nerve cells; no amount of detail on which cells are firing or at what rate could conceivably explain, or be taken to be the same as, pain. We shall encounter this notion of the irreducibility of mental phenomena in other theories of the mind. For dualists, the inference to be drawn is that different substances are involved in mental and physical events.

Other support for dualism—which has ancient origins—derives from mathematics. Many mathematicians believe that the truths of mathematics exist, independent of our knowledge of them, in a Platonic world, and that when they perceive the truth of some previously undiscovered proposition, their minds have accessed that world. Precisely this view has been argued recently[2] by the Oxford mathematician Sir Roger Penrose. And some—but not Penrose (whose account of mathematical intuition will be discussed in a later section)—argue that since minds can reach that non-physical world they cannot be mere physical entities.

Further final support comes from the widespread theological notion that we have immortal souls: if our souls are immortal, they cannot be made of perishable material substances.

The dominant current version of dualism supposes interaction between the substances. The alternative version—psychophysical parallelism—has never been able to provide any more plausible an account of the coincidence of the chain of events in the brain and mind worlds than that offered by Leibniz (the miracle of pre-established harmony—an account that is universally rejected). There are three principal difficulties with interactive dualism. First, where does the 'mind substance' come from? Second, how does it interact with matter? Third, why is there such a close correspondence between brain activity and mental activity?

Little progress has been made by dualists since Descartes in proposing plausible responses to the first two questions. The most popular account of the source of the 'mind substance' remains that it is created by a supernatural being who associates it with a human body at some early stage of development. This proposal bypasses the question of the *evolution* of mental activity. A supernatural being has singled out humans as a species to be quite different from our non-human ancestors. There seems no compelling theological reason (at least, not from western theology) for supposing that non-human animals have immortal souls, and the natural conclusion is simply that animals are, as Descartes supposed, automata without feelings.

Descartes' idea that the substances interact at the pineal gland has been abandoned and replaced, by some[3], by a site somewhere in the left cerebral hemisphere—in the regions that are specialized for speech. But that does not help us with the critical problem of how any interaction could possibly take place—a problem that is enhanced by the growing evidence for strong correlation between brain activity and mental activity.

Zeno Vendler[4], of the University of California at San Diego, has attempted to solve the problem of interaction by suggesting that voluntary decisions do not disrupt the chain of causality in the world (involving, in particular, the activities of neurons), but determine instead which of many possible chains of causality is actually realized. Alternative potential chains of causality extend backwards (and forwards) to infinity, so that an obvious problem with this suggestion is that it seems that decisions appear to act backwards in time. Vendler has argued that this problem may be resolved since the self is 'outside time'; but this is neither readily comprehensible nor plausible and so, has not been generally persuasive. The very fact that such a complex and seemingly implausible proposal has been advanced may, however, serve to emphasize the persistent difficulty of conceiving a way in which the two qualitatively different substances might interact. This difficulty remains the central, obstinate objection to dualism.

## Materialism

It might seem that rejection of dualism should bring about a general consensus about the relationship between brain and mind: if we are now (mostly) materialists—or to adopt a term now more widely used, 'physicalists'—there remains, surely, only the technical issue of showing how the matter of the brain gives rise to our mental lives. But in fact there are a bewildering number of rival accounts of how the dependence of mental life on physical events is to be accounted for. Contemporary philosophy of mind has generated a plethora of '-isms', and finding one's way around the rival 'isms' is not helped by the fact that philosophers cannot agree amongst themselves which 'ism' is embraced by which philosopher. Moreover, there are philosophers who, although rejecting dualism, deny that they are materialists. Their views will, nevertheless, be considered here under the general heading of 'materialism'.

## Logical behaviourism

We may begin with a school of thought that holds that there is, essentially, no real problem to solve—philosophers who maintain that the difficulty that we perceive in trying to reconcile physical events with mental events lies basically in our use (or abuse) of language. A major impetus for this school came originally from behaviourism, and its philosophy has come to be known as 'logical' or 'philosophical' behaviourism. One of its earliest and clearest exponents was the Oxford philosopher Gilbert Ryle (1900–82), whose 1949 book *The concept of mind*[5] had a huge impact (partly because of the entertaining way in which it was written).

Ryle attacked the dominant dualist approach to the mind by parodying what he called the 'official doctrine' that there was a 'ghost in the machine'—a non-physical entity that accompanied the actions of a person. (Actions have, according to this doctrine, two components: when, for example, a person says something, the body of the person does the saying while the ghost in the body does the thinking that lies behind the saying.) Ryle rejected not only this view, but also the unsophisticated behaviourist view that thinking and saying are *identical*. His proposal was that errors come about because we misunderstand the correct logical behaviour of mental concepts. Any attempt either to identify some mental event with a physical event (as a behaviourist would do) or to deny their identity (as a dualist would) is in error because the concepts involved belong to different categories. It is like being asked to say whether a square root is or is not green—a category mistake. There are, rather, two ways of talking about human actions: 'saying' belongs to one set of concepts, 'thinking' to another. Neither set is more appropriate or valid than the other, and so neither dualism nor materialism is 'correct'—but neither set should be used in conjunction with the other.

Ryle did not simply rule out as inadmissible any further discussion of mental terms. He attempted to provide a correct analysis of their logical behaviour, and it was this analysis that led to his being regarded as a behaviourist at heart. He argued that words normally regarded as referring to mental states should be regarded instead as 'dispositional terms'. To be angry, for example, means to have a disposition to respond to other people (animals and inert objects) in a particular (possibly violent) way. Similarly, the word 'brittle', when applied to glass, simply means that glass has a predisposition to shatter readily. And, Ryle argued, to have a dispositional property was *not* to be in a particular state. Mental states, in other words, do not exist.

Ryle attempted to distance himself from the behaviourism of psychologists, and from unsophisticated mechanistic doctrines like those of Hobbes (he actually ended *The concept of mind* by expressing more sympathy for Descartes than for Hobbes). According to Ryle, for example, intelligent actions differ in a profound way from unintelligent actions, even if the same *movements* are involved. Intelligent actions involve a person's intellectual competence which is, in turn, correctly seen as a propensity or disposition to act intelligently—a competence that is improved by experience.

Ryle's account of the mind has much in common with the Aristotelian view: the mind, for both, is in effect the sum of the capacities or functions of a person. However, unjust as it may be, Ryle is now largely seen as the philosophical representative of a failed materialist theory. Appealing as it would be to suppose that the mind–body problem can be disposed of as a 'pseudo-problem', the fact is that logical behaviourism has largely failed to convince the philosophical world. Being angry, to most of us, is *not* simply being likely to behave in such and such a way: it *is* an ongoing and internal experience that we find ourselves compelled to regard as a state of mind. A similar resistance is felt to the logical behaviourist claim that words associated with sensory experience—'blue' or 'pain', for example—do *not* refer to necessarily private, internal experiences. It is one thing to point to the logical absurdity of supposing that there is a 'mind's eye' inside my head, looking at images produced by my sensory system, but another to dismiss altogether the idea that there are private experiences.

Logical behaviourism fails to convince for essentially the same reason that the earlier, cruder psychological behaviourism failed: there *is* something private but real about conscious experience; something that calls for an explanation that must reconcile its existence with our current incomprehension of how it could arise from non-conscious material. It is, moreover, particularly unhelpful over the question of non-human consciousness, yielding only the suggestion that if an animal behaves as though it is in pain, then it *is* in pain (at least in so far as any human experiences pain). Most philosophers do not agree with Descartes' claim that animals are not conscious, but most do accept that there is a difficult issue to resolve here—one that cannot simply be dismissed by the unsophisticated argument that pain behaviour is inconceivable without pain[6].

## Anti-reductionists

The remaining contemporary materialists can be divided into two main groups—those who believe that conscious life can be explained entirely in terms of physical events, and those who, although accepting that nothing exists but 'physical particles in fields of force', nevertheless deny that mental events can in any sense be 'reduced to' physical events.

Anti-reductionism is a distinctly pessimistic approach to the mind–body problem, since it claims that the existence of consciousness can never be explained—at least not in the way that most of us are seeking. One particularly pessimistic view[7] is that although mental events are somehow dependent on physical events, the nature of that dependence will never become clear to us since our brains are simply too inadequate to understand it (just as rat brains will never grasp differential calculus).

A perhaps less pessimistic anti-reductionist view[8] is that states of consciousness are biological phenomena on a par with other biological phenomena, and are, similarly, physical features of the world. We simply observe that certain biological organisms (humans and some, if not all, animals) are conscious. This is an observation that does not call for further explanation, any more than any of the other fundamental features of the physical world need to be 'explained'. So, brain activity does *cause* mental activity, but there is no *necessary* link between nervous activity and consciousness—it simply is, the way the (physical) world is.

Although this 'naturalistic' view may have a certain common-sense appeal (and is in essence the view adopted by Darwin and Huxley), it is hardly likely to stop us looking for a more satisfying explanation. If nervous activity causes mental phenomena, we would want to know which types of nervous activity cause which types of conscious state. How do neurons have to be organized for consciousness to come about? It seems hard to believe either that questions of that kind cannot in principle be answered, or that answers to those questions would not transform our understanding of consciousness. The naturalistic view does not seem so much to provide a solution to the mind–body problem as to recommend a course of action—neurophysiological research—as the proper (and *only*) way to approach the problem.

## Neurophilosophy

Given the widespread rejection of dualism, it is to be expected that the dominant current approaches to the nature of mind attempt to explain mental life in terms of its physical underpinning. And it is not, of course, surprising that one such attempt seeks to reduce mental life to neurophysiological events.

One major source of evidence to support the plausibility of neural reductionism has been the neural network enterprise within artificial intelligence. But although the relative success of work in that field has shown that it is clearly *possible* for complex cognitive activities to be implemented in our known neural hardware, the neurophilosophical approach has found it much harder to produce specific examples of the neural bases of conscious (as opposed to non-conscious) activity. Given that both learning and perception may proceed unconsciously, we could in principle learn much about the neural basis of those activities without necessarily impinging on the issue of central interest—the neural basis of consciousness.

One current proposal has taken the bull by the horns and looked specifically for neurons whose activity constitutes conscious awareness. Francis Crick (awarded a Nobel prize for his work at Cambridge University on the structure of DNA, and now collaborating in California with the neuroscientist Christof Koch) has focused attention on conscious visual awareness. The suggestion is that we should look for those nerve cells within the visual system whose activity gives rise directly to conscious visual experience[9]. Crick and Koch assume that not all neocortical cells active at any one time contribute to immediate awareness, and that it should be possible to locate the subset of active cells that do so contribute. There is evidence, for example, that activity in the so-called primary visual cortex—the region of neocortex that receives direct input from sub-cortical visual regions, and projects in turn to regions of visual 'association' cortex—does *not* give rise directly to conscious experience[10]. Human observers can be shown very fine gratings of light and dark bars which do systematically affect subsequent psychophysical judgements (despite the fact that the subjects cannot discriminate between the gratings and a uniform grey stimulus). Neurons within the primary visual cortex respond differentially to these fine gratings—which presumably accounts for their psychophysical effects—but since we cannot discriminate consciously between the gratings and a blank field, it seems that active neurons in the primary visual cortex do not contribute directly to visual awareness. This work may rule out cells in the primary visual cortex, but it is much harder to 'rule in' any specific cells. Crick and Koch argue from general principles that the 'neural correlates of consciousness' cells should be expected to project out of the cortical sensory system to areas—such as the frontal lobes or motor centres—that have to do with initiating action based on the perceptions achieved. If we could identify sets of neurons whose activity invariably contributes directly to our conscious awareness, then we could investigate them to find out what properties (if any) they have in common, and so gain insight into the link between neurons and consciousness.

However odd it may seem that blindsight (see Chapter 6) should be a consequence of the destruction of an area (primary visual cortex) whose activity does not—according to Crick and Koch—in any case give rise to visual awareness, the idea has the advantage of a reasonable degree of specificity. But there is currently no *experimental* support for the idea that there will be attributes found that could discriminate between 'neural correlates of consciousness cells' and those other neurons—the great majority no doubt—whose activity does not directly contribute to our conscious experience. And it is probably true to say that most currently active neuroscientists would be more than a little surprised if there *was* any difference between 'neural correlate' and other neurons. Finally, it does not address the major objection of the anti-reductionist camp, namely, that it remains inconceivable that we could ever *identify* the activity of a subset of nerve cells with the phenomenal experience of, say, a patch of blue, or of pain.

How *could* the anti-reductionist's problem be resolved within the neurophilosophical approach? How can we move from the language of conscious experience to that of the world of neurons? One suggestion[11] is that as progress is made in neuroscience and we understand more of the neurophysiology of such activities as thinking and feeling, our ways of talking about mental life will change. Ultimately, we shall not have to translate our current mental terms into neurophysiological terms because our present way of talking about mental events will change—our 'folk psychology' will give way to a more sophisticated and accurate account of our activities. This too is a speculative suggestion, and one for which there is as yet little observational support. Work on the brain has succeeded in persuading us that there is, at the least, a close correlation between brain activity and mental activity—but it has not yet achieved much beyond that. Our languages for mental life and for the physical world remain stubbornly distinct.

The (very reasonable) presumption of the neurophilosophical approach is that, since mental events are neuronal events, the proper way to explore the mind–body problem is to explore the nervous system. But neurophilosophers do not believe that there is necessarily something special about nerve cells that brings about consciousness. No one supposes that all nerve cells are conscious, nor that a single nerve cell, isolated from a nervous system, could be conscious; nor is it believed that *any* large aggregate of interacting neurons would necessarily be conscious (the isolated spinal cord provides a nice counter-example).

If it is the case that consciousness is the product of nervous systems, it is the functional organization of the systems that is critical—consciousness presumably arises from systems that have evolved to behave in certain ways. If we could specify what types of organization give rise to consciousness, we could begin to understand the relationship between brains and minds. But as soon as we entertain the idea that functional organization is the critical factor, we are led to question the idea that *neural* activity is of particular relevance. Unless there is something special about nerve cells, there seems little reason for restricting our attention to those functional systems that are implemented by neurons as opposed to some other type of physical device. We would not rule out the possibility of mental life in some extraterrestrial alien species simply because they did not possess cells like human nerve cells. We would, of course, use their behaviour as a guide to their consciousness—we would, in other words, rely on the functional organization of whatever system they did possess.

## Functionalism

The idea that consciousness is a product of functional organization lies at the heart of what is now the most widely held materialist account of the mind–body problem—so widely held that it has been claimed[12] that functionalism now constitutes a virtual orthodoxy among psychologists and philosophers.

If functional organization is critical, then we are faced with the issue of how best to characterize this in an organism. The functionalist response is that the various internal or mental states should be characterized in terms of their causal relations with: (1) input from the external world (stimuli); (2) output—consisting, for organisms, of muscular or glandular activity (responses); and (3) other internal states. Once a state has been characterized in this way, any system with a process that has identical causal relationships will manifest the same state.

Functionalism does not restrict mental states to organisms—earthbound or alien. It allows the possibility that machines too could exhibit mental states—could, in other words, be conscious. One objection to functionalism is that, taken to extremes, it might imply that *any* device whose internal states can vary so as to produce different responses to the same input (depending, for example, on the sequence of preceding inputs) is a device with mental (conscious) states—it might imply, for example, that pocket electronic calculators are conscious[13]. It goes without saying that most functionalists reject this implication and suppose instead that true mental states will not be shown by machines until computers have been programmed successfully to simulate in considerable detail some higher cognitive process.

Despite the popularity of functionalism, the idea that machines might one day become conscious has met with vigorous opposition, and I shall now outline two of the more intriguing modern-day objections.

## The 'Chinese room' argument

One argument was advanced in 1980[14] by the philosopher John Searle, of the University of California at Berkeley, and specifically related to the idea that a computer might become conscious simply by implementing a program. (As a physicalist he accepts the idea that there *may* one day be a way of building a conscious machine.) Computers are pieces of hardware that run programs (software) according to formal rules; those rules constitute the syntax of the system (and so are comparable to the grammar of natural languages). Searle distinguished between syntax, of which computers are capable, and semantics (the achievement of mental content) or meaning—which is the mark of genuine thinking. Searle argues that although a computer might be programmed to generate a syntactically correct sentence, that sentence could not be meaningful to the computer (but might be meaningful to a human). He extends the argument to claim that even if a computer could be programmed to carry out a sensible conversation it still would not 'understand' its own utterances.

Searle asks us to imagine an English-speaking person being placed in a room, with people from outside the room handing him Chinese symbols (incomprehensible to the English speaker), which he then 'matches' according to a rule book (in English) with other Chinese symbols. The rule book is sufficiently complicated that the symbols handed back (the answers) are indistinguishable from the answers that a person understanding Chinese would give. The analogy is straightforward: the symbols are the arbitrary symbols that are input to computers; the English speaker is the computer; the rule book is the syntax of the system. In 1950 the British mathematical logician Alan Turing (1912–54) suggested[15] that a computer that could answer questions in a way that could not be discriminated from human performance would in fact possess a mind comparable to the human mind. But we see that, although the 'Chinese room' satisfies the Turing test, there is nothing in the room that understands Chinese— nothing comparable to a human mind that understands Chinese.

Before commenting on the 'Chinese room' argument, I shall introduce a second, quite different, objection to the idea that computers might act as minds do.

*Mathematical intuition*

I introduced earlier Sir Roger Penrose's adherence to the Platonic notion that the mind has access to an independent world of mathematical truths. That belief forms part of his assault on the idea that minds might function as computers. But the main force of his objection derives from another, related, argument. Computers are devices that proceed entirely according to formal rules, so that each succeeding state is determined by the previous state; these systematic procedures are known as algorithms. Computers can prove theorems within mathematics when given basic propositions (axioms) and the formal rules for manipulation of the symbols in the system. Some of the mathematical proofs achieved by computers have been original, in the sense that the steps used have differed from those previously used by mathematicians. But, for all their novelty, the method of derivation remains entirely predetermined: the machine employs algorithms. Not only do computers use algorithms, but also it can be shown mathematically that any *computable* proof could in principle be derived by the use of an algorithm. The trouble with the computer model of the mind analogy is that there are true mathematical propositions that are *not* computable.

The Czech-born logician Kurt Gödel (1906–78) shook the foundations of the mathematical world when, at a meeting in Königsberg in 1930, he made public his proof that within *any* consistent formal mathematical system there will be propositions that are well formed according to the rules of the system but whose truth or falsehood cannot be determined from those rules. All mathematical systems are, in that sense, necessarily incomplete: there are within them propositions that are systematically *not* computable. But humans *know* 'intuitively' whether these 'undecidable' propositions are true or false. There are, in other words, certain propositions within mathematics that we humans *know* are true, but which cannot be proved from the formal axioms and principles of the system —— which could not be derived by any algorithmic procedure. The Oxford philosopher John Lucas had used this observation to support the claim that minds could not be physical systems[16]. Penrose expands and develops the argument, but draws a different conclusion. He argues that human minds are not computers—although they *are* physical systems[17].

A major difficulty with Penrose's conclusion is that if the human mind is, as he believes, a physical system, then it would seem that its states *must* succeed each other in a lawful and predictable way, determined by the laws of physics. How can we escape the implication that our minds must in some sense rely on algorithms for the solution of problems? Penrose concedes that neither classical nor quantum physics allows any room for series of events that could not be described computationally. (He dismisses two obvious exceptions—chaotic series in classical physics, and randomness in quantum physics—as being unsuitable for the type of non-computational event required for consciousness.) He looks, therefore, to events at the boundary between the applicability of classical physics (concerned with the behaviour of large numbers of molecules) and of quantum physics (concerned with events at the scale of single atoms). At that boundary, where small aggregates of atoms are involved, he finds events that cannot be described computationally—events involving quantum coherence (and other phenomena that I am spectacularly incompetent to discuss). The question is, then, whether any events on this scale could plausibly be supposed to be critically involved in human thought?

Penrose, in collaboration with the University of Arizona anaesthesiologist Stuart Hameroff[18], has suggested that there are structures in the brain—microtubules inside neurons—that possess functional components (tubulin dimers) at the appropriate scale to escape the computational determinism of both classical and quantum physics. But the functional role of microtubules remains obscure (they are found in all bodily cells, not solely in nerve cells); they may play a part in the transport of neurotransmitters within neurons—but whether quantum coherence phenomena affect that or any other function is unknown, and what the functional consequences would be is in any case wholly unclear.

In assessment of Penrose's position, we need note only that speculation about microtubules may strengthen the plausibility of the suggestion that there are brain events that are systematically non-computable. The core of his argument remains the claim that the human capacity to intuit non-computable truths demonstrates that the mind cannot be a computer.

*Counter-arguments*

There have, inevitably, been rebuttals (and counter-rebuttals) of the arguments of both Searle and Penrose, and I shall outline here what is, for each argument, probably the most widely held objection.

One common response to the 'Chinese room' argument (characterized by Searle himself as the 'systems reply') points to the enormous complexity of the processes envisaged by Searle in the room[19]. In order for an appropriate response to be made to a series of Chinese symbols—the equivalent of, for example, some complex question—there would have to be processes (mediated by the 'rule book') that: parsed the question; that identified the referents of many of the 'words' in the question; that arrived at and selected one of the myriad possible responses; and so on. In effect, it would be the ensemble of those processes—the entire system—that simulated the mental processes of understanding and responding. The *system* would understand the input and generate a semantically appropriate output: individual components of the system—like the English speaker handling the Chinese characters—would not understand the interchange, just as nobody imagines that individual neurons or small assemblies of neurons could independently demonstrate understanding.

A common objection to Penrose's argument from human intuition is that it supposes that the processes involved in the human's intuiting the truth of apparently non-computable statements should be based on a formally consistent system[20]. Human intuition is, however, fallible—even sophisticated mathematicians may 'see' truths that turn out not to be truths. Given that whatever system we use for our intuitions of mathematical truths is fallible, there is no reason to suppose that it is consistent. Since Gödel's theorem applies only to consistent formal systems, the major objection to the computability of intuitions falls away.

Little would be gained by going into further detail here, either of other objections, or of counter-rebuttals. The important point is that these arguments have not been universally accepted; for many, if not most observers, the arguments do not have the force that their proponents would have us believe. Kant showed that it is not possible to define God into existence; similarly, we cannot decide by argument alone whether machines might have minds.

## Virtue of testability

After two and a half thousand years of effort, philosophers have not succeeded in explaining consciousness. Many have, of course, explained it to their own satisfaction; but none has succeeded in obtaining a general consensus of support. We might be justified in concluding that philosophy (argumentation) alone will never succeed in solving the mind–body problem.

One major virtue of the functionalist view is that it does at least offer a route to a universally accepted conclusion. If functionalist objections to Searle and Penrose are valid, then it may be possible to build a computer whose performance will in fact persuade all who encounter it that the computer is conscious. And if that does happen, then the problem will be solved; if we construct a conscious machine, we shall know what magic it is that is required for consciousness.

I have supposed here that if everyone believes that the machine is conscious, then it *will* be conscious; it will, after all, have had to overcome the scepticism of those, like dualists and anti-functionalist materialists, who currently believe that no such machine could exist. The converse of this armchair vision of ultimate success is, of course, that we may come to the point where everyone accepts that it is never going to be possible to construct a conscious machine. And if the impossibility of construction is based not on mere practical considerations but on violation of some universally accepted principle (a law of physics, for example), belief in functionalism will wither away and leave us with one less theory to brood over. Functionalism offers, then, a degree of testability, and the attempt to develop a conscious machine seems to promise the only realistic possibility of final resolution of an age-old problem.

### Congruence with cognitive psychology

Potential testability is not the only virtue of functionalism in the eyes of a psychologist: the program of functionalism is precisely the program of cognitive psychology. It requires that we specify causal relationships among inputs, outputs, and central states (whereas behaviourism supposed that psychology could proceed simply by formalizing relationships between inputs and outputs). In the concluding sections of this book, I shall rely on psychological observations detailed in earlier chapters in making a psychologist's attempt to show *which* functions are critical for the emergence of consciousness. I shall not, unfortunately, be able to produce computer programs that will manifest consciousness, nor indeed do anything more than point to what may be the key issues that must be solved before we can think at all seriously about writing and implementing such programs. But we should not lose sight of the long-term goal—the specification in detail of those cognitive processes that are necessary and sufficient for the emergence of consciousness in systems in which programs implement those processes.

## Consciousness and complexity

I shall finish this discussion of contemporary theories of the mind by returning once more to the question of non-human consciousness.

Although there are wide differences between contemporary approaches, there is one issue over which the rival materialist theorists are in general agreement: it is, that consciousness is manifested not only by humans but also by at least *some* animals, and that there are differences between the consciousness of different groups of animals. Some suppose that not all animals are conscious; others, that there is a continuum of consciousness, and that some animals are more conscious than others (humans being the most conscious of all). And although there is no consensus over which animals show consciousness and which do not, or over which animals are the most, and which the least, conscious, there is agreement about the sort of animals that are most likely to be the most conscious: they are the animals that show the most complex, flexible, and adaptable behaviour. Further than this, it seems, few attempt to go. But there is something unsatisfactory, something seriously incomplete in the claim that consciousness is associated with, or arises from, behavioural complexity (just as there was with the idea that consciousness arises from neuronal complexity).

If functionalism is to provide a satisfying solution to the mind–body problem, it has to specify the nature of the behavioural complexity that is associated with consciousness. That in turn requires a decision about *which* organisms experience consciousness. *Is* consciousness confined to mammals? To mammals and birds? To vertebrates? Or are *all* animals conscious? All living cells even? In the light of that decision, we can think productively about what complexity is shown by those organisms, as opposed to those that are not conscious.

The extreme difficulty of making a rational decision has been highlighted in earlier chapters. I argued in Chapter 1 that feeling-consciousness could not be demonstrated by observing an animal's behaviour (and I argued in Chapter 7 that it could not be demonstrated from physiology either). Chapter 6 discussed experiments on theory of mind in animals, and concluded that they have not yet succeeded in demonstrating a self-concept. Furthermore, Chapter 6 introduced experiments on humans that show that it is perfectly possible to suppose that complex cognitive activities such as learning and perception can proceed in the absence of conscious processing. What these arguments show, however, is that we cannot *prove* that consciousness—either self- or feeling-consciousness—exists in animals (in *any* animal). If it is so difficult to prove even that at least some animals are conscious, it is clearly going to be even more of a challenge to sort the more conscious from the less conscious species.

Failure to prove consciousness in animals is, of course, a very different thing from showing that animals are *not* conscious. We humans are just another animal species—more than 98 per cent of our genes are in common with the chimpanzee; and many animals—mammals in particular—respond to events that excite feelings in us in very much the way that we would respond (excepting only their lack of linguistic commentary). The empathy that we so naturally feel for animals does surely reflect the entirely plausible notion that their inner experience may not be so very different from ours, or, at the very least, that they do have some inner experience. Nevertheless, I believe that we should give serious consideration to the possibility that consciousness, in all its forms, is confined to humans. I would not do so, of course, if there were not problems with the conventional view that some (or all) animals are conscious. What are those problems?

The major problem was outlined in Chapter 1—if animals are conscious, then consciousness must have evolved: non-conscious elements in some way gave rise to consciousness. But unless consciousness serves some function, it is hard to see how it could have evolved. Organisms that were not conscious would be at no disadvantage to those who were. We cannot tell from the behaviour of an organism whether it is conscious or not, and unless we can find a function for consciousness it would seem to be systematically impossible to diagnose conscious from unconscious species.

The problem of finding a function for consciousness has been intensified by our consideration of experimental work. We have seen evidence that neither learning nor perception requires consciousness; and we have not found support for the idea that primates have developed a theory of mind that confers advantages in their social interactions. We have seen that cognitive activity may play a surprisingly large role in the feelings that we experience; but we have not seen any abrupt leap in cognitive capacity in any particular group of animals—the sort of leap that might suggest a transition from non-consciousness to consciousness. The only place in which we have seen an unexpected shift in cognitive capacity has been in the transition from non-humans to humans: humans have the capacity for language, and animals do not. The philosophical and experimental work discussed in this book supports two basic central conclusions: first, we have no proof that any non-human organism is conscious; second, only humans possess language. It is time now to speculate on the significance of those conclusions.

## From language to consciousness

In these final sections of the book I shall explore the possibility that the transition from animals to humans may have involved, not only the evolution of language, but the evolution also of consciousness. It may help to clarify the organization of these sections if I precede them with a summary of the proposal that will be sketched out there. I shall begin by suggesting that a crucial property of the human language-acquisition device is that it allows us to think of one representation as being 'about' another, and that this 'aboutness' relation is not available to animals. I shall then argue that the maturation in an infant of the ability to conceive the 'aboutness' relation is a prerequisite of the development of a 'self'; and, finally, that a self is a prerequisite of any conscious experience.

### About subjects and predicates

In Chapter 5 I introduced the idea that humans possess a species-specific language-acquisition device, which in some way innately encodes a universal grammar. Although this notion has attracted considerable support from both linguists and psychologists, there is little agreement on the details of the universal grammar. I want here, however, to focus on one feature of human language that seems certain to be at the heart of any psycholinguistic theory—namely, that the basic structure of propositions consists of a noun phrase and a verb phrase (of a subject and a predicate). In making statements, we identify some entity to which we are going to refer and say something *about* it. Somewhere in our minds we activate internal representations of the subject and the predicate, and place those in a relationship such that the predicate is understood to be *about* the subject.

### 'Aboutness' and associations

In Chapters 4 and 5 I discussed evidence to the effect that cognition in non-human animals is dominated by association formation, and that animals cannot acquire language. That case was made first, by showing that there are serious difficulties facing any claim that an association-forming organism could successfully learn the rules of grammar, and second, by the failure of studies using chimpanzees to show that they could acquire grammar. My argument here concerns the related issue of whether the subject–predicate relationship could be conceived of as an association.

Contemporary learning theorists do suppose that animals form internal representations, and that it is between those representations that associations are formed. But the relationship between the terms of an association is very different from that between a subject and a predicate. Imagine that an animal forms an association between, for example, (an internal representation of) a red light and (an internal representation of) food. The fact that, after conditioning, presentation of the light leads (via activation of its internal representation) to activation of the representation of the food does not require us to suppose that the activation of the association is equivalent to the animal 'thinking' or 'believing' that, for example, the light *is* food. It is well established that animals can learn associations between two neutral stimuli (a red light followed by a green light, for example)[21], but we would not believe that an animal that had formed an association between a red and a green light (so that presentation of the red light led to the animal's anticipation of a green light) was now entertaining the proposition 'red *is* green'.

I shall assume, then, that the relationship involved between internal representations when we think something *about* some object (or form subject–predicate propositions) is one that is a basic prerequisite for language acquisition. In the light of the evidence that animals cannot acquire language, I shall also assume that it a relationship that animals do not achieve.

### Intentionality and language

The notion that there is a close link between 'aboutness' and language has clear similarities to the approach to mental states taken by the psycholinguist and philosopher Jerry Fodor, of Rutgers State University. Fodor[22] argues that the key characteristic of the mental states involved in cognition (states like belief, knowledge, doubt) is that they are intentional[23]—that is, they have 'content', they are 'about' something. Fodor's goal is to provide an explanation of those states that first, acknowledges that they are properly seen as intentional, and second, shows how they could, at least in principle, be seen as the product of computational processes of the brain.

At the heart of Fodor's position is the notion that a person exhibiting a mental state is in a certain relationship to a 'sentential representation' in a 'language of thought'. A sentential representation is a sentence that embodies a particular proposition about the world; the language of thought is an unambiguous formal language—innate and common to all humans—sometimes referred to as 'mentalese'. The content of mentalese sentential representations depends upon the semantic properties of their mentalese components. Although the precise nature of mentalese cannot be specified, the argument is that operations in mentalese are computational operations, and that, in effect, thinking is properly seen as a causal process involving the computational processes that instantiate the language of thought.

Part of the case that I wish to argue here has, therefore, been made out in detail and developed by Fodor: all those mental states that fall under the general heading of cognition are states that rely upon sentential representations—subject–predicate expressions. But Fodor argues that some kind of mentalese must exist in non-verbal organisms also, basing this argument on the claim that non-verbal organisms can 'obviously' think. And in fact Fodor uses the assumption that animals think as further support for the view that thinking does not proceed in a natural language, like English or French.

The idea that at least some aspects of language are innate is common to both Fodor and (as we saw in Chapter 5) Chomsky. But Fodor argues that all the critical components of language—and not only the grammatical component—must be innate. He claims, for example, that all concepts must be innate. The arguments involved are complex, and will not be explored in detail. What we should note here is that, whereas Chomsky uses the fact that animals cannot acquire language as evidence that our language-acquisition device is specific to humans (an argument with which I concur), Fodor uses the evident intelligence of animals to support the conclusion that they too use 'mentalese', and this is an argument that I reject. Fodor supports his view that animals think by pointing to clear continuities between certain features of animal and human learning. But the evidence discussed in Chapters 5 and 6 acknowledges the continuity between animal and human cognitive processes—both animals and humans engage comparable associative processes—while finding a marked discontinuity in language capacity. And this discontinuity provides just as good a ground for denying mentalese to animals as the supposed continuity of thought provided a ground for attributing it to them. If animals can entertain sentential representations, why can they *not* acquire language?

*Imperative inference in instrumental conditioning?*

There are, however, other grounds for arguing that animals may entertain propositions, and to discuss these we need to return to some of the issues discussed in the concluding sections of Chapter 4. I argued there that classical conditioning procedures gave rise to S–S (stimulus–stimulus) associations, and instrumental procedures, to R–S (response–stimulus) associations, with the clear implication that these associations are sufficient to account for the occurrence of conditioned responding. This is a readily justifiable implication where classical conditioning is concerned: the sound of a bell, for example, comes to elicit the internal representation of food, and that representation directly elicits the observed response. But consider instrumental conditioning. Suppose that an animal has formed an R–S association between a press of a lever and food; this would indeed elicit a representation of food *whenever a press of the lever occurred*—but why *would* a press of the lever occur? There is in the R–S account of instrumental conditioning no event—no internal representation—that should elicit a representation of the response. So why should an animal respond? This is not a problem for the S–R account of instrumental learning, since the response in that account *would* be directly elicited by the stimuli of the situation; replacement of the S–R account by the R–S account means that we have to find an explanation of the initiation of learned responses.

One proposal[24] has been that learned instrumental responding is best explained by an intentional account that involves an 'imperative inference' based on two propositions entertained by an animal. One of these propositions incorporates the belief represented by the R–S association—a proposition like: 'pressing a lever leads to food'. The second proposition is engaged by the 'desire' of the animal for a given outcome (food, for example)—a proposition like: 'perform a response that leads to food'. The inferential process based on these propositions leads to the initiation of a press of the lever.

There is a striking contrast between the simple, almost mechanistic, relationship between associations and performance in classical conditioning and the inferential process supposed to mediate the contribution of associations to instrumental conditioning. If the inferential account is valid, then the idea that animal cognition is best interpreted largely in terms of associations—involving simply excitatory and/or inhibitory links between internal representations—must be rejected. But in fact an associationist account of instrumental conditioning *is* available: it complicates considerably the assertion that instrumental conditioning is mediated by an R–S association, but does allow an interpretation that is as 'mechanistic' as the associationist account of classical conditioning.

In brief, the proposal, described by Anthony Dickinson[25] as a 'mechanistic-cybernetic' account, is that the first event in initiating an instrumental response is the activation of an S–R link between the contextual stimuli and the response. Activation of this link will typically not be sufficient to obtain responding—except under particular conditions (after extended training, for example) when an S–R 'habit' will have been formed. Activation of the representation of the response will then activate the R–S link, and so lead to activation of the representation of the reward. Finally, it is assumed that activation of the representation of a reward will feed back to the response through a process of general facilitation of responding, so that a weakly active response will be potentiated sufficiently to generate overt responding. This feedback varies according to the value assigned to the reward, and this is the mechanism through which devaluation of a reward affects instrumental performance.

There is currently 'no reason to choose between the mechanistic/cybernetic and intentional approaches to instrumental action on empirical grounds'[26], and the view taken here will be that a mechanistic, associative account provides a satisfactory and parsimonious explanation of both classical and instrumental conditioning. The associationist account of instrumental responding is more complex than that of classical conditioning. But to claim that a rat pressing a lever for food demonstrates a form of learning so different from that shown when a dog salivates to a bell signalling food that it requires the postulation of a form of propositional inference is, perhaps, placing too heavy a burden on the humble press of a lever.

*Sentences and mental states*

Fodor's work is a complex and challenging brand of functionalism that points to specific ways in which computational processes could generate intentional states. Its particular importance in this context is that it emphasizes the relationship posited here between language and intentional mental states—and it remains my case that if animals cannot form sentences, they cannot exhibit cognitive mental states. (Whether the inability to form sentences rules out *all* mental states is an issue that will be addressed in later sections.) And although Fodor provides a compelling account of cognitive states, he has much less to say about consciousness—and in particular about feeling-consciousness.

## The self and its properties

When does the capacity to form 'aboutness' relationships emerge in humans, and what are its consequences—apart, of course, from making language possible? Given its intimate association with language, it is plausible to assume that it matures in children as they are about to acquire language—sometime around one year to eighteen months of age. One consequence of a maturing capacity to conceive of one internal representation as being *about* another might be expected to be the growth of a clear distinction between conceptions about oneself and conceptions about the world outside oneself. We saw in Chapter 6 that the development of the concept of self and of language are roughly contemporaneous, and the notion that a maturing capacity for use of the 'aboutness' relationship is necessary for both the self-concept and language makes good sense of their time course.

## From self-concept to self

I cannot, of course, pretend to be able to characterize in detail what it is to have a concept of self. In this account, the development of the concept leads to the construction of a cognitive structure that monitors and controls some, but not all, cognitive processes. Once the cognitive leap necessary for discriminating between self and non-self has been made—a leap that requires the ability to formulate thoughts 'about' representations—the organism has in effect, not only a concept of self, but a 'self'—a novel cognitive structure that stands above and outside the cognitive processes that are available to organisms without a self.

Central among the processes that are subject to inspection and control by the self are aspects of memory. To say that a representation is active is (according to contemporary consensus) to say that it is currently in the short-term memory store (introduced in Chapter 4). The development of a self enables self-conscious monitoring of short-term memory, and also allows the self to influence the representations present in short-term memory. The self can, for example, retrieve into that store material represented elsewhere; and can maintain, via active rehearsal, representations in the store that would otherwise decay.

### Self and memory

We also saw (in Chapter 6) that the development of a concept of self coincided with the development of conscious memory for past events. Infants can learn and retain information over relatively long periods, but appear to have no capacity for conscious recollection of the events of their lives. I suggested that infants and animals rely predominantly upon an implicit learning system, and that human adults, although still capable of using the implicit system, exhibit conscious recollection as a consequence of their reliance on an explicit system (and we saw evidence that a forerunner of the explicit system is available to infants and animals, but no evidence that it is, in them, accessible to consciousness).

My proposals rely upon the conclusion that there is a difference between human and non-human cognition, reflected in our species-specific ability to acquire language. A core feature of this cognitive difference is that we humans can establish a relationship of 'aboutness' between internal representations. Although this human ability is innate, it is not functional in infants, but matures as a necessary prerequisite to language acquisition. The maturation of this capacity leads to the establishment not only of language, but also of a concept of self, and so, to the existence of a self. These developments in turn involve access to the short-term and hippocampal memory systems, so that the self is now aware of its (the hippocampal system's) processes. These interlocking processes constitute human self-consciousness: the hippocampal system is in effect a preadaptation that has, with the evolution of language, determined much of the content of our self-consciousness—the cognitive processes of which we are aware.

## The hard problem

The arguments developed thus far have concerned the ways in which a human-specific capacity for language might have paved the way for the development of self-consciousness. And although the evidence clearly does not adequately validate the arguments—we are a long way from anything that might be regarded as 'proof' of the way in which self-consciousness evolved—I have cited a reasonable amount of positive experimental support. There are data to support the claim that animals cannot acquire language, and that the concept of self develops alongside language in humans; and we saw in Chapter 7 that the evidence to substantiate the notion that (some) animals develop a concept of self was less than compelling. These data can plausibly be interpreted as pointing to a significant link between language and self-consciousness. But I have also suggested that feeling-consciousness is the more interesting and the more important problem. Unfortunately, it is very much more difficult to produce an account of feeling-consciousness that carries the same degree of plausibility. Like many others, I am compelled to agree with the philosopher David Chalmers, of the University of California at Santa Cruz, that feeling-consciousness indeed is 'the hard problem'[27]. In what follows, I attempt to make sense of feeling-consciousness, well aware that for many (perhaps most) readers, it will make so little sense that it may seem more a *reductio ad absurdum* than an explanation.

*Feeling-consciousness: recapitulation*

I argued in Chapter 1 that I could find no plausible function for feeling-consciousness in animals, and so, no plausible account of how it could have evolved. In Chapter 7, I presented evidence that feelings—pain in particular—appear, however 'raw' they may feel, to be the consequence of cognitive operations. I used this conclusion to bolster the idea that humans, but not non-humans, might feel: humans *do* show a qualitative difference in cognition from animals, and it is at least possible that this difference could allow humans but not animals to feel.

In Chapter 6 and this chapter I have developed the notion that a capacity for acquiring language—which is the critical difference between animal and human cognition—might be responsible for the development of the self, and of self-consciousness. My case will be that feeling-consciousness is a consequence of self-consciousness, and I shall endeavour now to show that a plausible link can be found between self-consciousness and feeling-consciousness.

*The self and feeling-consciousness*

I shall introduce two arguments to support a link between the two aspects of consciousness. To avert possible disillusion, I should give advance notice that neither is particularly compelling.

The first argument is that it makes no sense to speak of a feeling in an organism that does not possess a self. Who or what would be having the experience? This is, of course, not a problem for a dualist, who would believe in any case *either* that non-humans do not have feelings *or* that non-humans *do* possess an immaterial substance whose function is precisely to be an aware 'self'. But how could a non-dualist model of the mind be constructed so that feelings could plausibly be located to some structure within it, unless that model included some representation of a self? A weakness of this argument is that it may seem to assume the validity of its own conclusion. If we do in the end accept the conclusion that a concept of self is a necessary prerequisite for feeling, then we would have to consider senseless the idea that something without self could feel. But until we know that self is a prerequisite, the force of the argument is rather that we cannot now make any coherent sense of feelings: perhaps they are, as some suggest, simply caused by brain events in a way that is unfathomable.

The second argument involves an 'armchair' experiment. My proposal is that before the concept of self develops, a person is not aware of the contents of his memory—whether short- or long-term. Now suppose that a drug is found that has no effect on a man's immediate response to noxious stimuli—he still withdraws limbs, even cries out—but has the effect that the person has no access to his explicit memory stores during the episode. Let us imagine that there is some antidote, so that a drugged person can be instantly released from that state. If we now ask him anything about the episode he will, of course, recall nothing. Physiologists and pharmacologists confirm that they can detect no effect of the drug on any of the pathways associated with processing the noxious stimulation. Suppose further that there were considerable benefits of the drug over conventional anaesthetic drugs (zero toxicity, no side-effects). Would *you* use the drug as an anaesthetic?

Two rival interpretations of the effects of the drug are opposed here. One is, that the drugged human still feels the pain, but does not remember it: this might lead you to refuse the drug in favour of a conventional anaesthetic. The second is, that a necessary property of pain is that it is explicitly recallable at some delay—however small—after its occurrence: no memory, no feeling. So, accept the drug.

Consider now the position of someone who has taken the drug, been exposed to noxious stimulation, and is no longer under the drug's influence. We ask him if he recalls the episode; he denies any recollection. We then suggest to him that it was at the time very painful; he can only say that if it was, he has no memory of it. We ask him if he would go through the experience again; clearly, if he had not been told of this alternative account, he would not hesitate to do so (as it would be no different from our normal willingness to undergo treatment with a general anaesthetic to eliminate both memory and pain). One way of characterizing the puzzle facing this person is that it would seem to him that *someone* might have experienced pain, but that it was not him. This in turn brings us back to the earlier argument—to the notion that feelings have to be referred to an identifiable subject; to a continuing centre of explicit experience; to, in other words, a self. A difficulty with this argument is that there is no consensus over the rational answer to whether or not to use the drug. It seems likely that at least some philosophers would refuse the drug[28].

There is a theme common to both these arguments, and it is perhaps most easily captured in the question: *where* does pain occur? When we experience a pain in, say, a finger, we do not suppose that the pain is occurring *in* the finger: for one thing, we know that the pain can be eliminated by drugs that act centrally, in the brain. But we are likely to be cautious about saying that it occurs 'in the brain'. In which neurons, we might ask; and we might then ask whether any one of the neurons involved, firing in the same way but maintained on its own in a culture medium, would then be feeling pain (Leibniz's mill problem (see Chapter 2) again). The neurons involved are those, we would say, that form part of complex networks, and it is the whole network that generates experience. Complex networks are not, however, enough to guarantee experience: what functions must those networks serve? One adequate answer to that question is, the networks that constitute the self: *I* feel pain; *I* have a pain in my finger—wherever 'I' am, that is where the pain is. There may be other answers to that question, but it seems more comfortable to answer it in terms of a self than in any other terms—and that may be because it is not sensible to think of an organism without a self as feeling anything.

*Virtue of parsimony*

One somewhat negative source of support for this account of feeling-consciousness is that it is parsimonious: both types of consciousness are explained by a single proposal. The gap between conscious and non-conscious organisms is explained in terms of a change that occurred during the transition from non-human to human—the evolution of language. The proposal is also parsimonious in that it requires only the minimal (but critical) conceptual precondition of language—namely, the ability to master the subject–predicate relationship. We need not suppose that a person actually has to learn to talk before becoming conscious. All that has to be supposed is that the gradual maturation of the subject–predicate device, to the stage at which a representation can be conceived of as being 'about' another representation, would be sufficient for the development of a self-concept. Under normal circumstances, talking and the self-concept should develop alongside each other; but in the absence of the normal environmental support for learning to talk, a self-concept—and so, a self—could develop independently of speech.

Finally, the proposal is parsimonious in that it assumes that the systems that mediate consciousness are present, as preadaptations, in our animal relatives. In particular, animals do construct internal representations of external events, and there is (in the hippocampal system) a forerunner of the explicit system to which we humans come to have conscious access. I assume that the processes managed by the implicit system remain comparable in humans to those managed by their animal forerunners. The general organization of cognition is, therefore, preserved—the changes being seen as entirely due to the evolution of the capacity for language.

## A modified Turing test

In introducing functionalism, I suggested that one of its virtues was that it is testable. The proposals that I have outlined are functionalist, and I have suggested that functionalism could gain widespread acceptance if it led to the construction of a machine that was, in the opinion of all, conscious. Two questions might now be asked. First, what pointers are provided here for the construction of a conscious machine? Second, how should the machine be tested—that is, what do I suppose a machine would have to do to convince people of its consciousness?

The answer to the first question is clear enough. In order to make a machine conscious, you must make it capable of forming propositions of the subject–predicate kind: the machine must be able to manipulate internal representations so that one representation is 'about' another. It might be supposed that there are machines already available that possess this capacity; you can find computers programmed so that they produce well-formed sentences in response to questions. But these computers are not in fact saying anything *about* the subjects of their sentences. The main reason for this is that they do not possess internal representations of things in the world. They manipulate symbols, but these symbols do not 'represent' anything for the machine. Any contemporary machine that produces a 'word'—for example, 'house'—is not using the word to represent or stand for a 'real' house; it has no experience of real houses, it knows nothing of them (however many predicates it may be able to attach correctly to the term). In order to achieve internal representations, the machine must build up, as we do, a structured model of the world that allows the possibility of meaningful reference. This could not be achieved without the use of something analogous to both our senses and also our motor system since, without drawing distinctions both between inputs from outside the machine and inputs from within it, and between changes in inputs caused externally and those caused by the machine's own 'actions', the machine could not detect the difference between self and non-self.

Of course, it will not be sufficient simply to add 'senses' and 'limbs' to develop a concept of self—modern robots possess crudely comparable capacities, but are not believed to be conscious. The 'sensory' inputs must be processed in such a way as to yield a structured model of the world, and it may be that the only appropriate processing is one that at least approximates to our system—much of which we share with animals. We would, then, have to build a machine whose sensorimotor capacities were sufficient to allow the possibility of its discriminating self from non-self. We would then also have to build into it a language-acquisition device that was, at minimum, powerful enough to achieve the subject–predicate relationship. Those would be the conditions necessary for the machine to achieve a self-concept. At least one further step would be critical for the development of feelings: the machine would need goals—rewards to attain, punishments to avoid, and response systems that behaved appropriately. The goals would have various priorities so that, for example, potentially damaging inputs would be given high priority in the competition to engage response systems, now controlled by the self.

How, then, should we test the machine to see whether indeed it is conscious? I suggest that conviction could be achieved only if the machine *talked* to us (and although it would not matter whether its output was typed or spoken, speech would no doubt be the more effective medium). But it does not seem necessary that the test should be the original Turing test, which required that the machine's responses be indistinguishable from human responses. If we *could* find an animal—or an alien—that talked, we would expect it to be acutely aware that it was *not* human, and the same would surely be true of a talking machine. The machine might have no idea what we were talking about when we, for example, talk of feeling thirsty; that might convince us that the machine was not human—but it would not demonstrate that it was not conscious. What we would require in the machine's conversation would be clear evidence that it (as we do) thought of itself as 'I', of the listener as 'you', and generally discriminated, just as we do, between itself and the rest of the world. If the machine achieved that, then there could be little reason to deny its possession of self-consciousness. But there remains, of course, the thorny question of whether it experiences feelings.

I introduced, earlier in this chapter, two (less than overwhelming) arguments to support the view that self-consciousness may be a necessary precondition of feeling-consciousness. But, even if those arguments are accepted, they do not tell us whether self-consciousness is *sufficient* for feeling. I would like to believe that this is an empirical matter, to be settled by the experience reported by a machine that has successfully been enabled to be self-conscious. It does not seem implausible that a self-conscious machine *would* report what we describe as 'private' experiences, because its constructed self would refer to representations in its short-term memory in the same way that we do. It would, then, make as much (and as little) sense for the machine as for us to query whether when it saw 'red' it was seeing what we see when we see red. A consequence of this view is that the experience of pain should be seen as an inescapable consequence of conscious access to representations which are linked to behavioural withdrawal systems. And if a (self-conscious) machine described the internal events that accompanied activation of withdrawal systems in ways comparable to those in which we talk about painful events, I have no doubt that we would feel morally obliged to help the machine avoid those events.

## Magic from language

We have seen in various parts of this book attempts to specify the 'magic' required to forge mind from matter. Descartes' answer was that a soul was added by God, and that the soul conferred the ability both to think (to talk) and to feel; animals had no soul, and could neither think nor feel. The magic that I propose has obvious similarities: animals are indeed Cartesian machines, and it is the availability of language that confers on us, first, the ability to be self-conscious, and second, the ability to feel. But whereas Descartes ascribed language to divine intervention, I, in common with most scientists, prefer to explain language as a capacity that evolved in accordance with Darwin's principle of natural selection.

I have, of course, endowed the 'self' with a range of functions that may seem gratuitously large. I have simply taken it to be a cognitive construction that is somehow, in an entirely unspecified way, able to stand apart from and to monitor other mental operations. I have 'solved' the problem of intentionality by characterizing it as a matter of grammar. And I have assumed that the problem of feeling-consciousness will simply go away when we succeed in constructing a self-conscious machine. I have, in other words, built much of the magic required into what is supposed to be an explanatory entity. What is provided here may be seen constructively as a framework that concentrates attention on three key issues. First, what precisely *is* it that convinces most—almost all—of us that animals and infants are conscious? Second, *is* there a plausible link between the evolution of grammar and the concept of self? Third, what is the link, if any, between self- and feeling-consciousness?

### The puzzle of function

The proposals that I have made in this chapter assume that consciousness is a consequence of the evolution of language—in particular, of the evolution of an 'aboutness' relationship that is the fundamental grammatical requirement for language. I consider, therefore, that benefits gained from the possession of consciousness were not necessarily instrumental in its evolution. The key to the evolution of consciousness lies in the evolution of language—and it is hardly necessary to point to the evolutionary advantages of being able to talk. But it is possible that one of the many advantages of language is precisely consciousness. It therefore makes sense to ask what functional benefits could be gained through consciousness.

### Function of self-consciousness

The construction of a person's self, and the self's access to and control of both short-term and long-term explicit memory has clear advantages in at least two ways, each of which has been emphasized by many others. First, by manipulation of the contents of the short-term store it allows the direction of cognitive effort (attention) to subjects of particular importance. So, for example, it allows the active consideration of past events in the search for solutions to current problems. More generally, it allows us to decide what we are going to think about—a view in good accord with William James' account of the function of consciousness (see Chapter 3). Second, by generating an understanding of our own thought processes, it allows us the better to predict the actions of others. It does, then, create a theory of mind (and this 'social' account of the origin of consciousness has enjoyed considerable popularity recently). If non- or prelinguistic organisms are not, as is suggested here, self-conscious, then they are denied those advantages.

### Function of feeling-consciousness

My case has been that feeling-consciousness is a by-product of self-consciousness—a proposal that does not throw up any functional advantage to be gained by feeling as opposed to not feeling. The causes of feelings could serve perfectly well if they caused the consequential behaviour directly rather than through the intermediary of feelings. It is simply the case that when the self contemplates inputs that are closely associated with behavioural priorities, those inputs are experienced as pleasant or painful. Feelings may make our world much better and much worse, but they are, in the end, functionless epiphenomena.

A natural and reasonable objection to this conclusion is that it was precisely the failure to conceive a function that led to the rejection of the possibility of consciousness evolving throughout animals. Why, then, should we not agree that feeling-consciousness *is* functionless, but suppose that it evolved far back in evolutionary history? The only answer to this objection is that it provides no account at all of any process of which feelings could be an epiphenomenon: we should again be left with the unsatisfactory vacuum in place of a link between feelings and some form of neuronal or behavioural complexity. Language is an instance of undeniable behavioural complexity (with clear adaptive advantages) from which it is possible to derive an account of the origins—via self-consciousness—of feeling-consciousness.

## A final caution: to err is human

An uncomfortable feature of the suggestions made here is that they may be seen to have unwelcome implications. People who are swayed towards accepting them may as a result maltreat animals and infants on the grounds that the latter do not feel anything. In fact, this seems a distinctly unlikely consequence, for a number of reasons. Consideration of one reason in particular will allow me finally to point to what is both a weakness and a strength of the proposals advanced here. We should all appreciate the fact that there is a huge degree of uncertainty attached to any current hypothesis for the origins of consciousness. This applies at least as much to the framework offered here as to any other explanatory scheme.

The probability of eventual outright rejection of this framework is, moreover, increased by the fact that it rests on a number of experimental findings, some of which may, of course, be overturned. If subsequent experiments succeed in persuading us that chimpanzees, for example, *can* master some basic grammar but *cannot* develop a concept of self, then my proposal would fall to the ground. Similarly, if further exploration proves that animals *do* develop a theory of mind but *cannot* acquire language, my account should be abandoned. If it was shown that some species could in fact *both* master language *and* develop a concept of self, my explanatory account could stand, but those animals would, of course, be assumed to be conscious. The demonstration of a major gap between the cognitive capacity of one animal species and those of others would immediately raise the question of whether language is the *only* behavioural complexity that might plausibly be put forward as a basis for consciousness. And if time proves right those sceptics who doubt that humans can show complex but implicit learning, then my case will be weakened. Clearly, there is a multitude of further examples, but the point has, I hope, been made. It is far from clear that the major contemporary accounts of consciousness could be subjected to experimental test, and this is one reason for the longevity of the mind–body problem (and for the plethora of available accounts). But there are potential experimental findings which would disprove my account—and this vulnerability is surely a virtue.

I hope that I have made it clear enough that—to put it mildly—doubt (strong doubt) remains the only sensible attitude. Where there is doubt, the only conceivable path is to act as though an organism *is* conscious, and *does* feel. To propose that animals *may* not be conscious can in no way be used as justification for treating them as though they *are* not conscious. To do so would be irrational, not to say psychopathic.

Moreover, I suspect that even if humans in general *did* come to believe that animals and infants were not sentient beings, our behaviour towards them would not change. There are many philosophical precedents for this course of events. Hume's demonstration of the absence of a logically necessary link between causes and effects has not led anyone—including Hume—to worry about the possibility that the laws of physics might suddenly change; and the conclusion reached by many, that free will is a logically absurd concept (actions surely are either caused or random), does not affect their *behaviour*—they are just as likely as anyone else to attribute praise and blame for the actions they observe. There are indeed Kantian constrictions on the way that we can interpret our world. The imperative to empathy with organisms whose behaviour resembles our own is so strong that we cannot but treat them as fellow sentient beings, which, of course, they may (or may not) be. We may reluctantly conclude that it is not, after all, like anything to be like a bat[29], but nevertheless maintain (with the immortal Rabbie Burns) that 'a bat's a bat for a' that'.

## Notes and references

1. For a more detailed introduction, see Searle (1992) or Churchland (1988).
2. Penrose (1989).
3. For example, Eccles (1977).
4. Vendler (1984).
5. Ryle (1949). The foremost—but regrettably the most obscure—exponent of logical behaviourism was Ludwig Wittgenstein (1889–1951), whose major work was his *Philosophical investigations* (Wittgenstein (1958)). For a contemporary approach to the philosophy of mind that falls within this tradition, see Dennett (1991).
6. For a sophisticated version of this argument, however, see Dennett (1991).
7. McGinn (1990).
8. Searle (1992).
9. Crick and Koch (1992).
10. Crick and Koch (1995).
11. Churchland (1986).

12. Searle (1992).
13. See Fodor (1981) for discussion of this problem; and see McCarthy (1979) for exposition of the claim that thermostats have beliefs.
14. Searle (1980).
15. Turing (1950).
16. Lucas (1961).
17. Penrose (1989, 1994).
18. Hameroff (1994).
19. For a clear exposition of a 'systems reply' see Dennett (1991), pp. 435–40.
20. For a version of this argument (and for the possibility that this is the view taken by Turing) see Grush and Churchland (1995).
21. As shown, for example, by the phenomenon of sensory preconditioning (introduced in Chapter 4).
22. Fodor (1975).
23. This is a technical use of the word 'intentional', somewhat removed from its normal everyday definition. In this chapter I shall use 'intentional' and 'intentionality' in this technical sense.
24. Mackintosh and Dickinson (1979); Heyes and Dickinson (1990).
25. Dickinson (1994).
26. Dickinson (1989).
27. Chalmers (1995).
28. See, for example, Dennett's discussion of a similar thought experiment (Dennett (1978), pp. 209–10).
29. See Nagel (1974) for the view that bats do have experiences, but that we cannot know what they are like.

# References

Adams, C. D. and Dickinson, A. (1981). Instrumental responding following reinforcer devaluation. *Quarterly Journal of Experimental Psychology*, 33B, 109–12.

Aiken, H. D. (1956). *The age of ideology: the 19th century philosophers*. Houghton Mifflin, New York.

Amsel, A. and Rashotte, M. E. (1984). *Mechanisms of adaptive behavior: Clark L. Hull's theoretical papers, with commentary*. Columbia University Press, New York.

Anderson, J. R. (1986). Mirror-mediated finding of hidden food by monkeys (*Macaca tonkeana* and *M. fascicularis*). *Journal of Comparative Psychology*, 100, 237–42.

Anderson, J. R. (1995). *Learning and memory: an integrated approach*. Wiley, New York.

Barnes, J. (1982). *Aristotle*. Oxford University Press, Oxford.

Barnes, J. (ed.). (1984). *The complete works of Aristotle: the revised Oxford translation*, Vol. 1. Princeton University Press, Princeton, NJ.

Bauer, P. J. (1996). What do infants recall of their lives — memory for specific events by one-year-olds to 2-year-olds. *American Psychologist*, 51, 29–41.

Berlin, I. (ed.). (1956). *The age of enlightenment: the 18th century philosophers*. The New American Library, New York.

Berry, D. C. and Broadbent, D. E. (1984). On the relationship between task performance and associated verbalizable knowledge. *Quarterly Journal of Experimental Psychology*, 36A, 209–31.

Bitterman, M. E. (1975). The comparative analysis of learning. *Science*, 188, 699–709.

Boakes, R. A. (1984). *From Darwin to behaviorism: psychology and the minds of animals*. Cambridge University Press, Cambridge.

Boakes, R. A. (1989). How one might find evidence for conditioning in adult humans. In *Aversion, avoidance, and anxiety* (ed. T. Archer and L.G. Nilsson), pp. 381–402. Lawrence Erlbaum Associates, Hillsdale, NJ.

Boring, E. G. (1950). *A history of experimental psychology*, (2nd edn.). Appleton-Century-Crofts, New York.

Brewer, W. F. (1974). There is no convincing evidence for operant and classical conditioning in human beings. In *Cognition and the symbolic processes* (ed. W. Weimer and D.J. Palermo), pp. 1–42. Lawrence Erlbaum Associates, Hillsdale, NJ.

Broadbent, D. E. (1971). *Decision and stress*. Academic Press, London.

Brook, A. (1994). *Kant and the mind*. Cambridge University Press, Cambridge.

Brown, P. L. and Jenkins, H. M. (1968). Auto-shaping of the pigeon's key-peck. *Journal of the Experimental Analysis of Behavior*, 11, 1–8.

Byrne, R. W. (1995). *The thinking ape: evolutionary origins of intelligence*. Oxford University Press, Oxford.

Byrne, R. W. and Whiten, A. (ed.). (1988). *Machiavellian intelligence: social expertise and the evolution of intellect in monkeys, apes, and humans*. Clarendon Press, Oxford.

Cabanac, M. and Duclaux, R. (1970). Obesity: absence of satiety aversion to sucrose. *Science*, 168, 496–7.

Chalmers, D. J. (1995). The puzzle of conscious experience. *Scientific American*, 273, 80–6.

Chomsky, N. (1959). Review of B. F. Skinner's *Verbal Behavior*. *Language*, 35, 26–58.

Chomsky, N. (1972). *Language and mind*, (enlarged edn.). Harcourt Brace Jovanovich, New York.

Churchland, P. M. (1988). *Matter and consciousness: a contemporary introduction to the philosophy of mind*, (revised ed.). MIT Press, Cambridge, MA.

Churchland, P. S. (1986). *Neurophilosophy*. MIT Press, Cambridge, MA.

Clark, W. C. and Clark, S. B. (1980). Pain responses in Nepalese porters. *Science*, 209, 410–12.

Corkin, S. (1984). Lasting consequences of bilateral medial temporal lobectomy: Clinical course and experimental findings in H.M. *Seminars in Neurology*, 4, 249–59.

Crick, F. and Koch, C. (1992). The problem of consciousness. *Scientific American*, 267, 153–9.

Crick, F. and Koch, C. (1995). Are we aware of neural activity in primary visual-cortex. *Nature*, 375, 121–3.

Dawkins, M. S. (1993). *Through our eyes only? The search for animal consciousness*. W. H. Freeman, Oxford.

De la Mettrie, J. O. (1953). *Man a machine* (translated by G.C. Bussey and M.W. Calkins). Open Court, La Salle, IL.

DeCasper, A. J. and Fifer, W. P. (1980). Of human bonding: Newborns prefer their mother's voices. *Science*, 208, 1174–6.

DeCasper, A. J.and Prescott, P. A. (1984). Human newborns perception of male voices — preference, discrimination, and reinforcing value. *Developmental Psychobiology*, 17, 481–91.

DeCasper, A. J. and Spence, M. J. (1986). Prenatal maternal speech influences newborns perception of speech sounds. *Infant Behavior and Development*, 9, 133–50.

Dennett, D. C. (1978). *Brainstorms*. Harvester Press, Hassocks, Sussex.

Dennett, D. C. (1991). *Consciousness explained*. Penguin, Harmondsworth.

Descartes, R. (1931–4). *The philosophical works of Descartes* (translated by E. S.

Haldane and G. R. T. Ross), Vols 1 and 2. Cambridge University Press, Cambridge.

Dichiara, G. (1995). Psychobiology of the role of dopamine in drug-abuse and addiction. *Neuroscience Research Communications*, 17, 133–43.

Dickinson, A. (1980). *Contemporary animal learning theory*. Cambridge University Press, Cambridge.

Dickinson, A. (1985). Actions and habits: the development of behavioural autonomy. *Philosophical Transactions of the Royal Society of London, Series B*, 308, 67–78.

Dickinson, A. (1989). Expectancy theory in animal conditioning. In *Contemporary learning theories: Pavlovian conditioning and the status of traditional learning theories* (ed. S. B. Klein and R. R. Mowrer), pp. 279–308). Lawrence Erlbaum Associates, Hillsdale, NJ.

Dickinson, A. (1994). Instrumental conditioning. In *Handbook of perception and cognition*, (2nd edn.) (ed. N. J. Mackintosh) *Vol. 9: Animal learning and cognition*, pp. 45–79. Academic Press, London.

Dickinson, A., Shanks, D. R., and Evenden, J. (1984). Judgment of act-outcome contingency: the role of selective attribution. *Quarterly Journal of Experimental Psychology*, 36A, 29–50.

Doty, B. A., Jones, C. N., and Doty, L. A. (1967). Learning-set formation by mink, ferrets, skunks, and cats. *Science*, 155, 1579–80.

Eccles, J. C. (1977). *The understanding of the brain*, (2nd edn.). McGraw-Hill, New York.

Epstein, R., Kirschnit, C. E., Lanza, R. P., and Rubin, L. C. (1984). 'Insight' in a pigeon: antecedents and determinants of an intelligent performance. *Nature*, 308, 61–2.

Epstein, R., Lanza, R. P., and Skinner, B. F. (1981). 'Self-awareness' in the pigeon. *Science*, 212, 695–6.

Fagan, J. F. (1973). Infants' delayed recognition memory and forgetting. *Journal of Experimental Child Psychology*, 16, 424–50.

Fancher, R. E. (1990). *Pioneers of psychology*, (2nd edn.). W. W. Norton & Company, New York.

Fodor, J. A. (1975). *The language of thought*. Thomas Y. Crowell &; Co., New York.

Fodor, J. A. (1981). The mind–body problem. *Scientific American*, 244, 124–32.

Fraenkel, G. S. and Gunn, D. L. (1940). *The orientation of animals*. Clarendon Press, Oxford.

Gallup, G. G. (1970). Chimpanzees: self-recognition. *Science*, 167, 86–7.

Gallup, G. G. (1982). Self-awareness and the emergence of mind in primates. *American Journal of Primatology*, 2, 237–48.

Giannakoulopoulos, X., Sepulveda, W., Kourtis, P., Glover, V., and Fisk, N. M. (1994). Fetal plasma cortisol and ß-endorphin response to intrauterine needling. *Lancet*, 344, 77–81.

Glanzer, M. and Cunitz, A. (1966). Two storage mechanisms in free recall. *Journal of Verbal Learning and Verbal Behavior*, 5, 531–60.

Griffin, D. R. (1984). *Animal thinking*. Harvard University Press, Cambridge, MA.

Grush, R. and Churchland, P. S. (1995). Gaps in Penrose's toilings. *Journal of Consciousness Studies, 2*, 10–29.

Guthrie, W. K. C. (1965). *A history of Greek philosophy. Vol. 2. The Presocratic tradition from Parmenides to Democritus*. Cambridge University Press, Cambridge.

Guthrie, W. K. C. (1967). *The Greek philosophers: from Thales to Aristotle*. Methuen &; Co. Ltd., London.

Guthrie, W. K. C. (1975). *A history of Greek philosophy. Vol. 4. Plato: the man and his dialogues. Earlier period*. Cambridge University Press, Cambridge.

Guthrie, W. K. C. (1981). *A history of Greek philosophy. Vol. 6. Aristotle: an encounter*. Cambridge University Press, Cambridge.

Hameroff, S. (1994). Quantum coherence in microtubules: A neural basis for emergent consciousness? *Journal of Consciousness Studies, 1*, 91–118.

Hampshire, S. (ed.). (1956). *The age of reason: the 17th century philosophers*. The New American Library, New York.

Heyes, C. and Dickinson, A. (1990). The intentionality of animal action. *Mind and language, 5*, 87–104.

Heyes, C. M. (1993). Anecdotes, training, trapping and triangulating — do animals attribute mental states? *Animal Behaviour, 46*, 177–88.

Heyes, C. M. (1994). Reflections on self-recognition in primates. *Animal Behaviour, 47*, 909–19.

Hilton, S. C. and Krebs, J. R. (1990). Spatial memory of four species of *Parus*: performance in an open-field analogue of a radial maze. *Quarterly Journal of Experimental Psychology, 42B*, 345–68.

Hobbes, T. (1840). *The English works of Thomas Hobbes of Malmesbury; now first collected and edited by Sir William Molesworth, Bart,*Vol. 4, (reprint of the 1840 edition). Scientia Verlag, Aalen.

Howe, M. L. and Courage, M. L. (1993). On resolving the enigma of infantile amnesia. *Psychological Bulletin, 113*, 305–26.

Howe, M. L., Courage, M. L., and Peterson, C. (1994). How can I remember when 'I' wasn't there: long-term retention of traumatic experiences and emergence of the cognitive self. *Consciousness and Cognition, 3*, 327–55.

Hudson, J. A. (1990). The emergence of autobiographical memory in mother-child conversation. In *Knowing and remembering in young children* (ed. R. Fivush and J. A. Hudson), pp. 166–96. Cambridge University Press, New York.

Hull, C. L. (1930). Knowledge and purpose as habit mechanisms. *Psychological Review, 37*, 511–25.

Hull, C. L. (1935). The conflicting psychologies of learning — a way out. *Psychological Review, 42*, 491–516.

Hull, C. L. (1937). Mind, mechanism, and adaptive behavior. *Psychological Review, 44*, 1–32.

Hull, C. L. (1945). The place of innate individual and species differences in a natural-science theory of behavior. *Psychological Review, 52*, 55–60.

Hume, D. (1956). *A treatise of human nature.* J.M. Dent, London.

Humphrey, N. K. (1976). The social function of intellect. In *Growing points in ethology* (ed. P. P. G. Bateson and R. A. Hinde), pp. 303–17. Cambridge University Press, Cambridge.

Huxley, T. H. (1893). *Method and Results: Essays.* Macmillan &; Co. Ltd., London.

Ince, L. P., Brucker, B. S., and Alba, A. (1978). Reflex conditioning in a spinal man. *Journal of Comparative and Physiological Psychology,* 92, 796–802.

James, W. (1890/1950). *The principles of psychology, Vol. 1* (2 Vols) (reprint of 1890 edn.). Dover Publications, Inc., New York.

Jaynes, J. (1993). *The origin of consciousness in the breakdown of the bicameral mind.* Penguin Books, London.

Jenkins, H. M. and Moore, B. R. (1973). The form of the auto-shaped response with food or water reinforcers. *Journal of the Experimental Analysis of Behavior,* 20, 163–81.

Jerison, H. J. (1973). *Evolution of the brain and intelligence.* Academic Press, New York.

Kamil, A. C., Balda, R. P. and Olson, D. J. (1994). Performance of 4 seed-caching corvid species in the radial-arm maze analog. *Journal Of Comparative Psychology,* 108, 385–93.

Karten, H. J. & Hodos, W. (1967). *A stereotaxic atlas of the brain of the pigeon (Columba livia).* Baltimore, MD: Johns Hopkins University Press.

Kemp Smith, N. (1929). *Immanuel Kant's Critique of Pure Reason.* Macmillan &; Co., London.

Knowlton, B. J., Ramus, S. J., and Squire, L. R. (1992). Intact artificial grammar learning in amnesia — dissociation of classification learning and explicit memory for specific instances. *Psychological Science,* 3, 172–9.

Kolb, B., Sutherland, R. J., and Whishaw, I. Q. (1983). A comparison of the contributions of the frontal and parietal association cortex to spatial localization in rats. *Behavioral Neuroscience,* 97, 13–27.

Köhler, W. (1925/1957). *The mentality of apes* (translation of 2nd revised edn. by E. Winter). Penguin Books, Harmondsworth.

Krebs, J. R., Sherry, D. F., Healy, S. D., Perry, V. H., and Vaccarino, A. L. (1989). Hippocampal specialization of food-storing birds. *Proceedings Of The National Academy Of Sciences Of The United States Of America,* 86, 1388–92.

Kummer, H., Anzenberer, G., and Hemelrijk, C. K. (1996). Hiding and perspective-taking in long-tailed macaques (*Macaca fascicularis*). *Journal Of Comparative Psychology,* 110, 97–102.

Ledbetter, D. H. and Basen, J. D. (1982). Failure to demonstrate self-recognition in gorillas. *American Journal of Primatology,* 2, 307–10.

Leibniz, G. W. V. (1902/1957). *Discourse on metaphysics (1685); Correspondence with Arnauld (1686–1690); Monadology (1714)* (translated by G. R. Montgomery). Open Court Publishing, La Salle, IL.

Leichtman, M. D. and Ceci, S. J. (1993). The problem of infantile amnesia: lessons from fuzzy-trace theory. In *Emerging themes in cognitive development. Volume 1: foundations* (ed. M. L. Howe and R. Pasnak), pp. 195–213). Springer-Verlag, New York.

Lenhoff, H. M.. and Lenhoff, S. G. (1988). Trembley's polyps. *Scientific American,* 258 (April), 86–91.

Locke, J. (1947). *An essay concerning human understanding* (abridged and edited by R. Wilburn). J.M. Dent &; Sons, London.

Lucas, J. R. (1961). Minds, machines and Gödel. *Philosophy,* 36, 120–4.

Mackintosh, N. J. (1983). *Conditioning and associative learning.* Clarendon Press, Oxford.

Macphail, E. M. (1982). *Brain and intelligence in vertebrates.* Clarendon Press, Oxford.

Macphail, E. M. (1987). The comparative psychology of intelligence. *Behavioral and Brain Sciences,* 10, 645–96.

Macphail, E. M. (1993). *The neuroscience of animal intelligence: from the seahare to the seahorse.* Columbia University Press, New York.

Marcel, A. J. (1980). Conscious and preconscious recognition of polysemous words: locating the selective effects of prior verbal context. In *Attention and performance VIII* (ed. R. S. Nickerson), pp. 435–57. Lawrence Erlbaum Associates, Hillsdale, NJ.

McCarthy, J. (1979). Ascribing mental qualities to machines. In *Philosophical perspectives in artificial intelligence* (ed. M. Ringle), pp. 161–95. Harvester Press, Brighton.

McDonough, L. and Mandler, J. M. (1994). Very long-term recall in infants — infantile amnesia reconsidered. *Memory,* 2, 339–52.

McDonough, L., Mandler, J. M., McKee, R. D., and Squire, L. R. (1995). The deferred imitation task as a nonverbal measure of declarative memory. *Proceedings Of the National Academy Of Sciences Of the United States Of America,* 92, 7580–4.

McGinn, C. (1990). *The problem of consciousness: essays towards a resolution.* Blackwell, Oxford.

McGonigle, B. O. and Chalmers, M. (1977). Are monkeys logical? *Nature,* 267, 694–6.

Melzack, R. (1993). Pain: past, present and future. *Canadian Journal of Experimental Psychology,* 47, 615–29.

Melzack, R. and Eisenberg, H. (1968). Skin sensory afterglows. *Science,* 159, 445–7.

Melzack, R. and Wall, P. D. (1965). Pain mechanisms: a new theory. *Science,* 150, 971–9.

Melzack, R. and Wall, P. D. (1996). *The challenge of pain,* (2nd, updated edn.). Penguin Books, Harmondsworth.

Melzack, R., Wall, P. D., and Weisz, A. Z. (1963). Masking and metacotrast phenomena in the skin sensory system. *Experimental Neurology,* 8, 35–46.

Menzel, E. W., Savage-Rumbaugh, E. S., and Lawson, J. (1985). Chimpanzee (*Pan troglodytes*) problem-solving with the use of mirrors and televised equivalents of mirrors. *Journal of Comparative Psychology*, 99, 211–17.

Michel, F. and Perronet, F. (1990). *Unawareness of auditory deficit in hemianacousia.* Poster presented at the Wellcome Trust Symposium 'Consciousness and cognition', St Andrews, UK.

Milner, P. M. (1991). Brain-stimulation reward — a review. *Canadian Journal of Psychology*, 45, 1–36.

Morgan, C. L. (1894). *An introduction to comparative psychology.* Walter Scott, London.

Myers, N. A., Clifton, R. K., and Clarkson, M. G. (1987). When they were very young: Almost-threes remember two years ago. *Infant behavior and development*, 10, 123–32.

Nagel, T. (1974). What is it like to be a bat? *Philosophical Review*, 83, 435–50.

Neisser, U. (1967). *Cognitive psychology.* Appleton-Century-Crofts, New York.

Nelson, K. (1990). Remembering, forgetting, and childhood amnesia. In *Knowing and remembering in young children* (ed. R. Fivush and J. A. Hudson), pp. 301–16. Cambridge University Press, New York.

Olds, J. and Milner, P. (1954). Positive reinforcement produced by electrical stimulation of septal area and other regions of the brain. *Journal of Comparative and Physiological Psychology*, 47, 419–27.

Oswald, I., Taylor, A. M., and Treisman, M. (1960). Discriminative responses to stimulation during human sleep. *Brain*, 83, 440–53.

Owens, M. E. (1984). Pain in infancy: conceptual and methodological issues. *Pain*, 20, 213–30.

Owens, M. E. and Todt, E. H. (1984). Pain in infancy: neonatal reaction to a heel lance. *Pain*, 20, 77–86.

Paillard, J., Michel, F., and Stelmach, G. (1983). Localization without content — a tactile analog of blind sight. *Archives Of Neurology*, 40, 548–51.

Papini, M. R and Bitterman, M. E. (1990). The role of contingency in classical conditioning. *Psychological Review*, 97, 396–403.

Pascalis, O. and Deschonen, S. (1994). Recognition memory in 3-day-old to 4-day-old human neonates. *Neuroreport*, 5, 1721–4.

Patterson, F. G. P. and Cohn, R. H. (1994). Self-recognition and self-awareness in lowland gorillas. In *Self-awareness in animals and humans: developmental perspectives* (ed. S. T. Parker, R. W. Mitchell, and M. L. Boccia), pp. 273–90. Cambridge University Press, Cambridge.

Paxinos, G. & Watson, C. (1986). *The rat brain in stereotaxic coordinates.* (2nd ed.). London: Academic Press.

Pavlov, I. P. (1927). *Conditioned reflexes* (translated from 1960 edn. (Dover, New York) by G. V. Anrep). Oxford University Press, Oxford.

Penrose, R. (1989). *The emperor's new mind: concerning computers, minds and the laws of physics.* Oxford University Press, Oxford.

Penrose, R. (1994). *Shadows of the mind: a search for the missing science of consciousness.* Oxford University Press, Oxford.

Pepperberg, I. M. (1981). Functional vocalizations by an African grey parrot (*Psittacus erithacus*). *Zeitschrift Fur Tierpsychologie — Journal Of Comparative Ethology*, 55, 139–60.

Pepperberg, I. M. (1983). Cognition in the African grey parrot — preliminary evidence for auditory vocal comprehension of the class concept. *Animal Learning and Behavior*, 11, 179–85.

Pepperberg, I. M. (1994). Numerical competence in an African grey parrot (*Psittacus erithacus*). *Journal Of Comparative Psychology*, 108, 36–44.

Pepperberg, I. M., Garcia, S. E., Jackson, E. C., and Marconi, S. (1995). Mirror use by African grey parrots (*Psittacus erithacus*). *Journal Of Comparative Psychology*, 109, 182–95.

Pepperberg, I. M. and Kozak, F. A. (1986). Object permanence in the African grey parrot (*Psittacus erithacus*). *Animal Learning and Behavior*, 14, 322–30.

Perruchet, P. (1985). A pitfall for the expectancy theory of human eyelid conditioning. *Pavlovian Journal of Biological Science*, 20, 163–70.

Pillemer, D. B. and White, S. H. (1989). Childhood events recalled by children and adults. In *Advances in child development and behavior* (ed. H. W. Reese), Vol. 21, pp. 297–340. Academic Press, San Diego, CA.

Pinker, S. (1994). *The language instinct: the new science of language and mind*. Penguin Books, Harmondsworth.

Plato. (1953). *The dialogues of Plato* (translated by B. Jowett), (4th edn.). 4 Vols. Tudor Publishing Company, New York.

Povinelli, D. J. (1993). Reconstructing the evolution of mind. *American Psychologist*, 48, 493–509.

Povinelli, D. J. (1994a). How to create self-recognizing gorillas (but don't try it on macaques). In *Self-awareness in animals and humans: developmental perspectives* (ed. S. T. Parker, R. W. Mitchell, and M. L. Boccia), pp. 291–300. Cambridge University Press, Cambridge.

Povinelli, D. J. (1994b). Comparative studies of animal mental state attribution: a reply to Heyes. *Animal Behaviour*, 48, 239.

Povinelli, D. J., Nelson, K. E., and Boysen, S. T. (1990). Inferences about guessing and knowing by chimpanzees. *Journal of Comparative Psychology*, 104, 203–10.

Povinelli, D. J., Parks, K. A., and Novak, M. A. (1991). Do rhesus monkeys (*Macaca mulatta*) attribute knowledge and ignorance to others? *Journal of Comparative Psychology*, 105, 318–25.

Povinelli, D. J. and Preuss, T. M. (1995). Theory of mind — evolutionary history of a cognitive specialization. *Trends in Neurosciences*, 18, 418–24.

Povinelli, D. J., Rulf, A. B., Landau, K. R., and Bierschwale, D. T. (1993). Self-recognition in chimpanzees (*Pan troglodytes*): distribution, ontogeny, and patterns of emergence. *Journal of Comparative Psychology*, 107, 347–72.

Premack, D. and Woodruff, G. (1978). Does the chimpanzee have a theory of mind? *Behavioral and Brain Sciences*, 1, 515–26.

Real, L. A. (1991). Animal choice behaviour and the evolution of cognitive architecture. *Science,* 253, 980–6.

Reber, A. S. (1993). *Implicit learning and tacit knowledge: an essay on the cognitive unconscious.* Clarendon Press, Oxford.

Reese, H. W. (1964). Discrimination learning set in rhesus monkeys. *Psychological Bulletin,* 61, 321–40.

Rescorla, R. A. (1968). Probability of shock in the presence and absence of CS in fear conditioning. *Journal of Comparative and Physiological Psychology,* 66, 1–5.

Rovee-Collier, C. and Shyi, G. (1992). A functional and cognitive analysis of infant long-term retention. In M. L. Howe, C. J. Brainerd, &; V. F. Reyna (Eds.), *Development of long-term retention* (ed. M. L. Howe, C. J. Brainerd, and V. F. *Reyna),* pp. 3–55. Springer-Verlag, New York.

Ryle, G. (1949). *The concept of mind.* Hutchinson, London.

Sahley, C. R. J. W., Rudy, J. W. and Gelperin, A. (1981). An analysis of associative learning in a terrestrial mollusc. 1: Higher -order conditioning, blocking and a transient US pre-exposure effect. *Journal of Comparative Physiology,* A144, 1–8.

Savage-Rumbaugh, E. S., Murphy, J., Sevcik, R. A., Brakke, K. E., Williams, S. L., and Rumbaugh, D. M. (1993). Language comprehension in ape and child. *Monographs of the Society for Research in Child Development,* 58.

Scoville, W. B. and Milner, B. (1957). Loss of recent memory after bilateral hippocampal lesion. *Journal of Neurology, Neurosurgery and Psychiatry,* 20, 11–21.

Scruton, R. (1982). *Kant.* Oxford University Press, Oxford.

Searle, J. R. (1980). Minds, brains, and programs. *Behavioral and Brain Sciences,* 3, 417–58.

Searle, J. R. (1992). *The rediscovery of the mind.* MIT Press, Cambridge, MA.

Shanks, D. R. (1993). Human instrumental learning: a critical review of data and theory. *British Journal of Psychology,* 84, 319–54.

Shanks, D. R. and St John, M. F. (1994). Characteristics of dissociable human learning systems. *Behavioral and Brain Sciences,* 17, 367–447.

Sherrington, C. S. (1906). *The integrative action of the nervous system.* Yale University Press, New Haven.

Skinner, B. F. (1938). *The behavior of organisms.* Appleton-Century-Crofts, New York.

Skinner, B. F. (1953). *Science and human behavior.* Macmillan, New York.

Skinner, B. F. (1957). *Verbal behavior.* Appleton-Century-Crofts, New York.

Skinner, B. F. (1961). *Cumulative Record.* Methuen &; Co. Ltd., London.

Skinner, B. F. (1969). *Contingencies of reinforcement: a theoretical analysis.* Appleton-Century-Crofts, New York.

Sobel, D. (1996). *Longitude.* Fourth Estate, London.

Stoerig, P. and Cowey, A. (1993). Blindsight — neurons and behavior. *Progress In Brain Research,* 95, 445–59.

Stoerig, P. and Cowey, A. (1995). Visual-perception and phenomenal consciousness. *Behavioural Brain Research,* 71, 147–56.

Suarez, S. D. and Gallup, G. G. (1981). Self-recognition in chimpanzees and orangutans, but not gorillas. *Journal of Human Evolution,* 10, 175–88.

Terrace, H. S., Pettito, L. A., Sanders, R. J., and Bever, T. G. (1979). Can an ape create a sentence? *Science,* 206, 891–900.

Thorndike, E. L. (1911/1970). *Animal intelligence.* Hafner, Darien, Connecticut.

Turing, A. M. (1950). Computing machinery and intelligence. *Mind,* 59, 433–60.

Vendler, Z. (1984). *The matter of minds.* Clarendon Press, Oxford.

Voltaire. (1759/1947). *Candide* (translated by J. Butt). Penguin Books, Harmondsworth.

Von Fersen, L., Wynne, C. D. L., Delius, J. D., and Staddon, J. E. R. (1991). Transitive inference in pigeons. *Journal of Experimental Psychology: Animal Behavior Processes,* 17, 334–41.

Wall, P. D. and McMahon, S. B. (1985). Microneuronography and its relation to perceived sensation. A critical review. *Pain,* 21, 209–29.

Walters, E. T., Carew, T. J., and Kandel, E. R. (1981). Associative learning in *Aplysia:* Evidence for conditioned fear in an invertebrate. *Science,* 211, 504–6.

Warren, J. M. (1965). Primate learning in comparative perspective. In *Behavior of nonhuman primates: modern research trends* (ed. A. M. Schrier, H. F. Harlow, and F. Stollnitz), Vol. 1, pp. 249–81. Academic Press, New York.

Watson, J. B. (1913/1994). Psychology as the behaviorist views it. *Psychological Review,* 101, 248–53.

Watson, J. B. (1930). *Behaviorism.* University of Chicago Press, Chicago.

Weiskrantz, L. (1986). *Blindsight: a case study and its implications.* Clarendon Press, Oxford.

Weiskrantz, L. and Warrington, E. K. (1979). Conditioning in amnesic patients. *Neuropsychologia,* 17, 187–94.

Whiten, A. and Byrne, R. W. (1988). Tactical deception in primates. *Behavioral and Brain Sciences,* 11, 233–73.

Williams, D. R. and Williams, H. (1969). Auto-maintenance in the pigeon: sustained pecking despite contingent non-reinforcement. *Journal of the Experimental Analysis of Behavior,* 12, 511–20.

Wise, R. A. and Rompre, P. P. (1989). Brain dopamine and reward. *Annual Review Of Psychology,* 40, 191–225.

Wittgenstein, L. (1958). *Philosophical investigations* (translated by G. E. M. Anscombe), (2nd edn.). Basil Blackwell, Oxford.

Wundt, W. (1894). *Lectures on human and animal psychology* (translated from the 2nd edn. of 1892 by J. E. Creighton and E. B. Titchener). Swan Sonnenschein & Co., London.

Zeldin, R. K. and Olton, D. S. (1986). Rats acquire spatial learning sets. *Journal of Experimental Psychology: Animal Behavior Processes,* 12, 412–19.

Zentall, T. R. and Sherburne, L. M. (1994). Transfer of value from S+ to S- in a simultaneous discrimination. *Journal of Experimental Psychology: Animal Behavior Processes,* 20, 176–83.

# Index